MYTHS, RITES, SYMBOLS:

A Mircea Eliade Reader

Edited by
WENDELL C. BEANE
and
WILLIAM G. DOTY

Volume 2

HARPER COLOPHON BOOKS
Harper & Row, Publishers
New York, Evanston, San Francisco, London

151

MYTHS, RITES, SYMBOLS: A MIRCEA ELIADE READER. Copyright © 1975 by Wendell C. Beane and William G. Doty. All rights reserved. Printed in the United States of America. No part of this book may be used or reproduced in any manner without written permission except in the case of brief quotations embodied in critical articles and reviews. For information address Harper & Row, Publishers, Inc., 10 East 53d Street, New York, N.Y. 10022. Published simultaneously in Canada by Fitzhenry & Whiteside Limited, Toronto.

First HARPER COLOPHON editions published 1976

LIBRARY OF CONGRESS CATALOG NUMBER: 75-7931

STANDARD BOOK NUMBER: 06-090510-7 (vol. 1)
STANDARD BOOK NUMBER: 06-090511-5 (vol. 2)

Designed by Stephanie Krasnow

76 77 78 79 80 10 9 8 7 6 5 4 3 2 1

Contents

VOLUME 1

CHAPTER 1

Myths—Sacred History, Time, and Intercommunication

CHAPTER 2

VOLUME 2

CHAPTER 3

Abbreviations and Acknowledgments

AR   *Australian Religions. An Introduction.* Ithaca, N.Y.: Cornell
        University Press, 1973. © 1973 by Cornell University Press.
        Originally: *History of Religions*, Vols. 6 (1966) and 7 (1967).
        Reprinted by permission of The University of Chicago Press,
        © 1966, 1967.

CH   *The Myth of the Eternal Return, or Cosmos and History.*
        Translated by Willard R. Trask. Bollingen Series 46. Princeton,
        N.J.: Princeton University Press, 1954. Copyright © 1954 by
        Bollingen Foundation. Reprinted by permission of Princeton
        University Press, a total of 8,130 words. Reprinted by permis-
        sion of Routledge & Kegan Paul, Ltd., London.

FC   *The Forge and the Crucible (The Origins and Structures of
        Alchemy).* Translated by Stephen Corrin. New York: Harper
        & Row, 1971; © English translation by Rider & Company, 1962;
        © by Ernest Flammarion, 1956. Reprinted by permission of
        Hutchinson Publishing Group, Ltd., London.

FPZ   *From Primitives to Zen. A Thematic Sourcebook of the His-
        tory of Religions.* New York: Harper & Row, 1967. © 1967 by
        Mircea Eliade. Reprinted by permission of Harper & Row,
        Publishers, Inc.

IS   *Images and Symbols. Studies in Religious Symbolism.* Translated
        by Philip Mariet. New York: 1969. © Librairie Gallimard, 1952.
        © in the English translation Harvill Press, 1961, published by
        Sheed and Ward, Inc., New York. Reprinted by permission of
        Harvill Press, Ltd., London, and Sheed and Ward, Inc., New
        York.

MDM   *Myths, Dreams, and Mysteries. The Encounter Between Con-
        temporary Faiths and Archaic Realities.* Translated by Philip
        Mairet. New York: Harper & Row, 1967. © 1957 Libraire Gal-
        limard; © 1960 in the English translation Harvill Press. Re-
        printed by permission of Harper & Row, Publishers, Inc.
        Reprinted by permission of Harvill Press, Ltd., London.

MR   *Myth and Reality.* Translated by Willard R. Trask. New York:
        Harper & Row, 1963. © 1963 by Harper & Row, Publishers, Inc.
        Reprinted by permission of Harper & Row, Publishers, Inc.

MRS   "Methodological Remarks on the Study of Religious Symbolism," in Mircea Eliade and J. M. Kitagawa, eds., *The History of Religions: Essays in Methodology*. Chicago: The University of Chicago Press, 1959, pp. 86–107. © 1959 by The University of Chicago. Reprinted by permission of The University of Chicago Press.

PCR   *Patterns in Comparative Religions* by Mircea Eliade. New York: 1958. © Sheed and Ward, Inc. 1958. Reprinted by permission of Sheed and Ward, Inc., New York.

Q   *The Quest. History and Meaning in Religion*. Chicago: The University of Chicago Press, 1969. © 1969 by The University of Chicago. Reprinted by permission of The University of Chicago Press.

RSI   *Rites and Symbols of Initiation. The Mysteries of Birth and Rebirth* (also as title: *Birth and Rebirth*). Translated by Willard R. Trask. New York: Harper & Row, 1965. © 1958 by Mircea Eliade. Reprinted by permission of Harper & Row, Publishers, Inc.

S   *Shamanism, Archaic Techniques of Ecstasy* by Mircea Eliade. Translated by Willard R. Trask. Bollingen Series 76. Princeton, N.J.: Princeton University Press, 1964. Copyright © 1964 by Bollingen Foundation. Reprinted by permission of Princeton University Press, a total of 10,670 words.

SMA   "The Sacred and the Modern Artist," *Criterion* 4, no. 2 (Spring, 1965): 22–24. Reprinted by permission of *Criterion*, The University of Chicago, The Divinity School.

SP   *The Sacred and the Profane. The Nature of Religion*. Translated by Willard R. Trask. New York: Harcourt Brace Jovanovich, 1959. Copyright © 1959 by Harcourt Brace Jovanovich, Inc. Reprinted by permission of Harcourt Brace Jovanovich. Reprinted by permission of Rowohlt Taschenbuch Verlag G.m.b.H. from *The Sacred and the Profane* by Mircea Eliade. Copyright © 1957, Rowohlt Taschenbuch Verlag G.m.b.H., Hamburg.

TO   *The Two and the One*. Translated by J. M. Cohen. New York: Harper & Row, 1965. © 1962 Editions Gallimard. © 1965 in the English translation by Harvill Press, London, Sheed and Ward, Inc., and Harper & Row, Publishers, Inc., New York. Reprinted by permission from Harvill Press, Ltd., London, and Sheed and Ward, Inc., New York.

Y   *Yoga: Immortality and Freedom*, by Mircea Eliade. Translated by Willard R. Trask, Bollingen Series 56. Princeton, N.J.:

Princeton University Press, 1970. Copyright © 1958 and © 1969 by Bollingen Foundation. Reprinted by permission of Princeton University Press, a total of 8,760 words.

Z   *Zalmoxis. The Vanishing God. Comparative Studies in the Religions and Folklore of Dacia and Eastern Europe.* Translated by Willard R. Trask. Chicago: The University of Chicago Press, 1972. © 1972 by The University of Chicago. © 1970, Payot, Paris. Reprinted by permission of The University of Chicago Press.

Preface

To begin, I should like to express my deep gratitude to the editors of this volume, Professors Wendell C. Beane and William G. Doty. They have gone to a great deal of trouble in excerpting selections from various publications that have spanned the last forty years, and I believe that they have been enormously successful in choosing passages that effectively and honestly present my essential ideas on the interpretation of religious ideology, behavior, and institutions. It is their hope and mine that such a compilation will prove useful to students and others interested in problems relating to the field of History of Religions.

Over the years, I have had occasion to publish numerous books and articles in which I sought to address myself to a variety of different audiences—usually scholars or specialists in studies of religion, Orientalists, anthropologists, and so on—but also readers interested in such broader fields as history of culture or ideas, literary criticism, psychology, and the arts. As a result, the structure and style of my writing has often shifted in accord with the intended audience, and I am afraid that this has made it more difficult than it might have been for Messrs. Beane and Doty to select out of my *oeuvre* materials for a unified reader such as this one. Yet, I feel that they have done a marvelous job in this respect. I am delighted with their choice of texts, and their careful editing has made them uniformly accessible for the use of the nonspecialist.

This is of great importance to me, for I have always been of the opinion that the results of the investigations made by those who practice History of Religions as their trade are of real interest to the modern reader, and transcend the boundaries of narrow scholasticism. For, at a certain level, the study of the History of Religions is a continuous encounter with things that are "wholly other" to us as modern Westerners: other cultures, other times, other systems of speculation and reflection. Such an encounter with the foreign or bewildering has great potential for catalyzing creative experiences of all types, as the discovery of African art forms by European artists at the turn of this century has so clearly demonstrated. But the delimitation of this experience within a limited preserve that is open only to scholars is no less stultifying than the dismissal of all that is foreign as "primitive" or "nonsense." It is my fondest hope that the encounter with archaic, Oriental, and exotic cultures can serve to provoke thought and understanding, deepening our appreciation of man and his imagination—religious and otherwise—while provoking our own. It is this which I meant in earlier works when I spoke of History of Religions opening doors toward a "new humanism."[1]

My own experience of the creative possibilities contained within the "other" began with India, and I have since had occasion to make studies touching on numerous other areas as well: Siberia, Australia, the Ancient Near East, South America, and others. As a result, my writings have not always borne the mark of a systematic scheme of organization on a grand scale. Rather, I have pursued various questions as they aroused my interest, turning to new problems on the basis of their intrinsic fascination and not because they fit neatly into a preconceived niche. This approach has served to keep my discipline always fresh and exciting for me, but I am afraid that it may have caused problems for my readers at times, and for this reason I am again most grateful to Professors Doty and Beane. The organization that they have set up for the selections included in this book is an extremely useful one, bringing together passages that are thematically very close, but often chronologically distant within the unfolding of my work. In this way, they may well have served to make my thinking more accessible to the reader, and for this I am extremely grateful.

University of Chicago   MIRCEA ELIADE
June 1975

1. See "History of Religions and a New Humanism," in *History of Religions* 1, no. 1 (Summer 1961), pp. 1–8, reprinted in *The Quest* (Chicago, 1969).

On Using These Volumes

WILLIAM G. DOTY

The origins of these volumes date back to several years ago when I told my new colleague, Wendell Beane, about my frustration in wanting to use more of Eliade's writings in my courses, but finding it almost impossible to select only one or two volumes from the sixteen or so Eliade had written. And when several volumes were used, students found themselves reading duplicate accounts of some materials—since Professor Eliade has often provided in a second book a résumé of an earlier work. Dr. Beane, even though he was a student of Mircea Eliade, could not be enticed into compiling the anthology I thought most helpful; eventually, however, we did agree to become collaborators, and have produced this book. We have jointly shared responsibility for making selections, writing continuity-material, and the completing of many hours of tedious checking, seeking permissions, and the like that are required by such a composite product.

We have not tried to replace the writings available (for the most part in inexpensive paperback translations), but rather to bring together in one volume many of the observations and insights Professor Eliade makes in the approximately 5,000 pages of his writings in English. For the beginning student, especially, we felt the need of a volume that would concentrate upon the "essential" Eliade, highlighting a wide range of his observations rather than arguing a particular method or series of results.

In each section we indicate in our footnotes further or parallel readings in the Eliade corpus, and of course the interested reader can find further elaboration by tracking down the context in the original volume from which a specific quotation is taken. The standard bibliography of books and essays by Professor Eliade (in Romanian, French, English, German, and nine other languages) is in J. M. Kitagawa and Charles H. Long, eds., *Myths and Symbols: Studies in*

Honor of Mircea Eliade.[1] At his suggestion, our selections are almost exclusively from his books, since his articles are usually reworked into volumes published sometime after the articles appear.

Before mentioning something about Eliade's context in the study of religions, there are conventions used in this book which the reader should have in mind:

1. Abbreviations follow the list of "Abbreviations and Acknowledgements" at the front of this volume. In footnotes, source notes, and text references abbreviations are separated from page numbers with a slash. For example, *SP*/15, refers to *The Sacred and the Profane: The Nature of Religion*, p. 15.

2. Footnotes in the text by the editors rather than by Professor Eliade are indicated by "Eds."

3. We have standardized spellings of technical terms in the history of religions, and have used this spelling throughout, rather than following the varying conventions in Eliade's many books; *The Two and the One* provided the model for most Sanskrit terms.

4. We have omitted most of the technical footnotes from the original publications, especially the extensive bibliographic materials given by Professor Eliade and cross-references to his own works, and we have reduced many footnotes in size, retaining only necessary references, as when a source or translation is cited in the text (interested readers will be able to pursue bibliographic references and comments in the original publications, but we did not have space for repeating this rich store of resources in this volume; see selection 145 for an example of the extent of cutting necessary).

5. The source of each selection is indicated at the bottom of the first page on which a selection begins.

6. Standard elipsis marks (. . .) or asterisks (***) indicate places where we have omitted materials from the original published versions; materials in brackets [   ] provide our own emendations; and the subtitles in this volume are a mixture of our own work and Eliade's original subtitles.

7. Throughout these two volumes, the design element of a solid black diamond is employed to introduce new sections prefaced by

1. (Chicago, 1969), pp. 415–33.

editorial commentary: two diamonds (◆ ◆) indicate the beginning of a main division; one diamond (◆) indicates a subdivision. Italic text that directly follows a selection title indicates editorial comment.

Professor Eliade met with the two editors in Chicago in October 1973, and has responded a number of times to queries about policies and details; before the work went to the publisher, he reviewed the entire manuscript and made critical suggestions. For his continued encouragement and assistance the editors are extremely grateful and sympathetic as well, for it must have been painful to see his writings cut up and pieced together into this totally new format.

We hope the book will provide a readable introduction for the individual reader as well as providing convenient access to Eliade's thought for classroom work. We know of interest in Eliade's studies that range from scholarly works in the history of religions, anthropology and literature departments, to communes that have sought guidance for their communal living in his analyses of earlier societies. Our hope, therefore, is that this volume will encourage further attention to this scholar's works, and that persons who disagree with something in a selection will frown at us and go to the original sources to see if the selection adequately represents Eliade's own work before frowning at him as well!

Thanks are due to our families, our students, and to the several persons who have assisted with the actual day-to-day mechanics of producing this volume: they have all shown marvelous patience, and have given us the needed encouragement and help to see it through.

Understanding Mircea Eliade
as Historian of Religions

WENDELL C. BEANE

It is not easy to introduce someone whose writings have concerned themselves with such a wide spectrum of human religiosity as Mircea Eliade. The threefold division of this book ("Myths," "Rites," and "Symbols") by no means reflects the complete picture;[1] thus we have thought to include some inferential remarks on his method of reflecting on the meaning of religious data. Nonetheless, the foregoing threefold division is chosen by us because these terms, simply, are the substance of any religious world view, whether it take the form of an intensely rationalized but unsystematic array of cultural traditions, or else a critically ratiocinated and systematized theology of culture. What we shall attempt to do here is merely to suggest some contours of contacts with other exemplary scholars of religion and culture whose thoughts may be taken as models of field perspectives and thereby to highlight some of the working principles of Eliade's own approach.

It should be recognized at once that it is hard to avoid a certain relativity of scholarly portraiture and inference regarding method, especially when it comes to intellectual giants. There is, then, some basis for saying that there is no universally recognized authority on the thought of Mircea Eliade. At any rate, for the student who wants to become more acquainted with Eliade's thought and works, it would be helpful to consider the following items.

First of all, Mircea Eliade, though aware of the fact that humankind has "evolved" in one way or another as cultural beings, is not

---

1. See, for example, discussions on Eliade, the novelist, in J. M. Kitagawa and Charles H. Long, eds., *Myths and Symbols: Studies in Honor of Mircea Eliade* (Chicago, 1969), pp. 327–414.

himself an "evolutionist" scholar in the sense of J. G. Frazer (*The Golden Bough*, 1890), E. B. Tylor (*Primitive Culture*, 1871), or R. Marett (*The Threshold of Religion*, 1909); nor is he a "degeneration-ist" (= supporting an original monotheism that later becomes poly-theism, ancestor worship, spiritism, etc.) in the sense of Andrew Lang (*The Making of Religion*, 1898), or Pater Wilhelm Schmidt (*Der Ursprung der Gottesidee*, 1912–15).[2] Rather, an idea which underlies the superabundance of sacred phenomena Eliade includes in his works is that the ancient world is characterized by a "multiplicity of hiero-phanies"; that is to say, many of the religious ideas and forms which have tended to become the subjects of scholarly debate in the quest to achieve the final generalization in the study of religion's origins, Eliade believes, *coexisted* (though not in every time and place) as parts of the primitive ethos or world-orientation. Hence (types of) monotheism: male- or female-symbol dominated; polytheism, ances-tor worship, animism, etc., might all be symbolizations of the amaz-ing varieties of religious experience characterizing humankind's sa-cred past. The significance of this guideline should be an important consideration to both the introductory and the advanced reader, in light of the comments by Eliade's critics that his works ignore the factor of sociocultural stratification; that is, the questionableness of placing (so-called) "primitive" and "high culture" religious phe-nomena in juxtaposition, or raising particular elements out of their peculiar context to the level of becoming mere "snippets of ethnog-raphy."[3] As our Reader will show, however, Eliade's own conten-tion is that "nothing can take the place of the example, the concrete fact" (*SP*/15); therefore, the student will find much to ponder as he or she finds among the reading selections an emphasis upon symbols that Eliade believes can allow persons of different cultural back-ground "to intercommunicate."

Second, Eliade's use of the phrase "the Sacred and the Profane" requires an important announcement concerning their *relation*: that they are not rigidly antithetical descriptions of the primitive and

2. For Schmidt, students might better profit from a reading of Wilhelm Schmidt, *The Origin and Growth of Religion: Facts and Theories*, trans. H. J. Rose (New York, 1931).

3. See, e.g., Thomas J. J. Altizer, *The Sacred and the Profane: Mircea Eliade and the Dialectic of the Sacred* (Philadelphia, 1963), p. 42 and *passim*. Also see Edmund Leach, "Man on a Ladder," *The New York Review of Books*, October 20, 1966, pp. 28–31.

modern worlds as religious environments. While it may be accurate to say that of the two worlds the "primitive" lends himself more appropriately to the occasion of being a model of the pan-sacralized mentality, this does not mean that the modern world knows nothing of sacred things. In fact, our author would have us know that both primitive *and* modern religious beings know the Sacred but the Profane as well. Hence the title: "The Sacred *and* the Profane," not "the Sacred *versus* the Profane." However, it is the "modern" human being that presents himself as more appropriately the model of the desacralized mentality. In between these two extremes, therefore, there is Eliade's discernment of the essential relation between a primitive rite of annual community- or world-renewal rooted in Primordial Time and a modern liturgical rehearsal of a redemptive revelation rooted in Historical Time. What these two *sacred worlds* have in common, then, despite their limitations as cultural situations in the profane sense, is that the participants in these sacred worlds both insist upon understanding their frames of reference and their centers of gravity as rooted in a transcendental reality: the Sacred, the Holy, the Religious. In a word, it is this Reality which enables them to live *in* history and time with a genuine sense of being *beyond* time and history.

Finally, there is Eliade's attitude toward the problem of the *interpretation* of religion in the face of what seems to be an utterly unmanageable maze of data in the form of myths, rites, and symbols. Here are three specific and useful directives that we can detect in Eliade's works as his way of interpreting a vast array of sacred phenomena:

1. The need to recognize, on the basis of cumulative investigations by scholars from various disciplines, that sacred words and things always point beyond themselves to what Eliade calls "a meta-empirical reality and purpose" (i.e., they are material means to *spiritual* ends).

2. The need to adopt an attitude of radical displacement of one's personal biases concerning what "ought" to be thought, said, and done by other religious peoples, in order to begin not only to understand *how* religious symbols relate to their historical environment, but also *what* such symbols *intend* as sacred realities worth discovering again and again.

3. The need to compare and integrate the elements of religious traditions as a means of arriving at even tentative generalizations about humankind's religious ways of being in the world, which may lead us to understand anew the essential relation between the *human* and the religious.

As an historian of religions Eliade, to be sure, does not stand in complete opposition to all that has gone before him, either in the area of comparative religion or, for that matter, other fields of inquiry such as anthropology. In a broad sense, it were better to say that his way of doing things is distinctively a matter of *emphasis* rather than discontinuity with other students of religion and culture.

For example, Bronislaw Malinowski (d. 1942) is still recalled today as the chief pioneer and advocate of a *pragmatic* approach to the intentionality of myth as a religious form. His definition of myth, again, is classical in religious field studies and defies improvement by any scholar. Indeed, Eliade himself shows admiration for that scholar's remarkable achievement in this regard by citing Malinowski's definition. (*MR*/19 f.). Malinowski himself, of course, was an advocate of firm ethnographic principles, such as being scientific-minded and knowing field values, showing fellow-feeling and a willingness to "live in" among the subjects (= beings) of one's interest, and knowing how to gather, control, and classify one's overall data.

Malinowski, however, had a vital interest in the economic dynamics of the primitive social world, and this influenced him decisively when it came to his comprehension of the relation, for instance, between primitive magic, science, and religion.[4] Following and, in a real sense, succeeding his original inspiration (i.e., Frazer's *The Golden Bough*), he saw primitive man as a practical being who resorted to magical rites only when his everyday "scientific" know-how proved to be an ineffective mode of activity. The primary value in Malinowski's work, nonetheless, was a "functional" one, which placed more emphasis on the role of myth as a socioeconomic reality than *a religious reality in itself*.

Claude Lévi-Strauss, on the other hand, having also lent himself to solid traditional ethnographic principles, has recently appeared to have by-passed the foregoing functionalist vogue and has developed

---

4. See Bronislaw Malinowski, *Magic, Science and Religion, and Other Essays* (New York, 1948).

what Edmund Leach refers to as "a revised form of 'symbolist' analysis that he calls structural." Lévi-Strauss's distinctive lesson for us as an attitude toward the study of myth, however, comes in the form of his understanding of myth not as a "disease of language" but as a religious-cultural art form. It is this nature of myth as such which permits us to uncover its own inherent genius and to understand it as a well thought out structural reality; although this perspective demands a detailed study of the words, images, and symbols of myth. When this is done, even apart from their distinct historical or social setting, the discovery can be made that these myths are ardent and deliberate attempts to overcome the contradictions that human beings find both in nature and society—indeed in themselves. Through a series of symbols which form complex interrelations in the mythic structure the aim is at bottom the resolution of life's anomalies and the transformation of natural disorder into culturally understandable values. Here we include but move ultimately beyond Malinowski's sheer pragmatic approach to an emphasis upon the rational, humanistic, and, even, existentialist concerns of "les sauvages"; but, moreover, we have an understanding that, despite the *recurrent usefulness of myth-telling*, the key to the meaning of myth as a religious form lies in its *linguistic* structure.[5]

Mircea Eliade, as historian of religions, brings us a view of myth which engulfs the pragmatism of Malinowski and the symbolic linguistics of Lévi-Strauss, though we must be careful not to infer that they have had any direct influence upon him as an historian of religions. On the one hand, Eliade entertains the notion of the "ambivalence of the sacred," which is an ongoing recognition of the practical reality (= concreteness) of an object that has become a sacred symbol (e.g., a stone or tree *remains* what it is even while becoming something "*wholly other*"). On the other hand, Eliade understands the existentialist function of myth as an art form, which is both an act of creative thought and an effort to make a "world" out of often chaotic natural reality. Yet Eliade's distinctive approach as historian of religions is best understood when we notice the pervasive attention that he gives to the element of religious experience in both myth and ritual as symbolic realities. He thus calls our attention to some-

5. See Claude Lévi-Strauss, *Structural Anthropology*, trans. C. Jacobsen and B. G. Schoepp (New York, 1963), Ch. XI, "The Structural Study of Myth."

thing in the life of primitive peoples that is critically important beyond the anthropological confirmation that they are indeed human beings with the art of common sense and a remarkable inclination toward myth-making. Eliade, in sum, insists that behind and beyond the linguistic structure and pragmatic function of myth lies the conception, gestation, and birth of myth *out of the depths of a genuine religious experience*. It is ultimately this element of religious experience of the Sacred which is the true source of its structure, practicality, and repeatability. In the final analysis myth is a "living" testimony not only to its capacity to be ritually reenacted as a presentation of sacred human convictions; but, also, in terms of method, it points to the necessity of leaving room for the interpretation of the *transcendental milieu of myth* as uniquely the essence of religion.

◆ ◆

Technicians of the Sacred

As Eliade notes in selection 109, not every religious person obtains to the heights of religious experience. But there are specialists who do, whether healers, medicine men, priests, or shamans. We focus here on the specialist in terms of ritual and group performances, especially emphasizing the medicine man and the shaman. Eliade's *Shamanism: Archaic Techniques of Ecstacy* is a respected classic in the technical literature. (The next section of the book turns then from the group leader to the individual technician, i.e., to the individual participant in the religious mysteries.)

◆

Prestige and Power of the Sacred Specialist

"How does someone become a medicine man?"—this question seems especially relevant in our culture, where physicians are trained in the same mechanistic ways as are electrical engineers or mathematicians. The medicine men and shamans we learn about in these extracts, however, receive a very clear "calling," whether from the depths of their own experience, or as encouraged by older medicine men and shamans. Some of the functions of these specialists are described: they are not just medical healers, but also the "intellectuals" of the community. And since the shaman is the one "who conducts the dead person's soul to the underworld, . . . he is the psychopomp (spirit guide) par excellence."[1]

109. AUSTRALIAN MEDICINE MEN

Provided he pursues his religious instruction, every male hopes to learn, in his old age, the sacred history of the tribe. This ultimately means re-establishing contact with the actors of a sacred history and, consequently, partaking of their creative powers. But, as everywhere else in the world, so is it in Australia that man's relations with the sphere of the sacred are not uniform. There are always some exceptionally gifted individuals longing, or destined, to

Source: *AR*/128–31.
1. *S*/182.

become "religious specialists." These medicine men, doctors, shamans, or, as Elkin aptly calls them, "men of high degree," play a central role in the life of the tribe.[1] They cure the sick, defend the community against black magic, discover those responsible for premature deaths, and perform important functions in the initiation ceremonies.

But the most specific characteristic of the medicine man is his relation with the Supernatural Beings and the other heroes of the tribe's sacred history. He is the only one who is *really* able to recover the glorious conditions of the mythical Ancestors, the only one who can do what the Ancestors did, for instance, fly through the air, ascend to heaven, travel underground, disappear and reappear. Moreover, only the medicine man can encounter the Supernatural Beings and converse with them, and only he can see the spirits and the ghosts of the dead. In sum, only the medicine man succeeds in surpassing his human condition, and consequently he is able to behave like the spiritual beings, or, in other words, to partake of the modality of a Spiritual Being.

As in so many other parts of the world, the medicine man in Australia is not the product of a spontaneous creation; he is "made," either by Supernatural Beings or by the medicine men of his tribe. One becomes a medicine man by inheriting the profession, by "call" or election, or by personal quest. But whatever way he has taken, a postulant is not recognized as a medicine man until he has been accepted by a certain number of "men of high degree" and been taught by some of them, and, above all, until he has undergone a more or less spectacular initiation. In most cases the initiation consists of an ecstatic experience, during which the candidate meets Supernatural Beings, undergoes certain operations, and undertakes ascents to heaven and descents to the subterranean world.

All these ecstatic experiences, as well as the scenarios of the "quest," follow traditional patterns. For instance, the aspirant to the profession goes to sleep in isolated places, especially near the grave of a medicine man, and he is expected to have visions or even initiatory revelations similar to those of all the "elected." The basic experience is an inspired vision, during which the future medicine man encounters the Supernatural Being who will bestow upon

1. *Aboriginal Men of High Degree* (Sydney, 1945).

him the sacred powers. The meeting is always dramatic, even in cases where (as among the southeastern tribes) the "making" does not include a ritual "killing" of the postulant (although still, even in such cases, the transmutation of the postulant's mode of being— from a human state to a "spiritual" one—implies, as we shall presently see, a "death" followed by a resurrection). The Supernatural Beings, or their representatives, radically change the bodily condition of the aspirant (by inserting sacred substances, etc.), and at the same time teach him how to bear himself as a "spirit" (how to fly, etc.). Among the tribes where the "making" comprises a ritual killing, the Supernatural Beings or their representatives perform certain operations on the lifeless body of the candidate; they remove the insides and substitute new ones, inserting also sacred substances, quartz or pearl-shells. Whatever the nature of the ecstatic experience, the aspirant comes back to life as another person: he has seen the Supernatural Beings face to face and been "made" and taught by them. What remains to be learned from the old masters is now of a more or less technical nature. His mystical initiation introduced him to a spiritual universe which henceforth will be his *real* world.

110. INITIATION OF A WIRADJURI MEDICINE MAN

Ultimately, the three ways of becoming a medicine man—(1) inheriting the profession, (2) "call" or election, (3) personal "quest" —result in a specific experience, without which a change in the novice's mode of being would not take place. This can be clearly seen in the process of initiation. Where the profession is inherited, the father carefully prepares his son before provoking the rapture which will transform his life. Howitt reports a characteristic example of a Wiradjuri medicine man who had been initiated by his father. When he was still a young boy, his father took him into the bush and placed two large quartz crystals against his breast. They vanished into his body, and he felt them going through him "like warmth." The old man also gave him "some things like quartz crystals in water. They looked like ice and the water tasted sweet."

SOURCE: *AR*/131–33.

After that, the boy could see ghosts. When he was about ten years old, after having his tooth out in the age-grading ceremony, his father showed him a piece of quartz crystal in his hand, "and when I looked at it he [his father] went down into the ground and I saw him come up all covered with red dust. It made me very frightened." The father asked him to try to produce a piece of crystal, and the boy brought one up (probably from his own body).

Then the father led his son through a hole in the ground to a grave. Going inside, the boy saw a dead man who rubbed him all over to make him "clever"; the dead man also gave him some crystals. When the father and son came out, the father pointed to a tiger snake and told the boy that it was his secret totem (*budjan*) and that from then on it would also be his son's. "There was a string tied to the tail of the snake, and extending to us." It was one of the strings which the medicine men draw out of themselves, of which more will be said later. The father took hold of the string, saying, "Let us follow him." The snake went through several tree trunks, and finally to a tree with a great swelling around its roots. There the snake went down into the ground, and they followed it coming up inside the tree, which was hollow.

After they came out from the tree, the snake took them into a great hole in the ground. Here there were many snakes which rubbed themselves against the boy to make him a "clever man." The father then said:

We will go up to Baiame's camp. He got astride of a Mauir (thread) and put me on another, and we held by each other's arms. At the end of the thread was Wombu, the bird of Baiame. We went through the clouds, and on the other side was the sky. We went through the place where the Doctors go through, and it kept opening and shutting very quickly. My father said that, if it touched a Doctor when he was going through, it would hurt his spirit, and when he returned home he would sicken and die. On the other side we saw Baiame sitting in his camp. He was a very great old man with a long beard. He sat with his legs under him and from his shoulders extended two great quartz crystals to the sky above him. There were also numbers of the boys of Baiame and of his people, who are birds and beasts.[1]

1. A. W. Howitt, *The Native Tribes of South-East Australia* (London, 1904), pp. 406–8.

In sum, the physical transformation of the novice begins with his assimilation of quartz crystals. After taking some of these crystals into his body, the boy can see the "spirits," invisible to noninitiates, and can travel underground. The dead man in the grave, who probably was a former medicine man, likewise gave him quartz crystals, and also rubbed against his body, as the snakes did later in order to infuse him with their powers. The initiation was completed by an ascension to heaven, where the boy and his father saw Baiame with two great quartz crystals extending from his shoulders. We shall repeatedly encounter these motifs, and their meanings will become clearer as we proceed with the description of different types of initiation. . . .

111. MEDICINE MAN AS INTERMEDIARY

Thanks to his "transmutation," the medicine man lives simultaneously in two worlds: in his actual tribal world and in the sacred world of the beginning, when the Primordial Beings were present and active on earth. For this reason the medicine man constitutes the intermediary par excellence between his tribe and the Heroes of his tribe's mythical history. More and better than other members of the tribe, he can reactivate the contact with the Dreaming Time and thus renew his world. And because he can reintegrate at will the fabulous epoch of the beginnings, he can "dream" new myths and rituals. Such new creations are eventually introduced into the religious tradition of the tribe, but without bearing the mark of personal innovation, for they belong to the same primordial, eternal source of the Dreaming Time.

All the public functions and duties of the medicine man are justified by his singular existential condition. He can cure the sick because he can see the magical objects that caused a sickness, and he can eliminate or annihilate them. He can be a rainmaker because he is able to go to heaven or summon the clouds. And when he defends his tribe against magical aggression, the medicine man acts as a black magician: no one can use the "pointing bone" better than he

SOURCE: *AR*/157–58.

or surpass him in "singing" a deadly poison into a victim. His social prestige, his cultural role, and his political supremacy derive ultimately from his magico-religious "power." Among the Wiradjuri it was believed that a very powerful doctor was capable even of reviving a dead man. Summarizing the role of the Wiradjuri medicine man, Berndt emphasizes his "deep knowledge of all tribal matters, particularly those relating to the traditional and religious life." He was par excellence the "intellectual" of the tribe, and at the same time a man of great social prestige. "It was possible for him to assume the chief headmanship and to play a leading part in the totemic ceremonial life; in this way he could become both temporal and spiritual leader of the group."[1]

◆

THE SHAMAN AS SPECIALIST PAR EXCELLENCE

After a definition of the shaman (selection 112) with which Eliade introduces the primary texts on shamanism in his massive source-book, *From Primitives to Zen: A Thematic Sourcebook on the History of Religions* (recently re-issued in four paperback parts by Harper & Row, Publishers, Inc.), we present extracts discussing the initiation of the shaman and the question of his psychological health (selections 113–15). Other extracts then focus upon the general significance of the shaman as an ecstatic being (selection 116), and the wider connections of shamanism in various cultures and in the life of the religious community (selections 117–81).

112. SHAMANS AND MEDICINE MEN

Shamanism is a religious phenomenon characteristic of Siberian and Ural-Altaic peoples. The word "shaman" is of Tungus origin (*saman*) and it has passed, by way of Russian, into European scientific terminology. But shamanism, although its most complete expression is found in the Arctic and central Asian regions, must

SOURCE: FPZ/423–24.
1. Ronald A. Berndt, "Wuradjeri Magic and 'Clever Men,'" Part I, *Oceania* 17 (1946–47): 332.

not be considered as limited to those countries. It is encountered, for example, in southeast Asia, Oceania, and among many North American aboriginal tribes. A distinction is to be made, however, between the religions dominated by a shamanistic ideology and by shamanistic techniques (as is the case with Siberian and Indonesian religions) and those in which shamanism constitutes rather a secondary phenomenon.

The shaman is medicine man, priest, and psychopompos; that is to say, he cures sickness, he directs the communal sacrifices, and he escorts the souls of the dead to the other world. He is able to do all this by virtue of his techniques of ecstasy, i.e., by his power to leave his body at will. In Siberia and in northeast Asia a person becomes a shaman by hereditary transmission of the shamanistic profession or by spontaneous vocation or "election." More rarely a person can become a shaman by his own decision or upon request of the clan, but the self-made shamans are regarded as weaker than those who inherit the profession or who are "elected" by the supernatural beings. In North America, on the other hand, the voluntary "quest" for the powers constitutes the principal method. No matter how the selection takes place, a shaman is recognized as such only following a series of initiatory trials after receiving instruction from qualified masters.

In North and Central Asia as a rule the trials take place during an indefinite period of time during which the future shaman is sick and stays in his tent or wanders in the wilderness, behaving in such an eccentric way that it could be mistaken for madness. Several authors went so far as to explain Arctic and Siberian shamanism as the ritualized expression of a psychomental disease, especially of Arctic hysteria. But the "chosen" one becomes a shaman only if he can interpret his pathological crisis as a religious experience and succeeds in curing himself. The serious crises that sometimes accompany the "election" of the future shaman are to be regarded as initiatory trials. Every initiation involves the symbolic death and resurrection of the neophyte. In the dreams and hallucinations of the future shaman may be found the classical pattern of the initiation: he is tortured by demons, his body is cut in pieces, he descends to the nether world or ascends to heaven and is finally resuscitated. That is to say, he acquires a new mode of being, which allows him to have relations with the supernatural worlds. The shaman is now enabled to "see" the spirits, and he himself behaves like a spirit; he is able to leave his body and to travel in ecstasy in all cosmic regions. However, the ecstatic experience alone is not sufficient to make a shaman. The neophyte must be instructed by masters in the religious traditions of the tribe, and he is taught to recognize the various diseases and to cure them.

Among certain Siberian peoples the consecration of the shaman is a public event. Among the Buriats, for example, the neophyte climbs a birch, a symbol of the world tree, and in doing this he is thought to ascend to heaven. The ascension to heaven is one of the specific characteristics of Siberian and central Asian shamanism. At the occasion of the horse sacrifice, the Altaic shaman ascends to heaven in ecstasy in order to offer to the celestial god the soul of the sacrificed horse. He realizes this ascension by climbing the birch trunk, which has nine notches, each symbolizing a specific heaven.

The most important function of the shaman is *healing*. Since sickness is thought of as a loss of the soul, the shaman has to find out first whether the soul of the sick man has strayed far from the village or has been stolen by demons and is imprisoned in the other world. In the former case the healing is not too difficult: the shaman captures the soul and reintegrates it in the body of the sick person. In the latter case he has to descend to the nether world, and this is a complicated and dangerous enterprise. Equally stirring is the voyage of the shaman to the other world to escort the soul of the deceased to its new abode; the shaman narrates to those present all the vicissitudes of the voyage as it takes place.

113. SHAMANIC INITIATIONS

We now come to shamanic initiations. . . .

It is primarily with the syndrome of the shaman's mystical vocation that we are concerned. In Siberia, the youth who is called to be a shaman attracts attention by his strange behavior; for example, he seeks solitude, becomes absent-minded, loves to roam in the woods or unfrequented places, has visions, and sings in his sleep.

SOURCE: *RSI*/87–89.

In some instances this period of incubation is marked by quite serious symptoms; among the Yakut, the young man sometimes has fits of fury and easily loses consciousness, hides in the forest, feeds on the bark of trees, throws himself into water and fire, cuts himself with knives. The future shamans among the Tungus, as they approach maturity, go through a hysterical or hysteroid crisis, but sometimes their vocation manifests itself at an earlier age—the boy runs away into the mountains and remains there for a week or more, feeding on animals, which he tears to pieces with his teeth. He returns to the village, filthy, bloodstained, his clothes torn and his hair disordered, and it is only after ten or more days have passed that he begins to babble incoherent words.

Even in the case of hereditary shamanism, the future shaman's election is preceded by a change in behavior. The souls of the shaman ancestors of a family choose a young man among their descendants; he becomes absent-minded and moody, delights in solitude, has prophetic visions, and sometimes undergoes attacks that make him unconscious. During these times, the Buriat believe, the young man's soul is carried away by spirits; received in the palace of the gods, it is instructed by his shaman ancestors in the secrets of the profession, the forms and names of the Gods, the worship and names of the spirits. It is only after this first initiation that the youth's soul returns and resumes control of his body.[1]

A man may also become a shaman following an accident or a highly unusual event—for example, among the Buriat, the Soyot, the Eskimos, after being struck by lightning, or falling from a high tree, or successfully undergoing an ordeal that can be homologized with an initiatory ordeal, as in the case of an Eskimo who spent five days in icy water without his clothes becoming wet. . . .[2]

. . . If shamanism cannot simply be identified with a psychopathological phenomenon, it is nevertheless true that the shamanic vocation often implies a crisis so deep that it sometimes borders on madness. And since the youth cannot become a shaman until he has resolved this crisis, it is clear that it plays the role of a *mystical initiation*. The disorder provoked in the future shaman by the agonizing news that he has been chosen by the gods or the spirits is by that very fact valuated as an initiatory sickness. The precariousness

1. Cf. *S*/18–20. Eds.
2. On the theme of such "magical heat," see also selections 77–79. Eds.

of life, the solitude and the suffering, that are revealed by any sickness are, in this particular case, aggravated by the symbolism of initiatory death; for accepting the supernatural election finds expression in the feeling that one has delivered oneself over to the divine or demonic powers, hence that one is destined to imminent death. We may give all these psychopathological crises of the elected the generic name of initiatory sicknesses because their syndrome very closely follows the classic ritual of initiation. The sufferings of the elected man are exactly like the tortures of initiation; just as, in puberty rites or rites for entrance into a secret society, the novice is "killed" by semidivine or demonic Beings, so the future shaman sees in dreams his own body dismembered by demons; he watches them, for example, cutting off his head and tearing out his tongue. The initiatory rituals peculiar to Siberian and central Asian shamanism include a symbolic ascent to Heaven up a tree or pole; in dream or a series of waking dreams, the sick man chosen by the Gods or spirits undertakes his celestial journey to the World Tree. . . .

I should like even now to stress the fact that the psychopathology of the shamanic vocation is not profane; it does not belong to ordinary symptomatology. *It has an initiatory structure and signification*; in short, it reproduces a traditional mystical pattern. The total crisis of the future shaman, sometimes leading to complete disintegration of the personality and to madness, can be valuated not only as an initiatory death but also as a symbolic return to the precosmogonic Chaos, to the amorphous and indescribable state that precedes any cosmogony. Now, as we know, for archaic and traditional cultures, a symbolic return to Chaos is equivalent to preparing a new Creation. It follows that we may interpret the psychic Chaos of the future shaman as a sign that the profane man is being "dissolved" and a new personality being prepared for birth.

114. INITIATORY ORDEALS OF SIBERIAN SHAMANS

Let us now find out what Siberian shamans themselves have to tell about the ordeals that they undergo during their initiatory sicknesses. They all maintain that they "die" and lie inanimate for from

SOURCE: *RSI*/90–93.

three to seven days in their yurt or in a solitary place. During this time, they are cut up by demons or by their ancestral spirits; their bones are cleaned, the flesh scraped off, the body fluids thrown away, and the eyes torn from their sockets. According to a Yakut informant, the spirits carry the future shaman to Hell and shut him in a house for three years. Here he undergoes his initiation; the spirits cut off his head (which they set to one side, for the novice must watch his own dismemberment with his own eyes) and hack his body to bits, which are later distributed among the spirits of various sicknesses. It is only on this condition that the future shaman will obtain the power of healing. His bones are then covered with new flesh, and in some cases he is also given new blood. According to another Yakut informant, black "devils" cut up the future shaman's body and throw the pieces in different directions as offerings, then thrust a lance into his head and cut off his jawbone. A Samoyed shaman told Lehtisalo that the spirits attacked him and hacked him to pieces, also cutting off his hands. For seven days and nights he lay unconscious on the ground, while his soul was in Heaven. From a long and eventful autobiography that an Avam-Samoyed shaman confided to A. A. Popov, I will select a few significant episodes. Striken with smallpox, the future shaman remained unconscious for three days, so nearly dead that on the third day he was almost buried. He saw himself go down to Hell, and, after many adventures, was carried to an island, in the middle of which stood a young birch tree which reached up to Heaven. It was the Tree of the Lord of the Earth, and the Lord gave him a branch of it to make himself a drum. Next he came to a mountain. Passing through an opening, he met a naked man plying the bellows at an immense fire on which was a kettle. The man caught him with a hook, cut off his head, and chopped his body to bits and put them all into the kettle. There he boiled the body for three years, and then forged him a head on an anvil. Finally he fished out the bones, which were floating in a river, put them together, and covered them with flesh. During his adventures in the Other World, the future shaman met several semidivine personages, in human or animal form, and each of them revealed doctrines to him or taught him secrets of the healing art. When he awoke in his yurt, among his relatives, he was initiated and could begin to shamanize.

A Tungus shaman relates that, during his initiatory sickness, his shaman ancestors pierced him with arrows until he lost consciousness and fell to the ground; then they cut off his flesh, drew out his bones, and counted them before him; if one had been missing, he could not have become a shaman. According to the Buriat the candidate is tortured by his shaman ancestors, who strike him, cut up his body with a knife, and cook his flesh. A Teleut woman became a shamaness after having a vision in which unknown men cut her body to pieces and boiled it in a pot. According to the traditions of the Altaic shamans, their ancestral spirits open their bellies, eat their flesh, and drink their blood. . . .

* * *

One of the specific characteristics of shamanic initiations, aside from the candidate's dismemberment, is his reduction to the state of a skeleton. We find this motif not only in the accounts of the crises and sicknesses of those who have been chosen by the spirits to become shamans but also in the experiences of those who have acquired their shamanic powers through their own efforts, after a long and arduous quest. Thus, for example, among the Ammasilik Eskimos, the apprentice spends long hours in his snow hut, meditating. At a certain moment, he falls "dead," and remains lifeless for three days and nights; during this period an enormous polar bear devours all his flesh and reduces him to a skeleton. It is only after this mystical experience that the apprentice receives the gift of shamanizing. The *angakuts* of the Iglulik Eskimos are able in thought to strip their bodies of flesh and blood and to contemplate their own skeletons for long periods. I may add that visualizing one's own death at the hands of demons and final reduction to the state of a skeleton are favorite meditations in Indo-Tibetan and Mongolian Buddhism. Finally, we may note that the skeleton is quite often represented on the Siberian shaman's costume.[1]

We are here in the presence of a very ancient religious idea, which belongs to the hunter culture. Bone symbolizes the final root of animal life, the mold from which the flesh continually arises. It is from the bone that men and animals are reborn; for a time, they maintain themselves in an existence of the flesh; then they die, and their "life" is reduced to the essence concentrated in the skele-

1. See selection 71, "Contemplating One's Own Skeleton." Eds.

ton, from which they will be born again. Reduced to skeletons, the future shamans undergo the mystical death that enables them to return to the inexhaustible fount of cosmic life. They are not born again; they are "revivified"; that is, the skeleton is brought back to life by being given new flesh. This is a religious idea that is wholly different from the conception of the tillers of the soil; these see the earth as the ultimate source of life, hence they assimilate the human body to the seed that must be buried in the soil before it can germinate. For, as we saw, in the initiatory rituals of many agricultural peoples the neophytes are symbolically buried, or undergo reversion to the embryonic state in the womb of Mother Earth. The initiatory scenario of the Asiatic shamans does not involve a return to the earth (e.g., symbolic burial, being swallowed by a monster), but the annihilation of the flesh and hence the reduction of life to its ultimate and indestructible essence.

115. BURYAT INITIATION

The most complex initiation ceremony is that of the Buryat; thanks especially to Khangalov and to the "Manual" published by A. M. Pozdneyev and translated by J. Partanen, it is also the best known.[1] Even here, the real initiation takes place before the new shaman's public consecration. For many years after his first ecstatic experiences (dreams, visions, dialogues with the spirits, etc.) the apprentice prepares himself in solitude, taught by old masters and especially by the one who will be his initiator and who is called the "father shaman." During all this period he shamanizes, invokes the gods and spirits, learns the secrets of his profession. Among the Buryat, too, the "initiation" is rather a public demonstration of the candidate's mystical capacities, followed by his consecration by the master, than a real revelation of mysteries.

When the date for consecration has been determined, there is a purification ceremony, which theoretically should be repeated from

SOURCE: S/115–22.

1. N. N. Agapitov and M. N. Khangalov, "Materialy dlya izuchenia shamanstva v Sibirii. Shamanstvo u buryat Irkutskoi gubernii," pp. 46–52, tr. and summarized by L. Stieda, "Das Schamanenthum unter den Burjäten," Globus, 70:6 (1887): 250 ff.

three to nine times but which in practice is performed only twice. The "father shaman" and nine young men, called his "sons," fetch water from three springs and offer libations of *tarasun*[2] to the spring spirits. On the way back they pull up young birches and bring them to the house. The water is boiled and, to purify it, wild thyme, juniper, and pine bark are thrown into the pot; a few hairs cut from a he-goat's ear are also added. The animal is then killed and some drops of its blood are allowed to fall into the pot. The flesh is given to the women to prepare. After divining by means of a sheep's shoulder bone, the "father shaman" invokes the candidate's shaman ancestors and offers them wine and *tarasun*. Dipping a broom made of birch twigs into the pot, he touches the apprentice's bare back. The "shaman's sons" repeat this ritual gesture in turn, while the "father" says: "When a poor man has need of you, ask him for little and take what he gives you. Think of the poor, help them, and pray God to protect them from evil spirits and their powers. When a rich man summons you, do not ask him much for your services. If a rich man and a poor man summon you at the same time, go to the poor man and afterward to the rich man." The apprentice promises to obey the rules, and repeats the prayer recited by the master. After the ablution libations of *tarasun* are again offered to the guardian spirits, and the preparatory ceremony is finished. This purification by water is obligatory for shamans at least once a year, if not every month at the time of the new moon. In addition, the shaman purifies himself in the same fashion each time that he incurs contamination; if the contamination is especially grave, purification is also performed with blood.

Some time after the initiation the first consecration ceremony, *khärägä-khulkhä*, takes place, the whole community sharing the expense. The offerings are collected by the shaman and his assistants (the "sons"), who go in procession on horseback from village to village.[3] The offerings are usually kerchiefs and ribbons, rarely money. In addition, wooden cups, bells for the "horse-sticks," silk, wine, and other objects are bought. In the Balagansk district the

2. *Tarasun*: an intoxicating drink of the Buryats. Eds.
3. A similar collection of gifts among the Buryat is found in the complex of ideas that suggests that the shaman meets his celestial bride while in his initial ecstatic states: the gifts that are given and the communal celebration preceding the public initiation have mystical connotations; see *S*/75–76. Eds.

candidate, the "father shaman," and the nine "shaman's sons" retire to a tent and fast for nine days, subsisting on nothing but tea and boiled flour. A rope made of horsehair, with small animal pelts fastened to it, is stretched around the tent three times.

On the eve of the ceremony a sufficient number of strong, straight birches is cut by the shaman and his nine "sons." The cutting takes place in the forest where the inhabitants of the village are buried, and to appease the forest spirit offerings of sheep's flesh and *tarasun* are made. On the morning of the festival the trees are put in their places. First a stout birch tree is set up in the yurt, with its roots in the hearth and its top protruding through the smoke hole. This birch is called *udesi-burkhan*, "the guardian of the door" (or "porter god"), for it opens the entrance to the sky for the shaman. It remains in the tent permanently, as a mark to distinguish the shaman's dwelling.

The other birches are set up far from the yurt, in the place where the initiation ceremony is to be performed, and they are planted in a particular order: (1) a birch under which *tarasun* and other offerings are placed and to whose branches ribbons are tied (red and yellow in the case of a "black" shaman, white and blue in the case of a "white" shaman, and of four colors if the new shaman intends to serve all kinds of spirits, good and bad); (2) another birch, to which a bell and the hide of a sacrificed horse are fastened; (3) a third birch, stout and firmly set in the ground, on which the novice will have to climb. These three birches, usually taken up with their roots, are called "pillars" (*särgä*). Then follow: (4) nine birches, grouped in threes, tied together by a rope of white horsehair and with ribbons of various colors fastened to them in a particular order —white, blue, red, yellow (the colors perhaps signify the various levels of the sky); on these birches the hides of the nine animals to be sacrificed and various foods will be displayed; (5) nine stakes to which the animals to be sacrificed are tied; (6) large birches set in order, from which the bones of the sacrificed animals, wrapped in straw, will later be hung. The chief birch—the one inside the yurt—is connected with all the others outside by two ribbons, one red, the other blue; these symbolize the "rainbow," the road by which the shaman will reach the realm of the spirits, the sky.

When these various preparations are completed, the neophyte and the "shaman's sons," all dressed in white, proceed to consecrate the shamanic instruments: a sheep is sacrificed in honor of the Lord and Lady of the Horse-stick, and *tarasun* is offered. Sometimes the stick is daubed with blood from the sacrificed animal; thereupon the "horse-stick" takes on life and becomes a real horse.

This consecration of the shamanic instruments is followed by a long ceremony that consists in offering *tarasun* to the tutelary divinities—the western Khans and their nine sons—and the ancestors of the "father shaman," to the local spirits and the tutelary spirits of the new shaman, to a number of famous dead shamans, to the *burkhan* and other minor divinities. The "father shaman" again offers a prayer to the different gods and spirits, and the candidate repeats his words; according to certain traditions, the candidate holds a sword in his hand and, thus armed, climbs the birch that is set inside the yurt, reaches its top, and, emerging through the smoke hole, shouts to invoke the aid of the gods. During this time the persons and objects in the yurt are constantly purified. After this, four "sons of the shaman" carry the candidate out of the yurt on a felt carpet, singing.

Headed by the "father shaman" leading the candidate and the nine "sons," the whole group of relatives and spectators sets out in procession for the place where the row of birches has been set up. At a certain point, near a birch, the procession halts; a he-goat is sacrificed and the candidate, stripped to the waist, is anointed with blood on the head, eyes, and ears, while the other shamans drum. The nine "sons" dip their brooms in water, strike the candidate's bare back, and shamanize.

Then nine or more animals are sacrificed, and while the meat is being prepared, the ritual ascent into the sky takes place. The "father shaman" climbs a birch and makes nine notches at the top of it. He comes down and takes up his position on a carpet that his "sons" have brought to the foot of the birch. The candidate ascends in his turn, followed by the other shamans. As they climb, they all fall into ecstasy. Among the Buryat of Balagansk the candidate, seated on a felt carpet, is carried nine times around the birches; he climbs each of them and makes nine notches at their summits. While at the top of each birch he shamanizes; meanwhile, the "father shaman" shamanizes on the ground, walking around the trees. According to Potanin, the nine birches are planted close to one another and the candidate, who is being carried on the carpet, jumps down before the last of them, climbs it to the top, and repeats the same ritual for each of the nine trees, which, like the nine notches, symbolize the nine heavens.[4]

By this time the meat is ready and, after offerings are made to the gods (by throwing pieces into the fire and into the air), the banquet begins. The shaman and his "sons" then withdraw into the yurt, but the guests continue to feast for a long time. The bones of the animals are wrapped in straw and hung on the nine birches. . . .

. . . Even where an initiation of this type is not known, we find shamanic rituals of ascent into the sky that depend upon similar conceptions. This fundamental unity of Central and North Asian shamanism will appear when we study the technique of séances. The cosmological structure of all these shamanic rites will then be elucidated. It is, for example, clear that the birch symbolizes the Cosmic Tree or the Axis of the World, and that it is therefore conceived as occupying the Center of the World; by climbing it, the shaman undertakes an ecstatic journey to the Center. We have already come upon this important mythical motif in connection with initiatory dreams, and it will become even more obvious in relation to the séances of Altaic shamans and the symbolism of shamanic drums.[5]

In addition, we shall see that ascent by means of a tree or post plays an important part in other initiations of the shamanic type; it is to be regarded as one variation on the mythico-ritual theme of ascent to heaven (a theme that also includes "magical flight," the myth of the "chain of arrows," of the rope, the bridge, etc.). The same symbolism of ascent is attested by the rope (bridge) that connects the birches and is hung with ribbons of different colors (the strata of the rainbow, the different celestial regions). These mythical themes and rituals, although distinctive of the Siberian and Altaic religions, are not peculiar to these cultures exclusively, since their area of dissemination far exceeds Central and Northeast Asia. It is even questionable if a ritual so complex as the initiation of the Buryat shaman can be an independent creation. For, as Harva noted over a quarter of a century ago, the Buryat initiation is strangely reminiscent of certain ceremonies of the Mithraic mysteries. The

4. On the motif of "ascent," cf. selections 98–100. Eds.
5. On the cosmic tree, see selections 153, 91–92. Eds.

candidate, stripped to the waist, is purified by the blood of a goat, which is sometimes killed above his head; in some places he must even drink the blood of the sacrificed animal. This ceremony resembles the *taurobolion*, the chief rite in the Mithraic mysteries. And the same mysteries made use of a ladder (*klimax*) with seven rungs, each rung made of a different metal. . . .[6]

116. TECHNIQUES OF ECSTASY

The shaman or the medicine man can be defined as a specialist in the sacred, that is, an individual who participates in the sacred more completely, or more truly, than other men. Whether he is chosen by Superhuman Beings or himself seeks to draw their attention and obtain their favors, the shaman is an individual who succeeds in having mystical experiences. In the sphere of shamanism in the strict sense, the mystical experience is expressed in the shaman's trance, real or feigned. The shaman is pre-eminently an ecstatic. Now on the plane of primitive religions ecstasy signifies the soul's flight to Heaven, or its wanderings about the earth, or, finally, its decent to the subterranean world, among the dead. The shaman undertakes these ecstatic journeys for four reasons: first, to meet the God of Heaven face to face and bring him an offering from the community; second, to seek the soul of a sick man, which has supposedly wandered away from his body or been carried off by demons; third, to guide the soul of a dead man to its new abode; fourth, to add to his knowledge by frequenting higher beings.

But the body's abandonment by the soul during ecstasy is equivalent to a temporary death. The shaman is, therefore, the man who can die, and then return to life, many times. This accounts for the many ordeals and teachings required in every shamanic initiation. Through his initiation, the shaman learns not only the technique of dying and returning to life but also what he must do when his soul abandons his body—and, first of all, how to orient himself in the unknown regions which he enters during his ecstasy. He learns to explore the new planes of existence disclosed by his ecstatic ex-

6. See selection 99, where Origen, *Contra Celsun*, VI. 22, is cited. Eds.

periences. He knows the road to the center of the world, the hole in the sky through which he can fly up to the highest Heaven, or the aperture in the earth through which he can descend to Hell. He is forewarned of the obstacles that he will meet on his journeys, and knows how to overcome them. In short, he knows the roads that lead to Heaven and Hell. All this he learned during his training in solitude or under the guidance of the master shamans.

Because of his ability to leave his body with impunity, the shaman can, if he so wishes, act in the manner of a spirit; e.g., he flies through the air, he becomes invisible, he perceives things at great distances, he mounts to Heaven or descends to Hell, sees souls and can capture them, and is incombustible. The exhibition of certain fakirlike accomplishments during the séances, especially the so-called fire tricks, is intended to convince the spectators that the shaman has assimilated the mode of being of spirits. The powers of turning themselves into animals, of killing at a distance, or of fore-telling the future are also among the powers of spirits; by exhibiting them, the shaman proclaims that he shares in the spirit condition. The desire to behave in the manner of a spirit signifies above all the desire to assume a superhuman condition; in short, to enjoy the freedom, the power, and the knowledge of the Supernatural Beings, whether Gods or spirits. . . .

117. SUMMARY: ASIATIC SHAMANISM

It is in [a] historico-ethnological perspective that we must place the southern influences on the religions and mythologies of the peoples of Central and North Asia. As for shamanism proper . . . magical techniques [and the] shamanic costume and drum also underwent southern influences. But shamanism in its structure and as a whole cannot be considered a creation of these southern contributions. The documents that we have collected and interpreted in the present volume[1] show that the ideology and the characteristic techniques of shamanism are attested in archaic cultures, where it would

SOURCE: *S*/501–7.
1. *Shamanism: Archaic Techniques of Ecstasy*, from which this selection is taken. Eds.

be difficult to admit the presence of paleo-Oriental influences. It is enough to remember, on the one hand, that Central Asian shamanism is part and parcel of the prehistoric culture of the Siberian hunters, and, on the other, that shamanic ideologies and techniques are documented among the primitive peoples of Australia, the Malay Archipelago, South America, North America, and other regions.

Recent researches have clearly brought out the "shamanic" elements in the religion of the paleolithic hunters. Horst Kirchner has interpreted the celebrated relief at Lascaux as a representation of a shamanic trance.[2] The same author considers that the "Kommandostäbe"—mysterious objects found in prehistoric sites—are drumsticks.[3] If this interpretation is accepted, the prehistoric sorcerers would already have used drums comparable to those of the Siberian shamans. In this connection we may mention that bone drumsticks have been found on Oleny Island, in Barents Sea, at a site dated ca. 500 B.C. Finally, Karl J. Narr has reconsidered the problem of the "origin" and chronology of shamanism in his important study "Bärenzermoniell und Schamanismus in der Älteren Steinzeit Europas."[4] He brings out the influence of notions of fertility ("Venus statuettes") on the religious beliefs of the prehistoric North Asian hunters; but this influence did not disrupt the paleolithic tradition.[5] His conclusions are as follows: Animal skulls and bones found in the sites of the European Paleolithic (before 50,000–ca. 30,000 B.C.) can be interpreted as ritual offerings. Probably about the same period and in connection with the same rites, the magico-religious concepts of the periodic return of animals to life from their bones crystallized, and it is in this "Vorstellungswelt"[6] that the roots of the bear ceremonialism of Asia and North America lie. Soon afterward, probably about 25,000, Europe offers evidence for the earliest forms of shamanism (Lascaux) with the plastic representations of the bird, the tutelary spirit, and ecstasy.

It is for the specialists to judge the validity of this chronology

2. "Ein archäologischer Beitrag zur Urgeschichte des Schamanismus," *Anthropos* 47 (1952): 271 ff.

3. *Ibid.*, pp. 279 ff. ("Kommandostäbe"=bâtons de commandement.) Cf. S. Giedion, *The Eternal Present. I: The Beginnings of Art* (London, 1962), pp. 162 ff.

4. *Saeculum*, 10 (1959): 233–72.

5. *Ibid.*, p. 260.

6. "Vorstellungswelt": complex of images. Eds.

proposed by Narr. What appears to be certain is the antiquity of "shamanic" rituals and symbols. It remains to be determined whether these documents brought to light by prehistoric discoveries represent the first expressions of a shamanism *in statu nascendi* or are merely the earliest documents today available for an earlier religious complex, which, however, did not find "plastic" manifestations (drawings, ritual objects, etc.) before the period of Lascaux.

In accounting for the formation of the shamanic complex in Central and North Asia, we must keep in mind the two essential elements of the problem: on the one hand, the ecstatic experience as such, as a primary phenomenon; on the other, the historico-religious milieu into which this ecstatic experience was destined to be incorporated and the ideology that, in the last analysis, was to validate it. We have termed the ecstatic experience a "primary phenomenon" because we see no reason whatever for regarding it as the result of a particular historical moment, that is, as produced by a certain form of civilization. Rather, we would consider it fundamental in the human condition, and hence known to the whole of archaic humanity; what changed and was modified with the different forms of culture and religion was the interpretation and evaluation of the ecstatic experience. What, then, was the historico-religious situation in Central and North Asia, where, later on, shamanism crystallized as an autonomous and specific complex? Everywhere in those lands, and from the earliest times, we find documents for the existence of a Supreme Being of celestial structure, who also corresponds morphologically to all the other Supreme Beings of the archaic religions. The symbolism of ascent, with all the rites and myths dependent on it, must be connected with celestial Supreme Beings; we know that "height" was sacred as such, that many supreme gods of archaic peoples are called "He on High," "He of the Sky," or simply "Sky." This symbolism of ascent and "height" retains its value even after the "withdrawal" of the celestial Supreme Being— for, as is well known, Supreme Beings gradually lose their active place in the cult, giving way to religious forms that are more "dynamic" and "familiar" (the gods of storm and fertility, demiurges, the souls of the dead, the Great Goddesses, etc.). The magico-religious complex that has come to be called "matriarchy" accentuates the transformation of a celestial god into a *deus otiosus*. The reduction or even the total loss in religious currency of uranian

Supreme Beings is sometimes indicated in myths concerning a primordial and paradisal time when communications between heaven
and earth were easy and accessible to everyone; as the result of
some happening (especially of a ritual fault), these communications
were broken off and the Supreme Beings withdrew to the highest
sky. Let us repeat: the disappearance of the cult of the celestial
Supreme Being did not nullify the symbolism of ascent with all its
implications. As we have seen, this symbolism is documented everywhere and in all historico-religious contexts. Now, the symbolism
of ascent plays an essential part in the shamanic ideology and
techniques.

. . . The shamanic ecstasy could be considered a reactualization of
the mythical *illud tempus* when men could communicate *in concreto* with the sky. It is indubitable that the celestial ascent of the
shaman (or the medicine man, the magician, etc.) is a survival, profoundly modified and sometimes degenerated, of this archaic religious ideology centered on faith in a celestial Supreme Being and
belief in concrete communications between heaven and earth. But,
as we have seen, the shaman, because of his ecstatic experience—
which enables him to relive a state inaccessible to the rest of mankind—is regarded, and regards himself, as a privileged being. Furthermore, the myths refer to more intimate relations between the
Supreme Beings and shamans; in particular, they tell of a First
Shaman, sent to earth by the Supreme Being or his surrogate (the
demiurge or the solarized god) to defend human beings against diseases and evil spirits.

The historical changes in the religions of Central and North
Asia—that is, in general, the increasingly important role given to
the ancestor cult and to the divine or semidivine figures that took
the place of the Supreme Being—in their turn altered the meaning
of the shaman's ecstatic experience. Descents to the underworld,
the struggle against evil spirits, but also the increasingly familiar
relations with "spirits" that result in their "embodiment" or in the
shaman's being "possessed" by "spirits," are innovations, most of
them recent, to be ascribed to the general change in the religious
complex. In addition, there are the influences from the south, which
appeared quite early and which altered both cosmology and the
mythology and techniques of ecstasy. Among these southern influences we must reckon, in later times, the contribution of Buddhism

and Lamaism, added to the Iranian and, in the last analysis, Mesopotamian influences that preceded them.

In all probability the initiatory schema of the shaman's ritual death and resurrection is likewise an innovation, but one that goes back to much earlier times; in any case, it cannot be ascribed to influences from the ancient Near East, since the symbolism and ritual of initiatory death and resurrection are already documented in the religions of Australia and South America. But the innovations introduced by the ancestor cult particularly affected the structure of this initiatory schema. The very concept of mystical death was altered by the many and various religious changes effected by lunar mythologies, the cult of the dead, and the elaboration of magical ideologies.

Hence we must conceive of Asiatic shamanism as an archaic technique of ecstasy whose original underlying ideology—belief in a celestial Supreme Being with whom it was possible to have direct relations by ascending into the sky—was constantly being transformed by a long series of exotic contributions culminating in the invasion of Buddhism. The concept of mystical death, furthermore, encouraged increasingly regular relations with the ancestral souls and the "spirits," relations that ended in "possession." The phenomenology of the trance, as we have seen, underwent many changes and corruptions, due in large part to confusion as to the precise nature of ecstasy. Yet all these innovations and corruptions did not succeed in eliminating the possibility of the true shamanic ecstasy; and we have been able to find, here and there, examples of genuine mystical experiences of shamans, taking the form of "spiritual" ascents and prepared by methods of meditation comparable to those of the great mystics of East and West.

118. THE SHAMAN AND THE COMMUNITY

There is no solution of continuity in the history of mysticism. More than once we have discerned in the shamanic experience a "nostalgia for paradise" that suggests one of the oldest types of Christian mystical experience. As for the "inner light," which plays

Source: S/508–11.

a part of the first importance in Indian mysticism and metaphysics as well as in Christian mystical theology, it is, as we have seen,
already documented in Eskimo shamanism.[1] We may add that the
magical stones with which the Australian medicine man's body is
stuffed are in some degree symbolic of "solidified light."

But shamanism is important not only for the place that it holds in
the history of mysticism. The shamans have played an essential role
in the defense of the psychic integrity of the community. They are
pre-eminently the antidemonic champions; they combat not only
demons and disease, but also the black magicians.[2] The exemplary
figure of the shaman-champion is Dto-mba Shi-lo, the mythical
founder of Na-khi shamanism, the tireless slayer of demons. The
military elements that are of great importance in certain types of
Asian shamanism (lance, cuirass, bow, sword, etc.) are accounted
for by the requirements of war against the demons, the true enemies
of humanity. In a general way, it can be said that shamanism defends
life, health, fertility, the world of "light," against death, diseases,
sterility, disaster, and the world of "darkness."

The shaman's combativeness sometimes becomes an aggressive
mania; in certain Siberian traditions shamans are believed to challenge one another constantly in animal form. But such a degree of
aggressiveness is rather exceptional; it is peculiar to some Siberian
shamanisms and the Hungarian *táltos*. What is fundamental and universal is the shaman's struggle against what we could call "the powers of evil." It is hard for us to imagine what such a shamanism can
represent for an archaic society. In the first place, it is the assurance
that human beings are not alone in a foreign world, surrounded by
demons and the "forces of evil." In addition to the gods and supernatural beings to whom prayers and sacrifices are addressed, there
are "specialists in the sacred," men able to "see" the spirits, to go up
into the sky and meet the gods, to descend to the underworld and
fight the demons, sickness, and death. The shaman's essential role in
the defense of the psychic integrity of the community depends
above all on this: men are sure that *one of them* is able to help them
in the critical circumstances produced by the inhabitants of the in-

1. See selections 131–35, on the Mystic Light. Eds.
2. On "black" and "white" shamans and the dualistic mythology implied by
the distinction, see *S*/184–86. Eds.

visible world. It is consoling and comforting to know that a member of the community is able to *see* what is hidden and invisible to the rest and to bring back direct and reliable information from the supernatural worlds.

It is as a further result of his ability to travel in the supernatural worlds and to *see* the superhuman beings (gods, demons, spirits of the dead, etc.) that the shaman has been able to contribute decisively to the *knowledge of death*. In all probability many features of "funerary geography," as well as some themes of the mythology of death, are the result of the ecstatic experiences of shamans. The lands that the shaman sees and the personages that he meets during his ecstatic journeys in the beyond are minutely described by the shaman himself, during or after his trance. The unknown and terrifying world of death assumes form, is organized in accordance with particular patterns; finally it displays a structure and, in course of time, becomes familiar and acceptable. In turn, the supernatural inhabitants of the world of death become *visible*; they show a form, display a personality, even a biography. Little by little the world of the dead becomes knowable, and death itself is evaluated primarily as a rite of passage to a spiritual mode of being. In the last analysis, the accounts of the shamans' ecstatic journeys contribute to "spiritualizing" the world of the dead, at the same time that they enrich it with wondrous forms and figures.

. . . The shaman's adventures in the other world, the ordeals that he undergoes in his ecstatic descents below and ascents to the sky, suggest the adventures of the figures in popular tales and the heroes of epic literature. Probably a large number of epic "subjects" or motifs, as well as many characters, images, and clichés of epic literature, are, finally, of ecstatic origin, in the sense that they were borrowed from the narratives of shamans describing their journeys and adventures in the superhuman worlds.

It is likewise probable that the pre-ecstatic euphoria constituted one of the universal sources of lyric poetry. In preparing his trance, the shaman drums, summons his spirit helpers, speaks a "secret language" or the "animal language," imitating the cries of beasts and especially the songs of birds. He ends by obtaining a "second state" that provides the impetus for linguistic creation and the rhythms of lyric poetry. Poetic creation still remains an act of perfect spiritual freedom. Poetry remakes and prolongs language; every poetic language begins by being a secret language, that is, the creation of a personal universe, of a completely closed world. The purest poetic act seems to re-create language from an inner experience that, like the ecstasy or the religious inspiration of "primitives," reveals the essence of things. It is from such linguistic creations, made possible by pre-ecstatic "inspiration," that the "secret languages" of the mystics and the traditional allegorical languages later crystallize.

Something must also be said concerning the dramatic structure of the shamanic séance. We refer not only to the sometimes highly elaborate "staging" that obviously exercises a beneficial influence on the patient. But every genuinely shamanic séance ends as a *spectacle* unequaled in the world of daily experience. The fire tricks, the "miracles" of the rope-trick or mango-trick type, the exhibition of magical feats, reveal another world—the fabulous world of the gods and magicians, the world in which *everything seems possible*, where the dead return to life and the living die only to live again, where one can disappear and reappear instantaneously, where the "laws of nature" are abolished, and a certain superhuman "freedom" is exemplified and made dazzlingly *present*.

It is difficult for us, modern men as we are, to imagine the repercussions of such a *spectacle* in a "primitive" community. The shamanic "miracles" not only confirm and reinforce the patterns of the traditional religion, they also stimulate and feed the imagination, demolish the barriers between dream and present reality, open windows upon worlds inhabited by the gods, the dead, and the spirits.

These few remarks on the cultural creations made possible or stimulated by the experiences of shamans must suffice. A thorough study of them would exceed the limits of this work. What a magnificent book remains to be written on the ecstatic "sources" of epic and lyric poetry, on the prehistory of dramatic spectacles, and, in general, on the fabulous worlds discovered, explored, and described by the ancient shamans. . . .

◆ ◆

Religious Societies and Mysticism

In the selections that follow we are presented with an array of initiatic ideas and performances which are really quests to enter into what Eliade often refers to as the "deeper zones of sacrality." The endeavor, therefore, is not merely to initiate persons into the general sacral-social order but finally to bring about the fusion of a sense of belonging to humankind *and* to the mysterious power that animates the cosmos at large. In the context of this book, then, this section witnesses to something beyond the "rites of passage" as modes of transitional awareness of sacred realities at critical moments in ordinary life; the events in these readings testify more radically to the perennial human desire to achieve the Pan-Sacred as a permanent state of being *in* and *beyond* the world. Hence the emphasis here is upon either the consummate personal transformation that surpasses intermittent entrées into sacred worlds, or upon the final transpersonalization of one's humanity (in the sense of the Buddhist Nirvana). In any case, whether it be under the form of initiatic secrecy, redemptive mystery, or mystic light-experiences, the aim is always certain: the attainment of the ultimate religious experience of the Sacred.

◆

WOMEN'S MYSTERIES

We begin with mysteries/societies associated with women, and we find again that the initiatory period is crucial. The rites and the societies work to provide women with "access to sacrality," as Eliade puts it—the physical experiences of women such as menstruation, giving birth, are related to "the mystic unity between life, woman, nature, and the divinity."

119. SECRET SOCIETIES

Even on the archaic levels of culture (for example, in Australia), the puberty initiation may entail a series of stages. In such cases the sacred history can be only gradually revealed. The deepening of the religious experience and knowledge demands a special vocation or an outstanding intelligence and will power. This fact explains the emergence of both the secret societies and the confraternities of shamans and medicine men. The rites of entrance into a secret society correspond in every respect to those of tribal initiations: seclusion, initiatory tests and tortures, "death" and "resurrection,"

SOURCE: *Q*/114–15.

imposition of a new name, revelation of a secret doctrine, learning of a new language, etc. We may point out, however, a few innovations characteristic of the secret societies: the great importance of secrecy, the cruelty of initiatory trials, the predominance of the ancestor cult (the ancestors being personified by masks), and the absence of a supreme being in the ceremonial life of the group. As to the *Weiberbünde*,[1] the initiation consists of a series of specific tests followed by revelations concerning fertility, conception, and birth.

120. THE GOAL OF WOMANHOOD

There are . . . initiations for girls and women. In these feminine rites and mysteries we must not expect to find the same symbolism, or, more precisely, the same symbolic expressions, as those found in men's initiations and confraternities. But it is easy to discern a common element: the foundation for all these rites and mysteries is always a deep religious experience. It is *access to sacrality*, as it is revealed to her who assumes the condition of womanhood, that constitutes the goal both of feminine initiation rites and of women's secret societies.

Initiation begins at the first menstruation. This physiological symptom imposes a break, the girl's forcible removal from her familiar world; she is immediately isolated, separated from the community. The segregation takes place in a special cabin, in the bush, or in a dark corner of the house. The catamenial[1] girl is obliged to remain in a particular and quite uncomfortable position, and must avoid exposing herself to the sun or being touched by anyone. She wears a special dress, or a sign or color allotted to her, and must eat only raw foods.

Segregation and seclusion out of daylight—in a dark hut, in the bush—suggest the symbolism of the initiatory death of boys isolated in the forest or shut up in huts. Yet there is a difference: among girls, segregation occurs immediately after the first menstruation, hence it is individual; whereas boys are segregated in a group.

SOURCE: *SP*/193–95.
1. *Weiberbünde*: women's secret societies. Eds.
1. Catamenial: menstruating. Eds.

But the difference is explained by the fact that in girls the end of childhood has a physiological manifestation. However, in the course of time the girls make up a group, and they are then initiated collectively by old women who act as their instructors.

As for the women's societies, they are always connected with the mystery of birth and fertility. The mystery of childbearing, that is, woman's discovery that she is *a creator on the plane of life*, constitutes a religious experience that cannot be translated into masculine terms. This makes it clear why childbirth has given rise to secret feminine rituals, which sometimes attain the complex organization of real mysteries. Traces of such mysteries are still preserved even in Europe.

As in the case of men's societies, women's associations are found in various forms, in which secrecy and mystery progressively increase. To begin, there is the general initiation that every girl and every young married woman undergoes; this eventually produces the institution of the women's societies. Next come the women's mystery associations, as in Africa or, in antiquity, the closed groups of the Maenads. Women's mystery associations of this type were long in disappearing. We need only think of the witches of the Middle Ages and their ritual meetings.

121. FEMININE SECRET SOCIETIES

The secret conclaves of woman are always concerned with the mystery of birth and fertility. . . . Several types of secret women's associations have remained in being to this day; their rites always include fertility symbols. . . .

To obtain a few details about the initiations in feminine secret societies, let us look more closely at certain African examples. The specialists are careful to warn us that very little is known of these secret rites; nevertheless, we can discern their general character. Here is what we know of the Lisimbu society among the Kuta of the north (Okondja). A great part of the ceremony takes place near, or even in, a river; and it is important to note henceforward the presence of aquatic symbolism in almost all the secret societies

Source: *MDM*/214–18; cf. *AR*/118–27, *RSI*/78–80.

of this part of Africa. In the river itself, they build a hut of branches and leaves: "It has only one entrance, and the summit of the hut is hardly a yard above the surface of the water."[1] The candidates, whose ages vary from twelve to thirty-two years, are brought down to the shore. Each is under the supervision of an initiate, called the "mother." They advance all together, walking in the water, crouching down with only head and shoulders out of the water. Their faces are painted with *pembe*, and each holds a leaf in her mouth (. . .). This procession goes down the river and, on arrival at the hut, they stand up suddenly and dive into the opening. Having entered into the hut they undress completely, and dive out again. Crouching down, they form a semi-circle around the entrance to the hut and proceed to perform the "fishing dance." One of the "mothers" afterwards comes out of the river, tears off her loin-cloth and, thus naked, dances a most salacious dance.[2] After the dance, the candidates have to go into the hut and it is here that their first initiation takes place. The "mothers" take away their clothes, "plunge their heads under water to the verge of suffocation," and rub their bodies with rough leaves. The initiation is continued in the village: the "mother" beats her "daughter," holds the latter's head close to a fire on which they have thrown a handful of pepper and, lastly, taking her by the arm, makes her dance and then pass between her legs. The ceremony includes also a number of dances, one of which symbolizes the sexual act. Two months later, another initiation is held, still on the bank of the river. In this case the neophyte undergoes the same ordeals, and, on the bank, her hair is cut all round in the distinctive fashion of the society. Before going back into the village the president breaks an egg over the roof of the hut: "This is to ensure that the hunters will catch plenty of game." When they are back in the village, each "mother" rubs the body of her "daughter" on the *kula*, divides a banana in two, gives one piece to the novice, keeps the other, and they both eat the fruit together. Then the "daughter" bows down and passes between the "mother's" legs. After a few more dances, some of which symbolize the sexual act, the candidates are held to be initiated. "They believe that the ceremonies of Lisimbu exert a favorable influence over the

1. Ephraim Andersson, *Contribution à l'Ethnographie des Kuta*, (Uppsala, 1953), 1: 216.
2. *Ibid.*, pp. 217–18.

whole life of the village; the plantations will give a good return, the hunting and fishing expeditions will be successful, epidemics and quarrels will be averted from the inhabitants."

We will not dwell upon the symbolism of the Lisimbu mystery. Let us only remember this: that the initiation ceremonies take place in the river, and that, as water symbolizes chaos, the hut represents the cosmic creation. To penetrate into the waters is to re-enter the pre-cosmic condition, the nonbeing. Afterwards, the girl is re-born by passing between the legs of the "mother," meaning that she is born to a new spiritual existence. The elements of cosmogony, of sexuality, of the new birth, of fecundity and of luck, all belong together. In other feminine secret societies in the same part of Africa, certain initiatory features in the rituals are still more in evidence. Thus, in the Gaboon, there are the societies called Nyembe or Ndyembe, who also celebrate their secret ceremonies near a stream of water. Among their initiatory ordeals we should note this: a fire must be kept burning continually, and for fuel the novices have to venture alone into the forest, often during the night or in a storm, to gather wood. Another ordeal is that of staring at the burning sun, while a song is being sung. Lastly, each novice has to plunge her hand into a snake-hole and catch a snake; and they bring these into the village coiled around their arms. During the period of an initiation, the women who are already members of the sisterhood perform nude dances, singing obscene songs. But there is also a ritual of death and initiatory resurrection which is performed in the last act of the mystery; this is the leopard dance. It is executed by the leaders, two and two, one representing the leopard, and her partner the mother. Around the latter a dozen of the young girls are assembled and "killed" by the leopard. But when it comes to the mother's turn, she attacks the leopard and kills it. The death of the wild animal is supposed to allow the young women to be liberated from its belly.[3]

Some special points emerge from all that has just been said. We are struck by the initiatory character of these *Weiberbünde* and secret feminine associations. To take part in them, one has to have successfully passed through an ordeal—and not one of a physiological order (like the first menstruation or parturition), but initiatory

3. *Ibid.*, pp. 219–21.

in the sense that it brings into play the whole being of the young woman or young wife. And this initiation is effected in a cosmic context. We have just seen the ritual importance of the forest, of the water, of the darkness and of the night. The woman receives the revelation of a reality that transcends her although she is a part of it. It is not the natural phenomenon of giving birth that constitutes the mystery; it is the revelation of the feminine sacredness; that is, of the mystic unity between life, woman, nature and the divinity. This revelation is of a transpersonal order; for which reason it is expressed in symbols and actualized in rites. The girl or the initiated woman becomes conscious of a sanctity that emerges from the innermost depths of her being, and this consciousness—obscure though it may be—is experienced in symbols. It is in "realizing" and in "living" this sacredness that the woman finds the spiritual meaning of her own existence, she feels that life is both *real* and *sanctified*, that it is not merely an endless series of blind, psychophysiological automatisms, useless and in the last reckoning absurd. For the women too, initiation is equivalent to a change of level, to the passing out of one mode of being into another; the young woman is brutally separated from the profane world; she undergoes a transformation of a spiritual character which, like all transformation, implies an experience of death. We have just seen how the ordeals of the young women resemble those that are symbolic of the initiatory death. But what is in question is always *a death to something which has to be surpassed*, not a death in the modern and de-sanctified sense of the term. One dies to be transformed and attain to a higher level of existence. In the case of the girls, this is death to the indistinct and amorphous state of childhood, in order to be reborn into personality and fecundity.

As with the men's, so also with the women's associations, we have to deal with a number of different forms of progressively greater secrecy and mystery. There are, to begin with, those general initiations through which every girl and every young wife passes, and which lead up to the institution of the women's secret societies (*Weiberbünde*). Then there are the women's associations for the enacting of the mysteries as we find them in Africa or, in antiquity, the closed groups of the Maenads. We know that some sisterhoods of the kind have taken a long time to disappear—such as those of the witches of the Middle Ages in Europe, with their ritual reunions and "orgies." Although the medieval trials for sorcery were in most cases inspired by theological prejudice, and although it is sometimes hard to distinguish the genuine, rural magico-religious traditions, deeply rooted in prehistory, from collective psychoses of a very complex character, it is nevertheless probable that "orgies" of witches did take place, not with the meaning ascribed to them by the ecclesiastical authorities but in the first, authentic sense that they were secret reunions including orgiastic rites—that is, ceremonies related to the mystery of fertility.

The witches, just like the shamans and the mystics of other primitive societies, were only concentrating, intensifying or deepening the religious experience revealed during their initiation. Just like the shamans, the witches were dedicated to a mystical vocation which impelled them to live, more deeply than other women, the revelation of the mysteries.

◆

MEN'S MYSTERIES

Any one who knows Eliade's works well refers to his treatment of the Kunapipi, an Australian secret cult; we provide a brief extract here in which Eliade shows the transformation in this cult of initiatory death—for the Kunapipi emphasize new birth rather than death and resurrection.

The other classical example of men's mysteries can be found in accounts of the American Indian healing societies, and the extract used here provides details of some of these societies, especially in relationship to shamanism.

122. THE KUNAPIPI CULT

Let us now examine an Australian secret cult, Kunapipi, which still flourishes in Arnhem Land and in the west-central Northern Territory. From the point of view of our investigation, its interest is twofold: first, although its most important ceremonies are confined to men, the ideology of Kunapipi is dominated by female religious symbolism, especially by the figure of the Great Mother,

SOURCE: *RSI*/47–51; cf. *PCR*/167–69, *SP*/144–57, *FC*/104–5, *S*/313–22.

source of universal fertility; second, although its initiatory scenario is of a structural type already known to us—for the chief moment is a ritual swallowing—it also offers some new elements. In other words, Kunapipi is an excellent point of departure for our comparative investigation into the continuity of initiatory patterns. Only young men who have already undergone the initiatory rites of puberty are eligible for initiation into the Kunapipi cult. Hence we have here not an age-grading ceremony but a higher initiation—which once again confirms primitive man's desire to deepen his religious experience and knowledge.

The ritual goal of Kunapipi is twofold: the initiation of the young men, and the renewal of the energies that ensure cosmic life and universal fertility. This renewal is obtained through the reenactment of the original myth. The sacred power possessed by the Supernatural Beings is released by the reactualization of the acts that they performed during the "Dreaming Period."[1] We here have, then, a religious conception with which we are already more or less familiar: an origin myth forms the basis for an initiatory ritual; to perform the ritual is to reactualize the primordial Time, to become contemporary with the Dreaming Period; the novices participate in the mystery, and on this occasion the entire community and its cosmic milieu are bathed in the atmosphere of the Dreaming Period; the cosmos and society emerge regenerated. It is clear, then, that the initiation of a group of young men affects not only their own religious situation but also that of the community. Here we find the seed of a conception that will be developed in higher religions—that the spiritual perfection of an elite exerts a beneficial influence on the rest of society.

Let us now turn to the cult proper. It is based on a rather complex myth, of which I need mention only the chief elements. In the Dreaming Period, the two Wauwalak Sisters, the older of whom had just borne a child, set out into the north. These two sisters are really the "dual Mothers." The name of the cult, Kunapipi, is translated "Mother" or "Old Woman." After a long journey, the Sisters stopped near a well, built a hut, and tried to cook some animals. But the animals fled from the fire and threw themselves into the well. For, the aborigines now explain, the animals knew that one

1. R. M. Berndt, *Kunapipi* (Melbourne, 1951), p. 34.

of the Sisters, being impure because of her "afterbirth blood," ought not to go near the well, in which the Great Snake Julunggul lived. And indeed Julunggul, attracted by the smell of blood, emerged from his subterranean home, raised his fore part threateningly—which brought on clouds and lightning—and crawled toward the hut. The younger Sister tried to keep him away by dancing, and her dances are reactualized in the Kunapipi ceremony. Finally, the Snake poured spittle all over the hut in which the two Sisters and the child had taken refuge, swallowed it, then straightened up to his full length, his head toward the sky. Soon afterwards he disgorged the two Sisters and the child. Bitten by white ants, they returned to life—but Julunggul swallowed them again, this time for good.

This myth provides the foundation for two other rituals besides Kunapipi, one of which, the *djunggawon*, constitutes the rite of puberty initiation. The aborigines explain the origin of all these rituals thus: a python, Lu'ningu, having seen Julunggul swallow and then disgorge the two Sisters, wanted to imitate him. He went wandering about the country, swallowing young men, but when he disgorged them they were dead and sometimes reduced to skeletons. In revenge, men killed him, and later they raised a monument representing him—the two posts called *jelmalandji*. To imitate the Snake's hissing, they made bull-roarers. Finally, the ceremonial headman cut his arm, saying: "We make ourselves like those two women."[2]

In the Kunapipi ritual, Berndt writes, the young novices, "leaving the main camp for the sacred ground are said to be swallowed by Lu'ningu, just as he swallowed the young men in the Dreaming Era; and in the old days they had to stay away from womenfolk from a period of two weeks to two months, symbolizing their stay inside the belly of the Snake."[3] But the two Snakes—Julunggul and Lu'ningu—are confused, for on their return to the main camp, the men tell the women, "All the young boys have gone today; Julunggul has swallowed them up."[4] But in any case, the symbolism of the ritual swallowing is more complex. On the one hand, the novices, assimilated to the two Sisters, are supposed to have been swallowed by the Snake; on the other hand, by entering the sacred ground,

2. *Ibid.*, p. 36.
3. *Ibid.*, p. 37.
4. *Ibid.*, p. 41.

they symbolically return into the primordial Mother's womb. We find that they are painted with ocher and with "arm-blood," representing the blood of the two Wauwalak Sisters; "that is," Berndt writes, "for the purpose of the ritual they become the Two Sisters, and are swallowed by Julunggul; and on their emergence from the ritual, they are revivified just as were the women."[5] But then too, according to the aborigines, the "triangular dancing place" represents the Mother's womb. To quote Berndt's account again: "As the neophytes leave the camp for the sacred ground, they themselves are said to become increasingly sacred, and to enter the Mother; they go into her uterus, the ring place, as happened in the beginning. When the ritual is completed the Mother 'lets them out'; they emerge from the ring place, and pass once more into ordinary life."[6]

The symbolism of return to the womb recurs during the course of the ritual. At a certain moment, the neophytes are covered over with bark and "told to go to sleep." They remain there, the aborigines say, "covered up in the hut like the Wauwalak Sisters."[7] Finally, after an orgiastic ritual, which includes an exchange of wives, the final ceremony is performed. Two forked posts, with a thick connecting pole between them, are set up between the sacred ground and the main camp. The pole is covered with branches, and the initiates are stationed behind the branches; wholly invisible from outside, they remain there clinging to the pole with their feet on the ground, supposedly "hanging from the pole." They are, that is, in the womb, and they will emerge reborn—"their spirit comes out new."[8] Two men climb up onto the forked posts, and there cry like newborn infants, for they are "the children of Wauwalak." Finally all return to the main camp, painted with ocher and arm-blood.

I have dwelt on this Kunapipi ritual because, thanks to the work of Ronald Berndt, we are in a position to know not only a number of valuable details but also the meaning that the aborigines attribute to them. It must be added that the Kunapipi ritual does not represent an archaic state of Australian culture; very probably it has

5. *Ibid.*, p. 38.
6. *Ibid.*, p. 14.
7. *Ibid.*, p. 45.
8. *Ibid.*, p. 53.

been influenced by more recent Melanesian contributions. The tradition that in the beginning women possessed all cult secrets and all sacred objects, and that men later stole them, indicates a matriarchal ideology. Obviously, a number of the ritual elements are pan-Australian—for example, the fire-throwing, the bull-roarer and the myth of its origin, the custom of covering women and neophytes with branches. The essential characteristic of Kunapipi, is, as we saw, the initiatory pattern of return to the womb. We found it more than once: when the neophytes enter the sacred ground; when they wait under the branches, "hanging from the pole"; finally, when they are considered to be in the two Sisters' hut. Their ritual swallowing by the Snake is also to be interpreted as a return to the womb —on the one hand, because the Snake is often described as female; on the other, because entering the belly of a monster also carries a symbolism of return to the embryonic state.

The frequent reiteration of the return to the primordial Mother's womb is striking. The sexual pantomimes and especially the ritual exchange of wives—an orgiastic ceremony that plays a leading role in the Kunapipi cult—further emphasize the sacred atmosphere of the mystery of procreation and childbirth. In fact, the general impression that we receive from the whole ceremonial is that it represents not so much a ritual death followed by resurrection as a complete regeneration of the initiate through his gestation and birth by the Great Mother. This of course does not mean that the symbolism of death is completely absent, for being swallowed by the Snake and even returning to the womb necessarily imply death to the profane condition. The symbolism of return to the womb is always ambivalent. Yet it is the particular notes of generation and gestation which dominate the Kunapipi cult. We here have, then, a perfect example of an initiatory pattern organized and constructed around the idea of a new birth, and no longer around the idea of symbolic death and resurrection.

123. SECRET BROTHERHOODS AND SHAMANISM

The problem of the relations between shamanism and the various North American secret societies and mystical movements is decidely complex and far from being solved. Yet it may be said that all these brotherhoods based on mysteries have a shamanic structure, in the sense that their ideology and techniques share in the great shamanic tradition. We shall soon give some examples drawn from secret societies (Midē'wiwin type) and ecstatic movements (Ghost-Dance-Religion type). They will clearly show the chief elements of the shamanic tradition: initiation involving the candidate's death and resurrection, ecstatic visits to the land of the dead and to the sky, insertion of magical substances in the candidate's body, revelation of secret doctrines, instruction in shamanic healing, and so on. The chief difference between traditional shamanism and the secret societies lies in the fact that the latter are open to anyone who displays some predisposition to ecstasy, who is willing to pay the required fee, and, above all, who consents to submit to the necessary apprenticeship and initiatory ordeals. A certain opposition, and even antagonism, is often observable between the secret brotherhoods and ecstatic movements on the one hand and the shamans on the other. The brotherhoods, like the ecstatic movements, oppose shamanism in so far as it has become assimilated to sorcery and black magic. Another cause for opposition is the exclusivistic attitude of certain shamanic circles; the secret societies and ecstatic movements, on the contrary, display a quite marked spirit of proselytism that, in the last analysis, tends to abolish the special privilege of shamans. All these brotherhoods and mystical sects work toward a religious revolution by the fact that they proclaim the spiritual regeneration of the entire community and even of all North American Indian tribes (cf. the Ghost-Dance Religion). Hence they are conscious of being at the opposite pole from the shamans, who on this point represent both the most conservative elements of the religious tradition and the least generous tendencies of the tribal spirituality.

But actually, things are far more complex. For, if all that we have just said is perfectly true, it is no less true that in North America the differences between "consecrated" men and the "profane" multitude are not so much qualitative as quantitative; they lie in the *amount* of the sacred that the former have assimilated. . . . Every Indian seeks religious power, that every Indian commands a guardian spirit acquired by the same techniques that the shaman uses to obtain his own spirits. The difference between layman and shaman is quanti-

tative; the shaman commands a greater number of tutelary or guardian spirits and a stronger magico-religious "power." In this respect
we could almost say that every Indian "shamanizes," even if he
does not consciously wish to become a shaman.

If the difference between the profane and the shamans is so indefinite, it is no clearer between shamanic circles and the secret
brotherhoods or mystical sects. On the one hand, the latter ex-
hibit supposedly "shamanic" techniques and ideologies; on the
other, the shamans usually share in the activities of the most important secret mystery societies, and sometimes take them over entirely. These relationships are very clearly demonstrated by the
Midē'wiwin, or, as it has been erroneously called, the "Grand Medicine Society," of the Ojibwa. The Ojibwa have two kinds of shamans: the *Wâbĕnō'* (the "Men of the dawn," the "Eastern men")
and the *jĕs' sakkīd'*, prophets and seers, also called "jugglers" and
"revealer[s] of hidden truths." Both categories are capable of shamanic exploits; the *Wâbĕnō'* are also called "fire-handlers," and can
touch burning coals and remain unhurt; the *jĕs' sakkīd'* perform
cures, the gods and spirits speak through their mouths, and they
are famous "jugglers," for they can instantly undo the ropes and
chains with which they are found.[1] Yet both voluntarily, join the
Midē'wiwin—the *Wâbĕnō'* when he has specialized in magical medicine and incantations, the *jĕs'sakkīd'* when he wants to increase his
prestige in the tribe. They are, of course, in the minority, for the
"Grand Medicine" fraternity is open to any who are interested in
spiritual matters and have the means to pay the entrance fees.
Among the Menomini, who in Hoffman's time numbered 1,500,
the Midē'wiwin had one hundred members, among them two *Wâbĕnō'* and five *jĕs'sakkīd'*.[2] But there could not have been many shamans who were not members.

The important aspect of the case is that the "Grand Medicine"
fraternity itself exhibits a shamanic structure. In fact, Hoffman
calls its members, the *midē*, "shamans," though other writers call
them at once shamans and medicine men, prophets, seers, and even
priests. All these terms are partly justified, for the *midē* act both as

1. W. J. Hoffman, "The Midē'winwin or 'Grand Medicine Society' of the
Ojibwa," *Reports of the Bureau of American Ethnology* (1885–86; pub. 1891),
7: 143–300, 157 ff.
2. *Ibid.*, p. 158.

healing shamans and seers and, to a certain extent, even as priests. The historical origins of the Midē′wiwin are unknown, but its mythological traditions are not far from the Siberian myths of the "first shaman." The myths tell that Mī′nabō′zho, the messenger of the Dzhe Manido (the Great Spirit) and intercessor between him and mankind, seeing the miserable state of sick and enfeebled humanity, revealed the most sublime secrets to the otter and inserted *mīgis* (symbol of the *midē*) in its body so that it should become immortal and be able to initiate and at the same time consecrate men.[3] Thus the otterskin pouch plays an essential part in the initiation of the *midē*; in it are placed the *mīgis*, the small shells that are believed to hold magico-religious power.[4]

The initiation of candidates follows the general pattern of all shamanic initiations. It includes revelation of the mysteries (that is, especially the myth of Mī′nabō′zho and the immortality of the otter), the death and resurrection of the candidate, and the insertion into his body of a large number of *mīgis* (which is strangely reminiscent of the "magical stones" with which the apprentice magician's body is stuffed in Australia and elsewhere). There are four degrees of initiation, but the last three are only a repetition of the first ceremony. The *midēwigan*, the "Great Medicine Lodge," a sort of enclosure twenty-five by eight yards, is constructed, with leafy branches between the posts to obviate eavesdropping. Some thirty yards away the *wigiwam*, or steam bath for the candidate, is built. The chief designates a teacher, who tells the candidate the origins and properties of the drum and rattles and shows him how to use them to invoke the Great God (Manidou) and exorcise demons. He is also taught the magical songs, the medicinal plants, therapy, and especially the elements of the secret doctrine. Beginning with the sixth or fifth day before the initiation the candidate purifies himself daily in the steam bath and then attends the demonstrations of magical power by the *midē*; assembled in the *midēwigan*, they make various wooden figurines and their own pouches move at a distance. The last night he spends alone with his teacher in the steam bath; the following morning, after another purification, and if the sky is clear, the initiation ceremony takes place. All the *midē* are

3. *Ibid.*, pp. 166 ff.; "Pictography and Shamanistic Rites of the Ojibwa," *American Anthropologist* 1 (1888): 209–29, 213 ff.
4. Hoffman, "The Midē′wiwin," pp. 217, 220 ff.

assembled in the "Great Medicine Lodge." After smoking in silence for a long time, they intone ritual songs revealing secret—and, for the most part, unintelligible—aspects of the primordial tradition. At a given moment, all the *midē* rise and, approaching the candidate, "kill" him by touching him with *mīgis*. The candidate trembles, falls to his knees, and, when a *mīgi* is placed in his mouth, lies lifeless on the ground. He is then touched with the pouch and "revives." Whereupon he is given a magical song, and the chief presents him with an otterskin pouch in which the candidate puts his own *mīgis*. To test the power of these shells, he touches all his fellow members one after the other, and they fall to the ground as if struck by lightning, then are resuscitated by the same touching process. He now has proof that his shells bestow both death and life. At the feast that ends the ceremony, the oldest *midē* narrates the tradition of the Midē'wiwin, and, in conclusion, the new member sings his song and drums.

The second initiation takes place at least a year after the first. The initiate's magical power is now increased by the large number of *mīgis* with which his body is stuffed, especially about the joints and the heart. With the third initiation, the *midē* obtains power enough to become a *jĕs'sakkīd'*, that is, he is able to perform all the various shamanic "juggleries," and, especially, he is now officially a master of healing. The fourth initiation introduces still more *mīgis* into his body.[5]

This example sufficiently shows the close relations between shamanism proper and the North American secret brotherhoods; both share the same archaic magico-religious tradition. . . .

Somewhat different is the Winnebago "Medicine Rite," whose complete initiation ceremony has been published by Paul Radin.[6] Here, too, we have a secret brotherhood to which admission is granted only after an extremely complex initiation ritual consisting principally in the candidate's "death" and resurrection from being touched by magical shells kept in otterskin pouches.[7] But here the resemblance of the Midē'wiwin of the Ojibwa and Menomini ends. Probably the rite of shooting shells into the candidate's body

5. *Ibid.*, pp. 204–76.
6. *The Road of Life and Death: a Ritual Drama of the American Indians* (New York, 1945).
7. *Ibid.*, pp. 5 ff., 283 ff., etc.

was incorporated at a late period (toward the end of the seventeenth century) into an earlier Winnebago ceremony rich in shamanic elements.[8] Since the Winnebago Medicine Rite shows various resemblances to the Pawnee "Ceremony of the Medicine Men," and since the distance between the two tribes excludes the possibility of direct borrowing, it may be concluded that both have preserved vestiges of an ancient ritual belonging to a cultural complex of Mexican origin.[9] It is also highly probable that the Ojibwa Midē'-wiwin is only a development of such a ritual.

In any case, the point to be emphasized is that the goal of the Winnebago Medicine Rite is the perpetual regeneration of the initiate. The mythical demiurge, the hare, sent to earth by the Creator to help mankind, was much struck by the fact that men died. To remedy the evil, he built an initiation lodge and turned himself into a small child. "If anyone repeats what [I] have done here," he declared, "this is the way he will look."[10] But the Creator interpreted the regeneration he had granted man differently: men can become reincarnated as many times as they wish.[11] And, basically, the Medicine Rite communicates the secret of a return to earth ad infinitum by revealing the right road to be taken after death and the words that the dead man must speak to the woman guardian of the beyond and to the Creator himself. Of course, the cosmogony and the origin of the Medicine Rite are also revealed, for in each case there is always a return to the mythical origins, an abolishing of time and thus a reinstatement of the miraculous moment of creation.

A number of shamanic elements are also preserved in the great mystical movements known as the Ghost-Dance Religion, which, though already endemic at the beginning of the nineteenth century, did not sweep through the North American tribes until toward its close.[12] Probably Christianity influenced at least some of its

8. *Ibid.*, p. 75.
9. *Ibid.*
10. *Ibid.*, p. 31.
11. *Ibid.*, p. 25.
12. Cf. James Mooney, "The Ghost-Dance Religion and the Sioux Outbreak of 1890," *Fourteenth Report of the Bureau of American Ethnology*, Part 2 (Washington, 1896), pp. 641–1136; Leslie Spier, "The Prophet Dance of the Northwest and Its Derivatives: the Source of the Ghost Dance," *General Series in Anthropology* I (Menasha, Wis., 1935); Cora A. Du Bois, "The 1870 Ghost Dance," *University of California Anthropological Records* 3:1 (Berkeley, 1939).

"prophets."[13] Messianic tension and the expectation of the imminent "end of the world" proclaimed by the prophets and masters of the Ghost-Dance Religion were easy to harmonize with an elementary and abortive Christian experience. But the actual structure of this important popular mystical movement is none the less autochthonous.[14] Its prophets had their visions in the purest archaic style; they "died" and ascended to the sky and there a celestial woman taught them how to approach the "Master of Life";[15] they received their great revelations in trances during which they journeyed through the beyond, and, after returning to normal consciousness, they told what they had seen;[16] during their voluntary trances they could be cut with knives, burned without feeling anything,[17] and so on.

The Ghost-Dance Religion prophesied the coming of universal regeneration: then all Indians, the dead and the living alike, would be called to inhabit a "regenerated earth"; they would reach this paradisal land by flying through the air with the help of magical feathers.[18] Some prophets—such as John Slocum, creator of the Shakers' movement—opposed the old Indian religion and especially the medicine men. This did not prevent the shamans from joining Slocum's movement; for in it they found the ancient tradition of celestial ascents and experiences of mystical light, and, like the shamans, the Shakers could resuscitate the dead.[19] The principal ritual of this sect consisted in prolonged contemplation of the sky and a continuous shaking of the arms, elementary techniques that are also found, in even more aberrant guises, in the ancient and modern Near East, always in connection with "shamanizing" groups. Other prophets also denounced the practice of sorcery and the tribe's medicine men, but did so rather to reform and regenerate them. An example is the prophet Shawano who, at about the age of thirty, was carried up to the sky and received a new revelation from the Master of Life, enabling him to know past and future events, and

13. Cf. Mooney, pp. 748 ff., 780, etc.
14. Autochthonous: indigenous, aboriginal. Eds.
15. Cf. Mooney, pp. 663 ff., 746 ff., 772 ff., etc.
16. *Ibid.*, pp. 672 ff.
17. *Ibid.*, pp. 719 ff.
18. *Ibid.*, pp. 777 ff., 781, 786.
19. See, for example, the case of four persons resuscitated, *ibid.*, p. 748.

who, though he denounced shamanism, declared that he had received the power to cure all illnesses and to withstand death itself
in the midst of battle.[20] In addition, this prophet regarded himself
as the incarnation of Manabozho, the first "Great Demiurge" of
the Algonquins, and wanted to reform the Midē'wiwin.[21]

But the astonishing success of the Ghost-Dance Religion was due
to the simplicity of its mystical technique. To prepare for the coming of the savior of the race, the members of the fraternity danced
continuously for five or six days and so went into trances during
which they saw and conversed with the dead. The dances were
ring dances around the fires, there was singing but no drumming.
The apostle confirmed the new priests by giving them an eagle's
feather during the dance. And he had only to touch one of the participants with such a feather for the dancer to fall lifeless; he remained in this state for a long time, during which his soul met the
dead and talked with them.[22] No other essential element of shamanism was lacking; the dancers became healers;[23] they wore
"ghost shirts," which were ritual costumes with representations of
stars, mythological beings, and even of visions obtained during
trances;[24] they adorned themselves with eagle feathers;[25] used the
steam bath;[26] and so on. Their dancing in itself represented a mystical technique that, if not exclusively shamanic, plays, as we have
seen, a decisive role in the shaman's ecstatic preparation.

Of course, the Ghost-Dance Religion reaches beyond shamanism
proper in all directions. The lack of an initiation and of a secret
traditional teaching, for example, suffices to separate it from shamanism. But we are dealing with a collective religious experience
crystallized around the imminence of an "end of the world"; the
source of this experience—communication with the dead—in itself implies, for one who obtains it, the abolition of the present
world and the reign, even though temporary, of a "confusion"
that constitutes both the closing of the present cosmic cycle and
the beginning of the glorious restoration of a new, paradisal cycle.

20. *Ibid.*, p. 672.
21. *Ibid.*, pp. 675–76.
22. *Ibid.*, pp. 915 ff.
23. *Ibid.*, p. 786.
24. *Ibid.*, pp. 789 ff., Pl. CIII, p. 895.
25. *Ibid.*, p. 791.
26. *Ibid.*, pp. 823 f.

The mythical visions of the "beginning" and the "end" of time being homologizable, since eschatology, at least in certain aspects, overlaps cosmology, the *eschaton* of the Ghost-Dance Religion reactualized the mythical *illud tempus* when communications with the sky, the Great God, and the dead were accessible to every human being. Such mystical movements differed from the traditional shamanism by the fact that, while preserving the essential elements of the shamanic ideology and techniques, they held that the time had come for the whole Indian people to obtain the shaman's privileged state, that is, to experience the re-establishment of "easy communication" with the sky, even as it existed at the dawn of time.

◆

CLASSICAL AND CHRISTIAN MYSTERIES

It is to Eliade's credit that he has been able to identify in so-called primitive societies rituals that have many parallels with the Hellenistic mysteries—the religious rites most frequently identified as "mysteries." In the following extracts he turns to the classical mysteries of Eleusis and Christianity, and it is informative now to see *them* in the light of the women's and men's mysteries presented above.

124. ELEUSIS AND THE HELLENISTIC MYSTERIES

The Eleusinian mysteries, the rites of Dionysus, Orphism, are exceedingly complex phenomena, whose importance in the religious and cultural history of Greece is considerable. . . . The Eleusinian mysteries, like the Dionysiac ceremonies, were founded on a divine myth; hence the succession of rites reactualized the primordial event narrated in the myth, and the participants in the rites were progressively introduced into the divine presence. To give an example: on the evening of their arrival at Eleusis, the initiands broke off their dances and rejoicings when they were told that Kore had been carried away. Torch in hand, crying and lamenting, they wandered everywhere, searching for Kore. Suddenly a herald announced that Helios had revealed where Kore was; and again all was gaiety, music, dancing. The myth of Demeter and Kore became contemporary once more; the rape of Kore, Demeter's laments, take place *here and now*, and it is by virtue of this nearness of the Goddesses, and finally of their *presence*, that the initiate (mystes) will have the unforgettable experience of initiation.

For, as Aristotle already noted (Frag. 15), the mystes[1] did not learn anything new; he already knew the myth, and he was not taught any really secret doctrine; but he performed ritual gestures and saw sacred objects. The initiation proper was performed in the place of initiation (telesterion) at Eleusis. It began with purifications. Then, his head covered by a cloth, the mystes was led into the telesterion and seated on a chair spread with an animal skin. For everything after this, we are reduced to conjecture. Clement of Alexandria (*Protrepticus*, II, 21) has preserved the sacred formula of the mysteries: "I fasted, I drank the *kykeon*, I took out of the chest, having done the act I put again into the basket, and from the basket again into the chest." We understand the first two parts of the rite—the fast and the drinking of the *kykeon*, which was a mixture of flour, water and mint that, according to the myth, Queen Metanira had offered to Demeter, exhausted by her long search for Kore.

For the rest of the sacred formula handed down by Clement, numerous interpretations have been proposed. . . . Some form of initiatory death, that is, a symbolic descent to Hell, is not improbable, for the play on words between "initiation" (*teleisthai*) and "dying" (*teleutan*) was quite popular in Greece.[2] "To die is to be initiated," Plato said. If, as seems likely, the mystical chest represented the nether world, the mystes, by opening it, symbolically descended to Hell. What we must note is that after this mysterious handling of the sacred objects, the mystes was born anew. We learn from Hippolytus that, at the culminating moment, the hierophant announced: "She who is Magnificent has given birth to a sacred child, Brimo (has engendered) Brimos."[3] Finally, the second degree of initiation included the *epopteia*; the mystes became the *epoptes*, "he who sees." We know that the torches were put out, a

1. Mystes: the person initiated. Eds.
2. Stobaeus, *Florilegium*, 120, 28, reproducing a fragment of Themistius or Plutarch.
3. Hippolytus, *Philososphoumena*, V, 8.

curtain raised, and the hierophant appeared with a box. He opened it and took out a ripe ear of grain. According to Walter Otto, "there can be no doubt of the miraculous nature of the event. The ear of wheat growing and maturing with a supernatural suddenness is just as much a part of the mysteries of Demeter as the vine growing in a few hours is part of the revels of Dionysus. . . . We find exactly the same plant miracles in the nature festivals of primitive peoples."[4] Soon afterward the sacred marriage between the hierophant and the priestess of Demeter took place.

It would be naïve to suppose that this brief treatment could convey the essentials of a mystery which, for over a thousand years, dominated the religious life of Greece and which, for at least a century, has given rise to impassioned controversies among scholars. The Eleusinian mysteries—like Dionysianism and Orphism in general—confront the investigator with countless problems, especially in regard to their origin and, hence, their antiquity. For in each of these cases we have to do with extremely archaic rites and beliefs. None of these initiatory cults can be regarded as a creation of the Greek mind. Their roots go deep into prehistory. Cretan, Asiatic, and Thracian traditions were taken over, enriched, and incorporated into a new religious horizon. It was through Athens that Eleusis became a Panhellenic religious center; but the mysteries of Demeter and Kore had been celebrated at Eleusis for centuries. The Eleusinian initiation descends directly from an agricultural ritual centered around the death and resurrection of a divinity controlling the fertility of the fields. The bull-roarer, which figured in the Orphic-Dionysiac ceremonies, is a religious object characteristic of primitive hunter cultures. . . . The myths and rites of Eleusis have their counterpart in the religions of certain tropical cultures whose structure is agricultural and matriarchal. The fact that such elements of archaic religious practice recur in the most central position in the Greek and the Greco-Oriental mysteries proves not only their extraordinary vitality but also their importance for the religious life of humanity. Undoubtedly we here have religious experiences that are at once primordial and exemplary.

For the purpose of our investigation, one thing is particularly of

4. W. F. Otto, "The Meaning of the Eleusinian Mysteries," in *The Mysteries. Papers from the Eranos Yearbooks* (New York, 1955), 2: 25, developing a conjecture of L. Deubner, *Attische Feste* (Berlin, 1932), p. 86.

interest—that these experiences are brought on by rites which, both in the Greco-Oriental and the primitive worlds, are initiatory, that is, pursue the novice's spiritual transmutation. At Eleusis, as in the Orphic-Dionysiac ceremonies, as in the Greco-Oriental mysteries of the Hellenistic period, the mystes submits himself to initiation in order to transcend the human condition and to obtain a higher, superhuman mode of being. The initiatory rites reactualize an origin myth, which relates the adventures, death, and resurrection of a Divinity. We know very little about these secret rites, yet we know that the most important of them concerned the death and mystical resurrection of the initiand. . . .

Everywhere there is this spiritual regeneration, a palingenesis, which found its expression in the radical change in the mystes' existential status. By virtue of his initiation, the neophyte attained to another mode of being; he became equal to the Gods, was one with the Gods. Apotheosis, deification, demortalizing (*apathanatismos*) are concepts familiar to all the Hellenistic mysteries. Indeed, for antiquity in general, the divinization of man was not an extravagant dream, "Know, then, that you are a God," Cicero wrote.[5] And in a Hermetic text we read: "I know thee, Hermes, and thou knowest me: I am thou and thou art I."[6] Similar expressions are found in Christian writings. As Clement of Alexandria says, the true (Christian) Gnostic "has already become God."[7] And for Lactantius, the chaste man will end by becoming *consimilis Deo*, "identical in all respects with God."[8]

The ontological transmutation of the initiate was proved above all through his existence after death. The Homeric *Hymn to Demeter*, Pindar, and Sophocles already praise the bliss of initiates in the Other World, and pity those who die without having been initiated.[9] In the Hellenistic period the idea that he who had been initiated into the mysteries enjoyed a privileged spiritual situation, both during life and after death, had become increasingly widespread. Those who submitted to initiation, then, sought thereby to

5. *De Republica*, VI, 17.
6. Cf. S. Angus, *The Mystery-Religions and Christianity* (London, 1925), p. 110, n. 5.
7. *Protrepticus*, VIII, 4.
8. *Institutiones Divinae*, VI, 21; Angus, *Mystery-Religions*, p. 106.
9. *Hymn to Demeter*, vv. 480–82; Pindar, *Threnoi*, Frag. X; Sophocles, Frag. 719 (Dindorf), 348 (Didot).

obtain a superhuman ontological status, more or less divine, and to ensure their survival after death, if not their immortality. And, as we have just seen, the mysteries employ the classic pattern: mystical death of the initiand, followed by a new, spiritual birth.

For the history of religion, the particular importance of the Greco-Oriental mysteries lies in the fact that they illustrate the need for a personal religious experience engaging man's entire existence, that is, to use Christian terminology, as including his "salvation" in eternity. Such a personal religious experience could not flourish in the framework of the public cults, whose principal function was to ensure the sanctification of communal life and the continuance of the State. In the great historical civilizations in which the mysteries proliferated, we no longer find the situation characteristic of primitive cultures; there, as we have noted more than once, the initiations of the youth were at the same time an occasion for the complete regeneration not only of the collectivity but also of the cosmos. In the Hellenistic period we find an entirely different situation; the immense success of the mysteries illustrates the break between the religious elites and the religion of the State, a break that Christianity will widen and, at least for a time, make complete.

But for our present investigation the interest of the mysteries lies in the fact that they demonstrate the perennial significance of the traditional patterns of initiation and their capacity for being indefinitely reanimated and enriched with new values. . . .

125. CHRISTIANITY AND INITIATION

From the end of the nineteenth century until about thirty years ago,[1] a number of scholars were convinced that they could explain the origins of Christianity by a more or less direct influence from the Greco-Oriental mysteries. Recent researches have not supported these theories. On the contrary, it has even been suggested that the renaissance of the mysteries in the first centuries of our era may well be related to the rise and spread of Christianity; that

SOURCE: *RSI*/115–20.
1. Eliade is referring to the initial form of *RSI* as The Haskell Lectures in 1956. Eds.

certain mysteries may well have reinterpreted their ancient rites in the light of the new religious values contributed by Christianity. . . . The presence of one or another initiatory theme in primitive Christianity does not necessarily imply the influence of the mystery religions. Such a theme could have been taken directly from one of the esoteric Jewish sects, especially the Essenes, concerning whom the Dead Sea manuscripts have now added sensationally to our knowledge.[2] Indeed, it is not even necessary to suppose that an initiatory theme was "borrowed" by Christianity from some other religion. As we have said, initiation is coexistent with any new revaluation of spiritual life. Hence there are two different problems involved, which it would be dangerous to confuse. The first raises the question of the initiatory elements (scenarios, ideology, terminology) in primitive Christianity. The second concerns the possible historical relations between Christianity and the mystery religions.

Let us begin by defining in what sense it is possible to speak of initiatory elements in primitive Christianity. Obviously, Christian baptism was from the first equivalent to an initiation. Baptism introduced the convert to a new religious community and made him worthy of eternal life. It is known that between 150 B.C. and A.D. 300 there was a strong baptist movement in Palestine and Syria. The Essenes too practiced ritual baths or baptisms. As among the Christians, it was an initiatory rite; but, unlike the Christians, the Essenes repeated their ritual baths periodically. Hence it would be useless to seek a parallel to Christian baptism in the lustration rites of the mysteries or other ceremonies of pagan antiquity. Not only the Essenes but other Jewish movements were familiar with it. But baptism could become a sacrament for the earliest Christians precisely because it had been instituted by Christ. In other words, the sacramental value of baptism derived from the fact that the Christians saw Jesus as the Messiah, the Son of God.

All this is already indicated by St. Paul (I Corinthians 10) and developed in St. John's Gospel: baptism is a free *gift* of God which makes possible a new birth from water and the Spirit (John 1:5).

2. For the following, we use the translations and commentaries of T. H. Gaster, *The Scriptures of the Dead Sea Sect* (New York, 1956), and especially the studies of Krister Stendahl, Oscar Cullmann, and Karl Georg Kuhn in K. Stendahl, ed., *The Scrolls and the New Testament* (New York, 1957).

As we shall soon see, the symbolism of baptism is much enriched after the third century. We shall then find borrowings from the language and imagery of the mysteries. But none of these borrowings occurs in primitive Christianity.

Another cult act whose structure is initiatory is the Eucharist, instituted by Jesus at the Last Supper. Through the Eucharist the Christian shares in the body and blood of the Lord. Ritual banquets were frequent in the mysteries, but the historical precedents for the Last Supper are not to be sought so far away. The Qumran texts have shown that the Essenes regarded meals taken in common as an anticipation of the Messianic Banquet. As Krister Stendahl points out, this idea is also found in the Gospels: ". . . Many will come from east and west and sit at table with Abraham, Isaac and Jacob in the Kingdom of Heaven" (Matthew 8:2). But here there is a new idea: the Christians regarded Jesus as already risen from the dead and raised to Heaven, whereas the Essenes awaited the resurrection of the Teacher of Righteousness as priestly Messiah together with the anointed of Israel. Even more important is the fact that, for the Christians, the Eucharist depended on a historical person and a historical event (Jesus and the Last Supper), but we do not find in the Qumran texts any redemptory significance accorded to a historical person. . . .[3]

The Qumran texts help us better to understand the historical context of the message of Jesus and of the development of the earliest Christian communities. We realize to what an extent primitive Christianity was bound up with the history of Israel and the hopes of the Jewish people. But even so, it is impossible not to realize all that distinguishes Christianity from the Essenes and in general from all other contemporary esoteric cults. Above all, there is the feeling of joy and newness. As has been pointed out, the terms designating newness and joy are characteristic of primitive Christian language.[4] The *newness* of Christianity is constituted by the historicity of Jesus; and the *joy* springs from certainty of his resurrection. For the earliest Christian communities, the resurrection of Jesus *could not be* identified with the periodic death and resurrection of the God of the mysteries. Like Christ's life, suffering, and death, his

3. Stendahl, *The Scrolls*, p. 10; Kuhn, in *ibid.*, p. 78.
4. A. D. Nock, "Hellenistic Mysteries and Christian Sacraments," *Mnemosyne*, Series 4, 5 (1952): 117–213, 199.

resurrection had occurred in history, "in the days of Pontius Pilate." The resurrection was an irreversible event; it was not repeated yearly, like the resurrection of Adonis, for example. It was not an allegory of the sanctity of cosmic life, as was the case with the so-called vegetation Gods, nor an initiatory scenario, as in the mysteries. It was a "sign" that formed part of the Messianic expectation of the Jewish people, and as such it had its place in the religious history of Israel, for the resurrection of the dead was an accompaniment of the coming of the Time. The resurrection of Jesus proclaimed that the last age (the *eschaton*) had begun. As St. Paul says, Jesus was resurrected as "the firstborn from the dead" (Colossians 1:18). This explains the belief which we find recorded in the Gospels, that many resurrections followed that of Jesus: "The graves were opened; and many bodies of the saints which slept arose" (Matthew 27:52). For the earliest Christians, the resurrection established a new era of history—the validation of Jesus as Messiah, and hence the spiritual transmutation of man and the total renewal of the world. This, of course, constituted a "mystery," but a mystery that was to be "proclaimed upon the housetops." And initiation into the Christian mystery was open to all.

In short, the initiatory elements in primitive Christianity simply demonstrate once again that initiation is an inseparable element in any revaluation of the religious life. It is impossible to attain to a higher mode of being, it is impossible to participate in a new irruption of sanctity into the world or into history, except by dying to profane, unenlightened existence and being reborn to a new, regenerated life. In view of the "inevitability" of initiation, it is surprising that we find so little trace of initiatory scenarios and terminology in primitive Christianity. St. Paul never uses *telete*, a specific technical term of the mysteries. It is true that he uses *mysterion*, but in the sense given it in the Septuagint, that is, "secret."[5] In the New Testament, *mysterion* does not refer to a cult act, as it does in the ancient religions. For St. Paul, the mystery is God's secret, that is, his decision to save man through his Son, Jesus Christ. The reference, then, is basically to the mystery of redemption. But redemption is an idea that is incomprehensible except in the context of the Biblical tradition; it is only in that tradition that man,

5. *Ibid.*, p. 100.

originally the son of God, had lost this privileged station by his sin.[6]

Jesus speaks of the "mysteries of the kingdom of Heaven" (Matthew 13:11; Mark 4:11; Luke 8:10), but the expression is only the counterpart of the "king's secret" of the Old Testament (Tobit 12: 7). In this sense, the mysteries concern the kingdom that Jesus opens to believers. The mysteries of the kingdom of heaven are the "secret counsels" that a king communicates only to his familiars (Judith 2: 2) and hides from others in the form of parables so that "they seeing see not; and hearing they hear not" (Matthew 13: 13). In conclusion, although Jesus' message also has an initiatory structure—and has it precisely because initiation is an integral part of any new religious revelation—there is no reason to suppose that primitive Christianity was influenced by the Hellenistic mysteries.

But with the spread of Christianity into all the provinces of the Roman Empire, especially after its final triumph under Constantine, there is a gradual change in perspective. The more that Christianity becomes a universalistic religion, the more its historicity recedes into the background. This does not mean that the Church abandons the historicity of Christ, as was done by certain Christian heresies and by Gnosticism. But by becoming paradigmatic for the entire inhabited world, the Christian message tended more and more to be couched in ecumenical terms. Primitive Christianity was bound up with a local history, that of Israel. From a certain point of view, any local history is in danger of provincialism. When a local history becomes sacred and at the same time exemplary, that is, a paradigm for the salvation of all humanity, it demands expression in a universally understandable language. But the only universal religious language is the language of symbols. The Christian writers will increasingly turn to symbols to make the mysteries of the Gospel intelligible. But the Roman Empire had two universalistic spiritual movements, that is, movements not confined within the frontiers of a local culture: the mysteries and philosophy. Victorious Christianity borrowed from both the former and the latter. Hence we find a threefold process of enrichment of primitive Christianity: (1) by archaic symbols which will be rediscovered and revalued by

6. H. Rahner, "The Christian Mystery and the Pagan Mysteries," in *The Mysteries, Papers from the Eranos Yearbooks*, 2 (New York, 1955): 337–401, 362.

being given new Christological meanings; (2) by borrowing from the imagery and initiatory themes of the mysteries; (3) by the assimilation of Greek philosophy.

For our purpose, all that is pertinent is the incorporation of initiatory motifs into victorious Christianity. But we must refer in passing to the Church Father's use of archaic and universally disseminated symbols. For example, we find the symbols of the Cosmic Tree and of the center of the world incorporated into the symbolism of the Cross. The Cross is described as a "tree rising from earth to Heaven," as "the Tree of Life planted on Calvary," the tree that "springing from the depths of the Earth, rose to Heaven and sanctifies the uttermost bounds of the universe." In other words, in order to convey the mystery of universal redemption through the Cross, Christian writers used not only the symbols of the Old Testament and the ancient Near East (reference to the Tree of Life) but also the archaic symbols of the Cosmic Tree set at the center of the world and ensuring communication between Heaven and earth. The Cross was the visible sign of the redemption accomplished by Jesus Christ; hence it must replace the ancient symbols of elevation to Heaven. And since the redemption extended to the whole of humanity, the Cross had to be set at the center of the world, that it might sanctify the entire universe. . . .

For our purpose it is important to note that, together with Neoplatonic philosophy, the first values to be accepted by Christianity were the initiatory themes and the imagery of the mysteries. Christianity took the place of the mysteries, as it took the place of the other religious forms of antiquity. The Christian initiation could not coexist with initiations into the mysteries. Otherwise the religion that sought to preserve at least the historicity of Christ would have been in grave danger of becoming indistinguishably confused with the countless syncretistic Gnosticisms and religions. The intolerance of Christianity in its hour of triumph is the most striking proof that no confusion with the Hellenistic mysteries was possible. For the fact is that even Christianity, a revealed religion which did not originally imply any secret rite, which had proclaimed and propagated itself in the broad light of day and for all men, came in the end to borrow from the liturgies and the vocabulary of the Hellenistic mysteries. Morphologically speaking, Christianity too comprises an initiatory pattern—if only by the fact that baptism symbolizes the catechumen's mystical death and resurrection in Christ. It would be needless to insist on the radical differences in religious content that separate the Christian *mysterion* from the Hellenistic mysteries; for, as the result of a succession of profound and thoroughly documented studies, those differences are today clear. But in estimating the role and the importance of initiation in the religious life of humanity, it is not without interest to record the fact that certain initiatory themes were taken over and revaluated by Christianity.

◆

MYSTICISM: YOGA AND THE MYSTIC LIGHT

Professor Eliade has devoted a massive study to yoga (*Yoga: Immortality and Freedom*), and that book has been important in disabusing many people of the idea that yoga is merely a form of weight-control or physical exercise. In the following extracts, we present some of the materials from *Yoga* that emphasize the mysteries-religion side of yoga, the advanced spiritual disciplines. And because certain aspects of the practice of yoga lead to the theme of the "mystic light," we conclude this section with that subject—the "highest form," if you will, of mystical experiencing of the sacred.

126. THE DOCTRINES OF YOGA

Four basic and interdependent concepts, four "kinetic ideas," bring us directly to the core of Indian spirituality. They are *karma*, *maya*, *nirvana*, and *yoga*. A coherent history of Indian thought could be written starting from any one of these basic concepts; the other three would inevitably have to be discussed. In terms of Western philosophy, we can say that, from the post-Vedic period on, India has above all sought to understand:

1. The law of universal causality, which connects man with the cosmos and condemns him to transmigrate indefinitely. This is the law of *karma*.

2. The mysterious process that engenders and maintains the cos-

mos and, in so doing, makes possible the "eternal return" of existences. This is *maya*, cosmic illustion, endured (even worse—accorded validity) by man as long as he is blinded by ignorance (*avidya*).

3. Absolute reality, "situated" somewhere beyond the cosmic illusion woven by *maya* and beyond human experience as conditioned by *karma*; pure Being, the Absolute, by whatever name it may be called—the Self (*atman*), *brahman*, the unconditioned, the transcendent, the immortal, the indestructible, *nirvana*, etc.

4. The means of attaining to Being, the effectual techniques for gaining liberation. This corpus of means constitutes Yoga properly speaking.

With these four concepts in mind, we can understand how the fundamental problem of all philosophy, the search for truth, presents itself to Indian thought. For India, truth is not precious in itself; it becomes precious by virtue of its soteriological function, because knowledge of truth helps man to liberate himself. It is not the possession of truth that is the supreme end of the Indian sage; it is liberation, the conquest of absolute freedom. The sacrifices that the European philosopher is prepared to make to attain truth in and for itself: sacrifice of religious faith, of worldly ambitions, of wealth, personal freedom, and even life—to these the Indian sage consents only in order to conquer liberation. To "free oneself" is equivalent to forcing another plane of existence, to appropriating another *mode of being* transcending the human condition. This is as much as to say that, for India, not only is metaphysical knowledge translated into terms of *rupture* and *death* ("breaking" the human condition, one "dies" to all that was human); it also necessarily implies a consequence of a mystical nature: *rebirth to a nonconditioned mode of being*. And this is liberation, absolute freedom.

In studying the theories and practices of Yoga we shall have occasion to refer to all the other "kinetic ideas" of Indian thought. For the present, let us begin by defining the meaning of the term *yoga*. Etymologically, *yoga* derives from the root *yuj*, "to bind together," "hold fast," "yoke," which also governs Latin *jungere*, *jugum*, French *joug*, etc. The word *yoga* serves, in general, to designate any *ascetic technique* and any *method of meditation*. Naturally, these various asceticisms and meditations have been differently evaluated by the many Indian philosophical currents and mystical movements. As we shall soon see, there is a "classic" Yoga, a "system of philosophy" expounded by Patanjali in his celebrated *Yoga-sutras*; and it is from the "system" that we must set out in order to understand the position of Yoga in the history of Indian thought. But, side by side with this "classic" Yoga, there are countless forms of "popular," nonsystematic yoga; there are also non-Brahmanic yogas (Buddhist, Jainist); above all, there are yogas whose structures are "magical," "mystical," and so on.

Basically it is the term *yoga* itself that has permitted this great variety of meanings, for if, etymologically, *yuj* means "to bind," it is nevertheless clear that the "bond" in which this action of binding is to result presupposes, as its preliminary condition, breaking the "bonds" that unite the spirit to the world. In other words, liberation cannot occur if one is not first "detached" from the world, if one has not begun by withdrawing from the cosmic circuit. For without doing so, one could never succeed in finding or mastering oneself. Even in its "mystical" acceptation—that is, as signifying *union*—Yoga implies a preliminary detachment from matter, emancipation with respect to the world. The emphasis is laid on man's *effort* ("to yoke"), on his self-discipline, by virtue of which he can obtain concentration of spirit even before asking (as in the mystical varieties of Yoga) for the aid of the divinity. "To bind together," "to hold fast," "to yoke"—the purpose of all this is to *unify* the spirit, to do away with the dispersion and automatism that characterize profane consciousness. For the "devotional" (mystical) schools of Yoga this "unification," of course, only precedes the true union, that of the human soul with God.

What characterizes Yoga is not only its *practical* side, but also its *initiatory* structure. One does not learn Yoga by oneself; the guidance of a master (*guru*) is necessary. Strictly speaking, all the other "systems of philosophy"—as, in fact, all traditional disciplines or crafts—are, in India, taught by masters and are thus initiations; for millenniums they have been transmitted orally, "from mouth to ear." But Yoga is even more markedly initiatory in character. For, as in other religious initiations, the yogin begins by forsaking the profane world (family, society) and, guided by his *guru*, applies himself to passing successively beyond the behavior patterns and values proper to the human condition. When we shall have seen to what a degree the yogin attempts to dissociate himself from the profane condition, we shall understand that he dreams of "dying to this life." We shall, in fact, witness a *death* followed by a *rebirth* to another mode of being—that represented by liberation. The analogy between Yoga and initiation becomes even more marked if we think of the initiatory rites—primitive or other—that pursue the creation of a "new body," a "mystical body" (symbolically assimilated, among the primitives, to the body of the newborn infant). Now, the "mystical body," which will allow the yogin to enter the transcendent mode of being, plays a considerable part in all forms of Yoga, and especially in tantrism and alchemy. From this point of view Yoga takes over and, on another plane, continues the archaic and universal symbolism of initiation—a symbolism that, it may be noted, is already documented in the Brahmanic tradition (where the initiate is called the "twice-born"). The initiatory rebirth is defined, by all forms of Yoga, as access to a nonprofane and hardly describable mode of being, to which the Indian schools give various names: *moksha, nirvana, asamskrita,* etc.

127. YOGA AND HINDUISM

It is hard—even with a little "free association"—to conceive of Hinduism without the element of Yoga. It is shown here as a pervasive, purifying, power-giving, and theistic enterprise which has gone into the making of Hinduism as a world religion. In watching the way Eliade notes the various Indian scholarly and literary responses to it, we see that Yoga is so very basic to Indian spirituality that it was possible to understand its purposes in different ways, although immortality and freedom in some sense always remained primary.

The gradual spread of Yoga practice, regarded as an admirable way of salvation, can be traced both in juridico-theological literature and in the didactic and religious portions of the *Mahabharata.* Yet it would be difficult to define the successive stages of this infiltration, which will finally result in the almost total conquest of

SOURCE: *Y*/143–46; cf. *Y*/47–95.

Indian spirituality by Yoga. We shall say only that we are dealing with works whose composition lies in the period between the fourth century B.C. and the fourth century of our era. A fact of greater interest for us is the coincidence between this triumph of yogic practices and the irresistible upsurge of popular mystical devotion. For this planting of Yoga technique in the very heart of Hinduism took place at a moment of crisis for orthodoxy; that is, at the very moment when the latter validated the "sectarian" mystical movements en bloc. In the course of its expansion, Brahmanism—like every victorious religion—was forced to accept a number of elements that had originally been foreign or even hostile to it. Assimilation of the forms in which autochthonous, pre-Aryan religious sentiment had found expression began very early, from the Vedic period (the god Shiva is an example). But this time— that is, at the beginning of the Indian Middle Ages (during the period that extends from the flowering of Buddhism to the *Bhagavad-Gita*)—assimilation assumes alarming proportions. We sometimes have the impression of a victorious revolution, before which Brahman orthodoxy can only bow. What is called "Hinduism" dates from the still little-known period when the ancient Vedic pantheon was eclipsed by the enormous popularity of a Shiva, a Vishnu, or a Krishna. There is no room here to study the causes of this profound and immense transformation. But let us note that one of its principal causes was precisely the need that the masses of the people felt for a more concrete religious experience, for a mystical devotion more easily accessible, more intimate, more personal. Now, the traditional (i.e., popular, "baroque," nonsystematic) practices of Yoga offered just this type of mystical experience; scorning rituals and theological science, they were based almost entirely on immediate, concrete data still hardly separated from their physiological substratum.

Naturally, this increasing infiltration of yogic techniques into orthodoxy did not take place without encountering a certain degree of resistance. From time to time voices were raised against the propaganda of the ascetics and "magicians," who claimed that neither final liberation (*mukti*) nor the "occult powers" (*siddhi*) could be gained except by adherence to their particular disciplines. Needless to say, this resistance appeared first in the official circles of orthodox Brahmanism, made up of Vedantist jurists and metaphysicians. Both groups adhered to the "golden mean" in respect to Yoga ascetic and contemplative techniques, which they considered to be exaggerated in some cases and contrary to the Vedantic ideal in others. Manu writes: "If he keeps both his organs and his consciousness under subjection, he can attain his ends without further tormenting his body by Yoga."[1] Shankara too writes in the same vein; Yoga, he warns, "leads to the acquirement of extraordinary powers," but "the highest beatitude cannot be obtained by the road of Yoga."[2] The true Vedantist chooses purely metaphysical knowledge.

But reactions of this kind are sporadic. In fact, if the Vedantic tradition continues to see Yoga practices only as a means for acquiring possession of magical powers or, at best, as a purification preliminary to true salvation, to which only metaphysical knowledge can lead, it nevertheless remains true that the majority of the juridico-theological treatises do in fact validate such practices and sometimes even praise them. The *Vaisishta Dharma Shastra*, for example, declares that "neither . . . through the daily recitation of the Veda, nor through offering sacrifices can the twice-born reach that condition which they attain by the practice of Yoga."[3] The magical and purifying power of this practice is incomparable: "If, untired, he performs three suppressions of his breath according to the rule, the sins which he committed during a day and a night are instantly destroyed."[4] And another theologico-juridic treatise, the *Vishnusmriti*, confirms the miraculous value of logic technique: "Whatever he meditates upon, that is obtained by a man: such is the mysterious power of meditation." It is true that the text immediately following contains the significant stipulation that the yogin's goal must be achieving final liberation, not enjoyment of the "powers" that his meditation will confer on him. "Therefore must he dismiss everything perishable from his thoughts and meditate

1. *Smriti*, II, 98; trans. G. Bühler, *The Laws of Manu*, p. 48.
2. Commentary on the *Vedanta-sutras*, trans. G. Thibaut, *The Vedanta Sutra. With Shankara's Commentary* (Sacred Books of the East, XXXIV), I, 223, 298.
3. XXV, 7; trans. G. Bühler, *The Sacred Laws of the Aryas* (Sacred Books of the East, XIV), p. 125.
4. *Ibid.*, XXVI, 1; trans. Bühler, p. 126.

upon what is imperishable only. There is nothing imperishable except Purusha. Having become united with him (through constant meditation), he obtains final liberation."[5] But this is precisely the counsel of the *yoga sutras*.

128. YOGA TECHNIQUES IN THE MAHÀBHARATA

In the *Mahabharata* Yoga, in contrast to Samkhya, designates any activity that leads the soul to Brahman and at the same time confers countless "powers." In the majority of cases this activity is equivalent to restraining the senses, asceticism, and various kinds of penance. Only occasionally does Yoga have the meaning that Krishna gives it in the *Bhagavad-Gita*—"renunciation of the fruits of one's acts." This fluidity in the meanings of the word has been brought out by Hopkins in an exhaustive study.[1] "Yoga" sometimes means "method,"[2] sometimes "activity,"[3] "force,"[4] "meditation,"[5] or "renunciation" (*sannyasa*),[6] etc. This variety of meanings corresponds to a real morphological diversity. If the word "yoga" *means* many things, that is because Yoga *is* many things. For the epic is the meeting place of countless ascetic and popular traditions, each with its own "Yoga"—that is, its particular mystical technique. The many centuries during which new episodes were interpolated allowed all these forms of "baroque" Yoga to find a place (and a justification), with the result that the epic was transformed into an encyclopedia.

In broad outline, we can distinguish three classes of data of possible interest to our study: (1) episodes involving asceticism (*tapas*),[7] and revealing practices and theories closely related to Vedic *ascesis*

SOURCE: *Y*/149–52.

5. XCVI, 11–14; trans. Julius Jolly, *The Institutes of Vishnu*, pp. 285–90.

1. "Yoga-Technique in the Great Epic," *Journal of the American Oriental Society* 22 (1901): 333–79.

2. E.g., *Bhagavad-Gita*, III, 3.

3. *Mokshadharma*, 11, 682.

4. *Ibid.*, 11, 675 ff.

5. *Ibid.*, 11, 691, etc.

6. *Bhagavad-Gita*, VI, 2.

7. *Tapas*: see selection 78. Eds.

but without references to Yoga, properly speaking; (2) episodes and discourses in which Yoga and *tapas* are synonymous and are both regarded as magical techniques; (3) didactic discourses and episodes in which Yoga is presented with a philosophically elaborated terminology of its own. It is especially the documents in this third category—most of them contained in the *Mokshadharma*—that we regard as of interest, for they reveal some forms of Yoga that are inadequately documented elsewhere.

We find, for example, extremely ancient "magical" practices, which yogins use to influence the gods and even to terrorize them. The phenomenology of this magical asceticism is archaic: silence (*mauna*), extreme torture (*ativatapas*), "desiccation of the body," are means employed not only by yogins but also by kings.[8] To move Indra . . . , Pandu stands on one foot for a day and thus obtains *samadhi*.[9] But this trance exhibits no yogic content; rather, it is a hypnosis provoked by physical means, and the relations between the man and the god remain on the level of magic. Elsewhere Yoga and pure asceticism, *tapas*, are confused.[10] *Yatin* (ascetic) and *yogin* become equivalent terms, and finally both come to designate any being "desirous of concentrating his mind" (*yuyuksat*) and whose object of study is not the scriptures (*Shastra*), but the mystical syllable *OM*. There is little doubt that the "study of the syllable *OM*" designates techniques concerned with mystical audition, with repetition and "assimilation" of particular magical formulas (*dharani*), with incantation, etc.

But, whatever the method chosen, these practices are crowned by the acquisition of a force that our texts call the "force of Yoga" (*yoga-balam*). Its immediate cause is "fixation of mind" (*dharana*), which is obtained both by "placidity and equanimity" (the "sword" of yogic equanimity)[11] and by progressively retarding the rhythm of respiration.[12] The latest interpolations in the *Mahabharata* are full of mnemotechnic schemata and summaries of yogic practices. Most of them reflect the traditional clichés: "A yogin who, devoted to the great vow . . . , skillfully fixes his subtle spirit [*suksh-*

---

8. *Mahabharata*, I, 115, 24; I, 119, 7 and 34.
9. *Ibid.*, I, 123, 26.
10. E.g., *ibid.*, XII, 153, 36.
11. *Mahabharata*, XII, 255, 7.
12. *Ibid.*, XII, 192, 13–14.

man atman] in the following places: navel, neck, head, heart, stomach, hips, eye, ear, and nose, quickly burning all his good and evil actions, were they like a mountain (in size), and seeking to attain the supreme Yoga, is released (from the snares of existence) if such be his will."[13]

Another text[14] magnifies the difficulty of these practices and draws attention to the danger that threatens him who fails: "Hard is the great path . . . and few are they who travel it to the end, but greatly guilty . . . is he called who, after entering the way of Yoga . . . , gives up his journey and turns back." This is the well-known danger inherent in all magical actions, which unleash forces capable of killing the magician if he is not strong enough to subdue them by his will and direct them in accordance with his desire. The yogin's ascetic practice has unleashed an impersonal and sacred force, similar to the energies released by any other magical or religious act.

The magical character of Yoga practices is also brought out on other occasions. One text, for example, explains that he who knows the most perfect carnal joys is not the Brahman but the yogin; even on earth, in the course of his ascetic conditioning, the yogin is attended by luminous women, but in heaven all the pleasures he has renounced on earth will be his to enjoy with tenfold intensity.[15]

129. YOGA TECHNIQUES IN THE BHAGAVAD-GITA

In addition to this Yoga within the reach of everyone, which consists in renouncing the "fruit of one's acts," the *Bhagavad-Gita* also briefly expounds a yogic technique in the strict sense, for the use of *munis* (VI, 11 ff.). Although morphologically (bodily postures, gazing at the tip of the nose, etc.) this technique resembles the one described by Patañjali, the meditation of which Krishna speaks is different from that of the *Yoga-sutras*. In the first place, *pranayama* is not mentioned in this context. Secondly, yogic meditation in the *Gita* does not achieve its supreme end unless the yogin concentrates on Krishna.

SOURCE: *Y*/159–61.
13. *Ibid.*, XII, 301, 39 ff.
14. *Ibid.*, V, 52 ff.
15. *Ibid.*, XIII, 107.

"With soul serene and fearless, constant in his vow to keep the way of chastity [*brahmacari*], his mind firm and steadfastly thinking of Me, he must practice Yoga, taking Me for the supreme end. Thus, with his soul continually devoted to meditation and his mind under control, the yogin obtains the peace that dwells in Me and whose final boundary is *nirvana*" (VI, 14–15). The mystical devotion (*bhakti*) of which Krishna is the object gives him an infinitely greater role than that which Ishvara played in the *Yoga-sutras*. In the *Gita*, Krishna is the only goal; it is he who justifies yogic meditation and practice, it is upon him that the yogin "concentrates," it is through his grace (and in the *Gita* the concept of grace already begins to take form, foreshowing the luxuriant development that it will undergo in Vishnuist literature) that the yogin obtains the *nirvana* that is neither the *nirvana* of late Buddhism nor the *samadhi* of the *Yoga-sutras*, but a state of perfect mystical union between the soul and its God.

A true yogin (. . . "freed from the corruption" of good and evil) easily attains the infinite bliss . . . produced by contact with Brahman. . . . This invoking of Brahman (VI, 28) in a text that is a vindication of Krishna need not surprise us. In the *Bhagavad-Gita*, Krishna is pure Spirit; the "great Brahman" is only the "womb" (*yoni*) for him (XIV, 3). "I am the father, the giver of the seed" (XIV, 4).[1] Krishna is the "foundation of Brahman," as he is of immortality, of the imperishable, of eternal order and perfect happiness (XIV, 27). But although in this context Brahman is put in the "feminine" condition of *prakriti*, his nature is spiritual. The *muni* attains him through Yoga (V, 6). The "infinite bliss" that results from union with Brahman allows the yogin to see "the soul [*atman*] in all beings and all beings in the *atman*" (VI, 29). And, in the following strophe, it is precisely the identification of the *atman* of beings with Krishna that provides the foundation for the mystical bond between the yogin and the God: "To him who sees me in everything and everything in me, I am never lost, and he is not lost to me. The devotee who worships me abiding in all beings, holding that all is one, lives in me, however he may be living" (VI, 30–31).[2]

1. Trans. Telang, p. 107.
2. *Ibid.*, p. 71.

We find the same motif as that of the verse just cited (VI, 30) in the *Isha Upanishad* (VI), which proves that the Upanishads contained theistic trends that they passed on to the *Gita*, where they flowered so magnificently. Krishna the personal god and source of true mystical experiences (*bhakti*), is here identified with the Brahman of the purely speculative metaphysics of the earliest Upanishads.

Nevertheless, the *Gita* reserves its highest praise not for the yogin completely detached from the pain and illusions of this world, but for him who regards another's pain and joy as his own (VI, 32). This is a leitmotiv of Indian mysticism, and particularly of Buddhist mysticism. The author of the *Bhagavad-Gita* bestows all his sympathy on him who practices this kind of Yoga. If he fails in this life, he will be reborn in a family of talented yogins, and, in another life, will succeed in accomplishing what he could not achieve in this (VI, 41). Krishna reveals to Arjuna that the mere fact of having attempted the way of Yoga raises the yogin above the man who has confined himself to practicing the rites prescribed by the Vedas (VI, 44). Finally, Krishna does not fail to say that, among the ways to salvation, the best and most commendable is the way of Yoga: "Yoga is higher than asceticism [*tapas*], higher even than knowledge [*jnana*], higher than sacrifice" (VI, 46).

The triumph of yogic practices is here complete. Not only are they accepted by the *Bhagavad-Gita*, the apogee of Indian spirituality; they are elevated to first place. It is true that this Yoga is purified from the last traces of magic (rigorous asceticism, etc.), and that the most important of its ancient techniques, *pranayama*, is reduced to a very minor role. It is true, too, that meditation and concentration here become instruments of an *unio mystica* with a God who reveals himself as a person. Nevertheless, the acceptance of yogic practices by the Vishnuist mystical and devotional trend proves the considerable popularity of these practices as well as their universality in India. Krishna's discourse amounts to a validation, for all Hinduism, of Yoga technique regarded as a purely Indian means of obtaining mystical union with a personal God. By far the greater part of the modern yogic literature published in India and elsewhere finds its theoretical justification in the *Bhagavad-Gita*.

130. YOGA AND BUDDHISM

Eliade's comments on yoga and its relation to Buddhism (granting the uncertain nature of Buddha's own techniques) represents a kind of "revalorization" of Hindu conceptions. Yoga, then, gains acceptance in Buddhism—at least among the less "popular" strains —only as a means of realizing the nonacceptance *of any idea of permanency in life. Neither union nor communion was thus the Buddhist goal, but that state (= Nirvana) which defies definition by leaving far behind all the methods and meanings that had become attached to the quest for salvation or liberation.*

We must remember that the Buddha's message was addressed to suffering man, to man caught in the net of transmigration. For the Buddha, as for all forms of Yoga, salvation could be gained only as the result of a personal effort, of a concrete assimilation of truth. It was neither a *theory* nor an escape into one or another kind of *ascetic effort.* "Truth" must be *understood* and at the same time *known experimentally.* Now, as we shall see, the two roads were attended by dangers; "understanding" ran the risk of remaining mere speculation, "experimental knowledge" might overwhelm ecstasy. But, for the Buddha, one can be "saved" only by attaining *nirvana*—that is, by going beyond the plane of profane human experience and re-establishing the plane of the unconditioned. In other words, one can be saved only by *dying* to this profane world and *being reborn* into a transhuman life impossible to define or describe.

This is why the symbolisms of death, rebirth, and initiation persist in Buddhist texts. The monk must create a "new body" for himself, be "reborn," as in other initiations, after being "dead." The Buddha himself proclaims it: "Moreover, I have shown my disciples the way whereby they call into being out of this body [composed of the four elements] another body of the mind's creation . . . , complete in all its limbs and members, and with transcendental faculties. . . . It is just like a man who should draw a reed from its sheath—or a snake from its slough—or a sword from its scabbard,—recognizing that the reed, the snake, or the sword was

Source: *Y*/164–73.

one thing and the sheath, slough, or scabbard was another," etc.[1] The initiatory symbolism is obvious; the image of the snake and its cast skin is one of the oldest symbols of mystical death and resurrection, and occurs in the literature of Brahmanism.[2] Ananda Coomaraswamy has shown that the Buddhist ordination continued the Vedic initiation (*diksha*) and adhered to the schema of initiations in general. The monk gave up his family name and became a "son of Buddha" (*shakyaputto*), for he was "born among the saints" (*ariya*); so Kassapa, speaking of himself, said: "Natural Son of the Blessed One, born of his mouth, born of the Dhamma, fashioned by the Dhamma, and an heir of the Dhamma," etc.[3] The importance of the *guru* as initiatory master is no less great in Buddhism than in any other Indian soteriology.

To obtain the state of the unconditioned—in other words, to die completely to this profane, painful, illusory life and to be reborn (in another "body"!) to the mystical life that will make it possible to attain *nirvana*—the Buddha employs the traditional yogic techniques, but correcting them by the addition of a profound effort to "comprehend" truth. Let us note that the preliminaries of Buddhist *ascesis* and meditation are similar to those recommended by the *Yoga-sutras* and other classic texts. The ascetic should choose a retired spot (in the forest, at the foot of a tree, in a cave, in a graveyard, or even on a heap of straw in the open fields), assume the *asana* position, and begin his meditation. "Putting away the hankering after the world, he abides with unhankering heart, and purifies his mind of covetousness. Putting away the canker of ill-will, he abides with heart free from enmity, benevolent and compassionate towards every living thing, and purifies his mind of malevolence. Putting away sloth and torpor, he abides clear of both; conscious of light, mindful and self-possessed, he purifies his mind of sloth and torpor. . . . Putting away doubt, he abides as one who has passed beyond perplexity; no longer in suspense as to what is good, he purifies his mind of doubt."[4]

1. *Majjhima-nikaya*, II, 17; trans. Robert Chalmers, *Further Dialogues of the Buddha*, II, 10.

2. *Jaiminiya Brahmana*, II, 134, etc.

3. *Samyutta-nikaya*, II, 221; trans. Coomaraswamy.

4. *Udumbarika Sihanada Suttanta, Digha-nikaya*, III, 49; trans. T. W. and C. A. F. Rhys Davids, *Dialogues of the Buddha*, III, 44. See also *Dialogues*, II, 327 ff.; *Vinaya Texts*, I, 119, etc.

Although containing "moral" elements, this meditation is not ethi-cal in intent. Its purpose is to purify the ascetic's consciousness, to prepare it for higher spiritual experiences. Yogic meditation, as interpreted by the Buddha in some texts of the *Digha-nikaya*, defi-nitely aims at "remaking" the ascetic's consciousness—that is, at creating for him anew "direct experience" of his psychic life and even of his biological life. Through all of his concrete actions—gait, bodily posture, respiration, etc.—the ascetic must concretely rediscover the "truths" revealed by the Master; in other words, he turns all his movements and actions into pretexts for meditation. The *Maha Sattipatthana Suttanta*[5] specifies that the *bhikku*, after choosing a solitary spot for his meditation, should become con-scious of all those physiological acts he had previously performed automatically and unconsciously. "Whether he inhale a long breath, let him be conscious thereof; or whether he exhale a long breath, let him be conscious thereof [etc.]. . . . Let him practice with the thought 'Conscious of my whole body will I inhale . . . will I ex-hale.' Let him practice with the thought 'I will inhale tranquillizing my bodily organism . . . I will exhale tranquillizing,' " etc.[6]

This procedure is not simply a *pranayama* exercise; it is also a meditation on the Buddhist "truths," a permanent experiencing of the unreality of matter. For that is the purpose of this meditation—to assimilate the fundamental "truths" completely, to transform them into a "continual experience," to diffuse them, as it were, through the monk's entire being. For the same text of the *Digha-nikaya* (II, 292) later states: a *bhikku*, "whether he departs or returns, whether he looks at or looks away from, whether he has drawn in or stretched out [his limbs], whether he had donned under-robe, over-robe, or bowl, whether he is eating, drinking, chewing, reposing, or whether he is obeying the calls of nature . . . in going, standing, sitting, sleeping, watching, talking, or keeping silence, he knows what he is doing."[7]

It is easy to comprehend the aim of this lucidity. Always, and whatever he may be doing, the *bhikku* must understand both his body and his soul, so that he may continually realize the fragility of the phenomenal world and the unreality of the "soul." The

5. *Digha-nikaya*, II, 327 ff.
6. Trans. Rhys Davids, *Dialogues*, II, 328.
7. Trans. Rhys Davids, *Dialogues*, II, 329.

Sumangala Vilasini commentary draws the following conclusion from this kind of meditation on the actions of the body: "They say it is a living entity that walks, a living entity that stands; but is there any living entity to walk or to stand? There is not."[8]

But this permanent attention to one's own life, this technique for destroying illusions created by a false conception of the "soul," are only the preliminaries. Real Buddhist meditation begins with experiencing the four psychic states called *jhanas* (cf. Skr. *dhyana*).

We do not know exactly what meditational technique the Buddha chose and practiced. The same formulas are often used to express various contents. (We may recall the troublingly diverse meanings of the word *yoga* throughout all the Indian literatures.) It is, however, probable that at least a part of the meditational technique employed by the Buddha was preserved by his disciples and transmitted by the primitive ascetic tradition. How should so rich and coherent a corpus of spiritual exercises be lost, or how should it suffer mutilation, in a tradition in which the Master's direct teaching plays such an important part? But, according to the texts collected by Caroline Rhys Davids,[9] it is clear that the Buddha was a fervent *jhain* and that he sought neither the Cosmic Soul (*brahman*) nor God (Ishvara) through the *jhana* that he practiced, nor exhorted others to seek them. For him, *jhana* was a means of "mystical" experimentation, a way of access to suprasensible realities, and not an *unio mystica*. This yogic experience prepared the monk for a "superknowledge" (*abhijna*) whose final goal was *nirvana*.

It is in the *Potthapada-sutta* (10 ff.)[10] that the technique of Buddhist meditation was formulated, if not for the first time (which is highly probable), at least in the clearest fashion. We shall give several long extracts from thi simportant text: "When he (the *bhikku*] has realized that these Five Hindrances [*nivarana*] have been put away from within him, a gladness springs up within him, and joy arises to him thus gladdened, and so rejoicing all his frame becomes at ease, and being thus at ease he is filled with a sense of peace, and in that peace his heart is stayed. Then estranged from lusts, aloof from evil dispositions, he enters into and remains

8. H. C. Warren, *Buddhism in Translations*, p. 358 n.
9. "Dhyana in Early Buddhism," *Indian Historical Quarterly* 3 (1927): 689–715.
10. *Digha-nikaya*, I, 182 ff.

in the First Rapture [*jhana*] . . . a state of joy and ease born of detachment [*vivekaja*: "born of solitude"], reasoning and investigation going on the while. Then that idea . . . of lusts, that he had before, passes away. And thereupon there arises within him a subtle, but actual, consciousness of the joy and peace arising from detachment, and he becomes a person to whom that idea is consciously present."

Then, "suppressing all reasoning and investigation, [the *bhikku*] enters into and abides in the Second Rapture [*jhana*] . . . a state of joy and ease, born of the serenity of concentration [*samadhi*], when no reasoning or investigation goes on, a state of elevation of mind, a tranquillization of the heart within. Then that subtle, but actual, consciousness of the joy and peace arising from detachment . . . , that he just had, passes away. And thereupon there arises a subtle, but actual, consciousness of the joy and peace born of concentration. And he becomes a person conscious of that."

Then the *bhikku*, "holding aloof from joy, becomes equable; and, mindful and self-possessed, he experiences in his body that ease which the Arahats [*arya*] talk of when they say: 'The man serene and self-possessed is well at ease.' And so he enters into and abides in the Third Rapture . . . [*jhana*]. Then that subtle, but yet actual, consciousness, that he had just had, of the joy and peace born of concentration, passes away. And thereupon there arises a subtle, but yet actual, consciousness of the bliss of equanimity."

After that, the *bhikku*, "by the putting away alike of ease and of pain, by the passing away of any joy, any elation, he had previously felt, enters into and abides in the Fourth Rapture . . . [*jhana*] a state of pure self-possession and equanimity [*sati*], without pain and without ease. Then that subtle, but yet actual, consciousness, that he just had, of the bliss of equanimity, passes away. And thereupon there arises to him a subtle, but yet actual, consciousness of the absence of pain, and of the absence of ease. And he becomes a person conscious of that."[11]

We shall not add further texts on the subject of these four *jhanas*. The stages are quite clearly defined in the passages already given: (1) to purify the mind and the sensibility from "temptations"

11. *Digha-nikaya*, I, 182 ff.; trans. Rhys Davids, I, 247–49.

—that is, to isolate them from external agents; in short, to obtain a first autonomy of consciousness; (2) to suppress the dialectical functions of the mind, obtain concentration, perfect mastery of a rarefied consciousness; (3) to suspend all "relations" both with the sensible world and with memory, to obtain a placid lucidity without any other content than "consciousness of existing"; (4) to reintegrate the "opposites," obtain the bliss of "pure consciousness."

But the itinerary does not end here. The *jhanas* are followed by four other spiritual exercises, called *samapattis*, "attainments," which prepare the ascetic for the final "enstasis." Despite the detailed description that the texts give of them, these "states" are difficult to understand. They correspond to experiences too far removed not only from those of normal consciousness but also from the extrarational (mystical or poetic) experiences comprehensible to Occidentals. However, it would be wrong to explain them as hypnotic inhibitions. As we shall see, the monk's lucidity during the course of his meditation is constantly verified; in addition, hypnotic sleep and trance are obstacles with which Indian treatises on meditation are perfectly familiar and against which they constantly warn the aspirant. The four last *dhyanas* (in the terminology of asceticism, *samapattis*) are described as follows: "And again . . . the *Bhikkhu*, by passing beyond the consciousness of form, by putting an end to the sense of resistance [*patigha*, the contact from which all sensation results], by paying no heed to the idea of distinction, thinking: 'The space is infinite,' reaches up to and remains in the mental state in which the mind is concerned only with the consciousness of the infinity of space. . . . And again . . . by passing quite beyond the consciousness of space as infinite, thinking: 'Cognition is infinite,' [he] reaches up to and remains in the mental state in which the mind is concerned only with the infinity of cognition [N.B., consciousness proves to be infinite as soon as it is no longer limited by sensory and mental experiences]. . . . And again, by passing quite beyond the consciousness of the infinity of cognition, thinking: 'There is nothing that really is,' [he] reaches up to and remains in the mental state in which the mind is concerned only with the unreality of things ['nihility']. Then that sense of everything being within the sphere of infinite cognition, that he just had, passes away. And there arises in him a consciousness, subtle but yet actual, of unreality as the object of his thought. And he becomes a person conscious of that."[12]

It would serve no purpose to comment on each of these stages, making use of the plentiful texts in the literature of later Buddhism, unless we were interested in reconstructing the psychology and metaphysics of Buddhist scholasticism. But since what concerns us here is essentially the morphology of meditation, we shall proceed to the ninth and last *samapatti*. "So from the time . . . that the Bhikkhu is thus conscious in a way brought about by himself [being in *dhyana*, he cannot receive ideas from outside; he is *sakasanni*], he goes on from one stage to the next . . . until he reaches the summit of consciousness. And when he is on the summit it may occur to him: 'To be thinking at all is the inferior state. 'Twere better not to be thinking. Were I to go on thinking and fancying, these ideas, these states of consciousness, I have reached to, would pass away, but others, coarser ones, might arise. So I will neither think nor fancy any more.' And he does not. And to him neither thinking any more, nor fancying, the ideas, the states of consciousness, he had, pass away; and no others, coarser than they, arise. So he falls into trance."[13] Another text of a later period, still more directly indicates the major importance of the ninth and last *samapatti*: "Venerable monks, acquire the *samapatti* that consists in the cessation of all conscious perception. The *bhikku* who has acquired it has nothing more to do."[14]

131. INDIA: THE LIGHT AND THE ATMAN

In Indian religions and philosophies, as might be expected, the mystique of the Light is [extremely] complex. In the first place there is the basic idea that light is creative. "Light is procreation" (*jyotir prajanaman*) says the *Satapatha Brahmana* (VIII, 7, 2, 16–17). It "is the procreative power" (*Taittirya Samhita*, VIII, 1, 1, 1). Already the *Rig Veda* (1,115,1) affirmed that the Sun is the Life or the *atman*—the Self—of all things. The Upanishads particularly

SOURCE: *TO*/26–28.
12. *Digha-nikaya*, I, 183 ff.; trans. Rhys Davids, I, 249–50.
13. *Digha-nikaya*, I, 184; trans. Rhys Davids, I, 251.
14. *Shantideva, Shiksasamuccaya*, ed. Cecil Bendall, p. 48.

insist on this theme: that being manifests itself by the pure Light and that man receives knowledge of being by an experience of supernatural Light. Now, says the *Chandogya Upanishad* (III, 13, 7), the light that shines beyond this Sky, beyond all things, in the highest worlds beyond which there are none higher, is in fact the same light that shines within a man (*antah puruse*).

Consciousness of the identity between the interior light and the super-cosmic light is accompanied by two well-known phenomena of subtle physiology: a rise in the temperature of the body and the hearing of mystical sounds (*ibid.*, III, 13, 8). There are signs that the revelation of the *atman-brahman* in the form of Light is not simply an act of metaphysical cognition but a deeper experience to which a man commits his existential governance. The supreme gnosis brings a modification of his way of being. In the words of the *Brihadaranyaka Upanishad* (I, 3, 28): "from nonbeing (*asat*) lead me to being (*sat*), from darkness lead me to the light (*tamaso ma jyotir gamaya*), from death lead me to immortality."

The light then is identical with being and immortality. The *Chandogya Upanishad* (III, 17, 7) cites two verses of the *Rig Veda* which speak of the contemplation of the "Light that shines above the Sky", and adds: "By contemplating (this) Very-high Light, beyond the Darkness, we attain the Sun, the god of gods . . ." According to the famous expression of the *Brihadaranyaka Upanishad* (IV, 3, 7) the *atman* is identified with the entity that is to be found at the heart of man, in the form of "a light in the heart" (*hrdy antarjyotih purusah*). "This calm being, rising from his body and reaching the highest light, appears in its own form (*svena rupenabhinispadyate*). It is the *atman*. It is the immortal, the fearless. It is Brahman. In fact the name of Brahman is *The True*" (*Chandogya Upanishad*, VIII, 3, 4). At the moment of death, the *Chandogya Upanishad* (VIII, 6, 5) goes on to tell us, the soul rises upwards on the rays of the Sun. It approaches the Sun, "the Gate of the World." Those who know how can enter, but the Gate is closed for those who do not know.

We are concerned therefore with a science of a transcendental and initiatory character, for he who gains it not only gains knowledge but also, and principally, a new and superior way of being. The revelation is sudden; that is why it is compared to lightning —and we have analyzed in another context the Indian symbolism of "instantaneous illumination." The Buddha himself received his illumination in a moment outside time—when at dawn, after another night passed in meditation, he raised his eyes to the sky and suddenly perceived the morning star. In Mahayana philosophy the light of the sky at dawn, when there is no moon, has come to symbolize the "Clear Light named the Universal Void." In other words, the Buddha state, the condition of one who is free of all relativity, is symbolized by the Light that Gautama perceived at the moment of his illumination. This Light is described as "clear," "pure," that is to say not only without spot or shadow, but also colorless, and without qualities. For this reason it is called "the Universal Void," since the term void (*sunya*) exactly signifies that it is free of all attributes, of all differentiation: it is the *Urgrund*, the ultimate reality. Comprehension of the Universal Void, like the act of knowledge of the identity of brahman and atman in the Upanishads, is an instantaneous action, comparable to the lightning-flash. Just as nothing precedes the dazzling flash that suddenly rends the mass of darkness, nothing appears to precede the experience of illumination; it belongs to another contextual plane, there is no continuity between the time before it and the timeless moment in which it takes place.

132. YOGA AND THE "MYSTIC LIGHTS"

According to certain Indian schools, however, the change of level effected by illumination may be anticipated. The ascetic prepares himself by long meditations and Yoga, and in the course of his spiritual journey meets occasional signs warning him of the approach of the final revelations. Among these premonitory signs, the experience of different coloured lights is the most important. The *Shvetasvatara Upanishad* (II, 11) carefully notes the "preliminary forms (*rupani purassarani*) of Brahman" which reveal themselves during yogic practice in the form of luminous manifestations. These are mist, smoke, sun, fire, wind, phosphorescent insects, lightning, crystal and moon. The *Mandala Brahmana Upanishad* (II, 1) gives quite a different list: the form of a star, a diamond mirror, the orb of the full moon, the sun at midday, a circle of fire, a crystal, a dark circle, then a point (*bindu*), a finger (*kala*), a star (*naksatra*), and again the sun, a lamp, the eye, the radiance of the sun and of the nine jewels.

As can be seen, there is no fixed rule for the sequence of experiences of light. Moreover, the order in which luminous manifestations are recorded does not correspond to a progressive increase of visual intensity. According to the *Shvetasvatara Upanishad* the light of the moon is perceived long after that of the sun. In the *Mandala Brahmana Unpanished* the succession of luminous manifestations is still more perplexing. This seems to me a further proof that we are not concerned with physical lights belonging to the natural world, but with experiences of a mystical nature.

The various schools of Yoga mention the manifestations of inner light. In commenting on the *Yoga-sutra* (I, 36), for instance, Vyasa speaks of "a concentration in the lotus of the heart" which leads one to an experience of pure light. In another context (III, 1) he mentions the "light of the head" as one of the objects on which the yogin should concentrate. Buddhist treatises insist on the potential importance of a luminous sign for the success of a meditation. "Do not let go of the sign of the light," one reads in the *Sravaka-bhumi*, "which may be that of a lamp, or the glow of a fire or the solar orb!"[1]

Needless to say, these luminous signs serve only as points of departure for the various yogic meditations. Yogavacara's treatise describes in detail the color-succession of mystical lights experienced by the monk in the course of his discipline. The particular subject of the book is meditation on the cosmic elements; it sets out a considerable number of exercises, each one in three parts, and each part distinguished by the experience of a different colored light. We have discussed elsewhere the method of Yogavacara's treatise,[2] and there is no point in returning to the subject. Let us say only that penetration into the ultimate structure of each cosmic element —penetration achieved by means of Yoga meditation—is accompanied by the experience of a different colored light. We can understand the significance and soteriological value of this immersion

1. Ms. cited by A. J. Wayman, "Notes on the Sanskrit Term jnana," *Journal of the American Oriental Society* 75 (1955): 253–68, 261, n.
2. *Yoga, Immortality and Freedom* (Paris, 1954), pp. 194 ff.

in the ultimate structure of the cosmic substance if we recall that for the Mahayana the cosmic elements—the *skandha* or *dhatu*—are identical with the Tathagatas; the Yogin's meditation on the cosmic elements is in fact a method of attaining a revelation of the very essence of the Tathagatas, that is to say of advancing on the path of deliverance. Now the ultimate reality of the Tathagatas is the Light in various colors. "All the Tathagatas are the five Lights," writes Candrakirti.[3] The *dharmadhatu*, that is to say the transcendental form of Vajradhara, is the Pure Light, the Light perfectly devoid of color. Candrakirti writes: "The *dharmadhatu* is the bright Light —and yogic concentration is its perception."[4] This amounts to saying that being can only be apprehended by an experience of the mystical order—and that the apprehension of being is accompanied by an experience of an absolute Light. One recalls that in the Upanishads brahman or the atman are identified with the Light.

We are dealing, therefore, with an all-Indian conception which could be resumed in these terms: pure being, the ultimate reality, can be known particularly through an experience of the pure Light; the process of the cosmic revelation ultimately consists of a series of luminous manifestations, and cosmic reabsorptions repeats the manifestations of these differently colored lights. According to a tradition conserved in the *Dighanikaya* (I, 2, 2), after the destruction of the World there remained only radiant beings named Abhassara: they had ethereal bodies, they flew in the air, they gave out their own light and lived indefinitely. A reabsorption on the microcosmic scale also takes place at the moment of death—and as we shall soon see, the process of death consists in fact of a number of experiences of light.

Certain corollaries follow from the all-Indian metaphysic of the Light, particularly (1) that the most adequate revelation of divinity is effected by the Light; (2) that those who have reached a high stage of spirituality—that is to say, in Indian terms, have realized or at least approached the condition of a "liberated one" or Buddha— are also capable of giving out the Light; (3) finally, that the cosmogony is comparable to a photic revelation. . . .

3. Text quoted by G. Tucci, *Some Glosses upon Guhyasamaja* ("Mémoires Bouddhiques et Chinoises," 3 [1935]: 339–53), p. 348.
   4. *Ibid.*, p. 348.

133. INDIAN EXPERIENCES OF THE MYSTIC LIGHT

Considered as a whole, the different experiences and appraisals of the interior Light advanced in India and in Indo-Tibetan Buddhism can be integrated into a perfectly consistent system. Experience of the Light signifies primarily a meeting with ultimate reality: that is why one discovers the interior Light when one becomes conscious of the Self (*atman*), or when one penetrates into the very essence of life and the cosmic elements, or, last of all, at one's death. Under all these conditions the veil of illusion and ignorance is torn. Suddenly a man is blinded by the Pure Light; he is plunged into being. From a certain point of view one may say that the profane world, the conditioned world, is transcended—and that the spirit breaks out on to the absolute plane, which is at once the plane of being and of the divine. Brahman, and the Buddha also, are at once a sign of the divine and of being, of the supreme reality. Indian thought identifies being, the divine and the mystic consciousness, the act by which one becomes conscious of reality. That is why one meets the Light both in meditating on being—the practice of the Upanishads and of Buddhism—and in trying to attain a revelation of the divine, the method followed in certain forms of yoga and the mystic schools. Since being is identical with the divine essence, divinities are necessarily luminous or reveal themselves to their worshippers in manifestations of light. But men also radiate light when they have destroyed the system of conditions under which worldly life is lived; that is to say when they have acquired supreme knowledge and attained the plane of liberty. In Indian thought, liberty is inseparable from knowledge; the man who knows, the man who has discovered the profane structures of being, is a man delivered in this life, he is no longer conditioned by cosmic laws. Henceforth he has immediate enjoyment of the divine, he no longer moves like a human automaton obedient to the laws of cause and effect, but "plays" like the gods—or like the flames of a fire.

To reach a conclusion: for Indian thought the Light mystically perceived denotes transcendence of this world, of profane and conditioned existence, and the attainment of another existential plane—that of pure being, of the divine, of supreme knowledge and abso-

SOURCE: *TO*/43–45.

lute freedom. It is a certain sign of the revelation of ultimate reality —of reality devoid of all attributes. This is why it is experienced as a dazzling white Light, into which one gazes blinded and into which one finally disappears, dissolving and leaving no trace. For traces are linked with the personal history of the individual, with the memory, therefore, of transitory and, in the long run, unreal events— elements which have nothing at all to do with being. One who reaches the Light and recognizes himself in it reaches a mode of transcendent being beyond the reach of the imagination. All that we can understand is that he is finally dead to our world—and that he is dead also to all other possible worlds of after-death existence.

134. COSMIC ILLUMINATION

Striking parallels between the experiences of the mystic light in yogic practice and in the life of an American businessman and a Canadian psychiatrist, Dr. R. M. Bucke, are presented by Eliade in The Two and the One. *They are parallels, rather than identical experiences, and by bringing together such parallels, Eliade seeks to create "a historico-religious commentary on the spontaneous experience of the inner light" (TO/21). It is this type of comparative study that has evoked criticism of Eliade from those anthropologists who favor a model of analysis that concentrates upon only one cultural example at a time: we leave it to the reader to see if this type of study provides more or less interpretive value in the long run.*

About the middle of last century an American merchant, aged thirty-two, had the following dream: "I was standing behind the counter of my shop in the middle of a bright, sunshiny afternoon, and instantly, in a flash, it became darker than the darkest night, darker than a mine; and the gentleman who was talking with me ran out into the street. Following him, although it was so dark, I could see hundreds and thousands of people pouring into the street, all wondering what had happened. Just then I noticed in the sky, in the far south-west, a bright light like a star, about the size of the

SOURCE: *TO*/19–20, 67–68.

palm of my hand, and in an instant it seemed to grow larger and larger and nearer and nearer, until it began to light up the darkness. When it got to the size of a man's hat, it divided itself into twelve smaller lights with a larger one in the center, and then very rapidly it grew much larger, and instantly I knew that this was the coming of Christ and the twelve apostles. By this time it was lighter than the lightest day that could possibly be imagined, and as the shining host advanced towards the zenith, the friend with whom I was talking exclaimed: 'That is my Saviour!' and I thought he immediately left his body and ascended into the sky, and I thought I was not good enough to accompany him. Then I awoke."

For some days the man was so impressed that he could not tell his dream to anyone. At the end of a fortnight he told it to his family and afterwards to others. Three years later, someone well known for his profound religious life said to this gentleman's wife: "Your husband is born again and don't know it. He is a little spiritual baby with eyes not yet open, but he will know in a very short time." In fact, about three weeks afterwards, when he was walking with his wife in Second Avenue (N.Y.) he suddenly exclaimed: "A—, I have eternal life." He felt at that moment that Christ had just arisen in him and that he would remain in everlasting consciousness.

Three years after this event, whilst on a boat and in a crowd of people, he had a new spiritual and mental experience: it seemed to him that his whole soul, *and his body too*, were suffused with light. But in the autobiographical account that we have just given, he adds that these experiences in the waking state never made him forget the first, the experience he had known in dream.[1]

* * *

This is how Dr. Bucke describes in the third person what happened to him in the early spring, at the beginning of his thirty-sixth year: He and two friends had spent the evening reading Wordsworth, Shelley, Keats, Browning, and especially Whitman. They parted at midnight, and he had a long drive in a hansom (it

1. This autobiological account was published by R. M. Bucke, *The Cosmic Consciousness* (Philadelphia, 1901), pp. 261–62. See other experiences of the light in dreams and their psychological interpretation in C. G. Jung, *Psychology and Alchemy* (New York, 1953), pp. 86, 89, 165, 177.

was an English city). "He was in a state of quiet, almost passive enjoyment. All at once, without warning of any kind, he found himself wrapped round as it were by a flame-colored cloud. For an instant he thought of fire, some sudden conflagration in the great city; the next he knew the light was within himself. Directly afterwards came upon him a sense of exaltation, of immense joyousness accompanied or followed by an intellectual illumination impossible to describe. Into his brain streamed one momentary lightning-flash of Brahmic splendor, leaving thenceforward for always an aftertaste of Heaven . . . He saw and he knew that the Cosmos is not dead matter but a living Presence; that the soul of man is immortal . . . that the foundation principle of the world is what we call love and that the happiness of everyone is, in the long run, absolutely certain. He claims that he learnt more within the few seconds during which the illumination lasted than in previous months or even years of study, and that he learnt much that no study could have taught him."[2]

Dr. Bucke adds that for the rest of his life he never had a similar experience. And these are the conclusions he comes to: the realization of cosmic consciousness comes as a sense of being immersed in a flame or in a rose-colored cloud, or, perhaps rather a sense that the mind is itself filled with such a cloud or haze. This sensation is accompanied by an emotion of joy, assurance, triumph, "salvation," and with this experience comes, simultaneously or instantly afterwards, an intellectual illumination quite impossible to describe. The instantaneousness of the illumination can be compared with nothing so well as with a dazzling flash of lightning in the middle of a dark night, bringing the landscape that had been hidden into clear view.[3]

There is much that could be said about this experience. Let us be content to make a few observations: (1) the inner light is at first perceived as coming from without; (2) not until he understands its subjective nature does Dr. Bucke feel inexplicable happiness and receive the intellectual illumination which he compares to a lightning-flash passing through his brain; (3) this illumination definitely changed his life, bringing a spiritual rebirth. Typologically, one

2. Bucke, *Cosmic Consciousness*, pp. 7–8.
3. *Ibid.*, pp. 60–62.

could relate this case of illumination to the illumination of the Eskimo shaman and, to a certain extent, to the self-illumination of the *atman*. A friend and admirer of Whitman, Dr. Bucke speaks of "cosmic consciousness" and of "Brahmic splendor": these are retrospective conceptions, derived from his own ideology. The character of the experience—its transcendence of the personality and its association with love recall rather a Buddhist climate of thought. A Jungian psychologist or a Catholic theologian would say that it was a realization of selfhood. But the fundamental point, in our opinion, is that, thanks to this experience of the inner light, Dr. Bucke had access to a spiritual world the existence of which he had not even suspected till then, and that the access to this transcendental world constituted for him an *incipit vita nova*.[4]

135. FINAL OBSERVATIONS: THE MYSTIC LIGHT

At the end of Eliade's essay on "Experiences of the Mystic Light," in The Two and the One, *he draws together some final observations about the various beliefs and experiences of the Light that he has presented from people of various cultures.*

. . . Let us now try to see in what respects these experiences are alike, and in what respects they differ. First of all it is important to differentiate between the subjective light and the phenomena of light objectively perceived by other people. In the Indian, Iranian and Christian traditions the two categories of experience are lumped together; and fundamentally the justifications offered for this failure to distinguish are alike: the divinity (or in India the being) being Light or emanating from light, sages (in India) or those who attain the *unio mystica* give out light (*Bhagavad-Gita*, *bhakti*; shamanism).

The morphology of the subjective experience of Light is extremely large. Certain of the more frequent forms can however be noted:

1. The Light may be so dazzling that it somehow blots out the

SOURCE: *TO*/75–77.
4. *Incipit vita nova*: beginning of a new life. Eds.

surrounding world; the man to whom it appears is blinded. This was the experience of Saint Paul, for instance, on the road to Damascus, and of many other saints—also, up to a point, of Arjuna in the *Bhagavad-Gita*.

2. There is the Light that transfigures the World without blotting it out: the experience of a very intense supernatural light, which shines into the depths of matter, but in which forms remain defined. This is like the Heavenly Light which reveals the World as it was in its primal perfection—or, according to the Judaeo-Christian tradition, as it was before Adam's fall. In this category lie the majority of experiences of the light undergone by mystics, Christian and non-Christian.

3. Rather close to this type is the illumination (*qaumanek*) of the Eskimo shaman, which enables him to see far into the distance, but also to perceive spiritual entities: an extra-retinal vision, as one might say, which permits him to see not only very far, but in all directions at once, and finally reveals to him the presence of spiritual beings, or unveils to him the ultimate structure of matter, and brings him a staggering growth of understanding. Here one must also note the difference between the various Universes mystically perceived during the experience: the Universe whose structure seems to be like that of the natural Universe, with the difference that now it is truly understood—and the Universe that reveals a structure beyond the reach of the intelligence in the waking state.

4. A distinction must also be made between the instantaneous experience and the various types of progressive perception of the light, in which the growing intensity is accompanied by a feeling of deep peace or a certainty that the soul is immortal, or a comprehension of a supernatural kind.

5. Finally we must distinguish between a light which reveals itself as a divine, personal Presence and a light which reveals an impersonal holiness: that of the World, Life, man, reality—ultimately, the holiness one discovers in the Cosmos contemplated as a divine creation.

It is important to stress that whatever the nature and intensity of an experience of the Light, it always evolves into a religious experience. All types of experience of the light that we have quoted have this factor in common: they bring a man out of his worldly Universe or historical situation, and project him into a Universe different in quality, an entirely different world, transcendent and holy. The structure of this holy and transcendent Universe varies according to a man's culture and religion—a point on which we have insisted enough to dispel all doubt. Nevertheless they share this element in common: the Universe revealed on a meeting with the Light contrasts with the worldly Universe—or transcends it—by the fact that it is spiritual in essence, in other words only accessible to those for whom the Spirit exists. We have several times observed that the experience of the Light radically changes the ontological condition of the subject, by opening him to the world of the Spirit. In the course of human history there have been a thousand different ways of conceiving or evaluating the world of the Spirit. That is evident. How could it have been otherwise? For all conceptualization is irremediably linked with language, and consequently with culture and history. One can say that the meaning of the supernatural light is directly conveyed to the soul of the man who experiences it—and yet this meaning can only come fully to his consciousness clothed in a pre-existent ideology. Here lies the paradox: the meaning of the light is, on the one hand, ultimately a personal discovery and, on the other, each man discovers what he was spiritually and culturally prepared to discover. Yet there remains this fact which seems to us fundamental: whatever his previous ideological conditioning, a meeting with the Light produces a break in the subject's existence, revealing to him—or making clearer than before—the world of the Spirit, of holiness and of freedom; in brief, existence as a divine creation, or the world sanctified by the presence of God.

3

Symbols—Patterns, Transitions, and Paradises

Introduction

Symbols may be understood as the central kernels of myths and rites. As opposed to signs, which refer to one specific meaning, symbols are polyvalent and multivocal, that is, they are words or things that open out onto a plurality of possible meanings, and still have a superplus of meaning left over. Signs "work," but symbols are lived and reinterpreted. A sign can be changed (remember when "Stop" signs were yellow and black?), but a symbol's essence underlies its modifications in such a way as to resist easy manipulation. (Think of the swastika, the very ancient Indo-European sign of good fortune: even the Hitler regime could not eliminate its earlier positive meaning entirely.)

Eliade's religious phenomenology has centered upon many of the great symbolic expressions of the world's religions. He takes up something like the Cosmic Tree (cross, axis of the world, bridge between heaven and earth, and hence ladders, etc.) and traces its appearances around the world. This sort of universal viewing is infinitely more sophisticated than that of Sir James Frazer, since (as we saw in Chapter One) Eliade stresses the importance of the historical contexts in which the symbol (or myth or rite) is "at home." Nonetheless, Frazer and Eliade are often tarred with the same feathers by contemporary "descriptive" anthropologists—unfairly, as far as Eliade is concerned, although for his treatments of symbols in this chapter, the reader will often have to go to the original versions to study the historical and ethnographic contexts, which we have had to omit because of space limitations.

Freud and Jung's names appear in Eliade's works, primarily in references to the parallels between psychoanalysis and archaic techniques of "going back to the beginnings" as therapy. An extended dialogue with Jung, especially, might clarify Eliade's opinions of Jung's concept of universal propensities toward symbolic patterns ("archetypes"), but it is clearly not accurate to characterize Eliade as a "Jungian," a judgment often heard from religion scholars. Both are truly concerned with the underlying symbolic valences that constellate symbolic expressions, but clearly Eliade remains more the chronicler and observer, Jung more the theorist. One of the desired items on the future agenda of the historian of religion, the psycho-theorist, and the philosophical interpreter, should be an attempt to clarify and to interrelate these approaches, working toward a universal symbolics.

◆ ◆

The Nature and Function of Religious Symbolism

We may be on the border of a new era with respect to metaphor and symbol! Again and again contemporary discussions turn toward these more emotive, less arid, forms of human expression, whether it be in literary or philosophical works. A University of Chicago colleague of Eliade, Paul Ricoeur, has now followed the earlier works of Cassirer, Langer, and others, in attempting to catch sight of the "aura of meaning" that surrounds symbolic expression.[1]

Eliade comments on the ways we are beginning to rediscover symbolism, and turns his attention to means of studying symbols in the history of religions. Selection 139 has struck both editors of this volume as a crucial analysis that opens up perspectives on symbols in a richly reflective and provocative way—we finally decided against using its six points as an explicit outline for Chapter Three. It is in this selection that we see Eliade's close relationship to phenomenology (for example, TO/201: "The World 'speaks' in symbols, 'reveals' itself through them. . . ."), and the three divisions of this part of the Reader (World-Patterning Symbols, Symbols for Transitions in Life, and Symbols Concerning Paradise) are our attempt to structure the selections around key modes in which Eliade sees the World "appearing" to humankind.

136. THE REDISCOVERY OF SYMBOLISM

The surprising popularity of psychoanalysis has made the fortunes of certain key-words: image, symbol and symbolism have now become current coin. At the same time, systematic research

SOURCE: IS/9–11.
1. See *The Symbolism of Evil*, trans. E. Buchanan (Boston, 1969); *Freud and Philosophy: An Essay in Interpretation*, trans. D. Savage (New Haven, 1970); *The Conflict of Interpretation: Essays in Hermeneutics*, ed. D. Ihde (Evanston, 1974).

devoted to the mechanisms of "primitive mentality" has revealed the importance of symbolism in archaic thinking and also the fundamental part it plays in the life of any and every primitive society. The obsolescence of "scientism" in philosophy, the revival of interest in religion since the first world war, many poetic developments and, above all, the researches of surrealism (with the rediscovery of occultism, of the "black" literature, of "the absurd," etc.) have, on various levels and with unequal effects, drawn the attention of the public in general to the symbol, regarded as an autonomous mode of cognition. The development in question is a part of the reaction against the nineteenth century's rationalism, positivism and scientism which became such a marked characteristic of the second quarter of the twentieth. But this conversion to the various symbolisms is not really a "discovery" to be credited to the modern world: in restoring the symbol to its status as an instrument of knowledge, our world is only returning to a point of view that was general in Europe until the eighteenth century and is, moreover, connatural to the other, non-European cultures, whether "historic" (like those of Asia or Central America for instance) or archaic and "primitive." . . .

A fortunate conjunction in time . . . has enabled Western Europe to rediscover the cognitive value of the symbol at the moment when Europeans are no longer the only peoples to "make history," and when European culture, unless it shuts itself off into a sterilizing provincialism, will be obliged to reckon with other ways and other scales of values than its own. In this respect, all the discoveries and successive fashions concerned with the irrational, with the unconscious, with symbolisms, poetic experience, exotic and non-representational art, etc., have been, indirectly, of service to the West as preparations for a more living and therefore a deeper understanding of non-European values, and in particular for a dialogue with the non-European peoples. One has only to reflect upon the attitude that nineteenth-century ethnography took up towards its subject, and above all to consider the results of its researches, to measure the progress made by ethnography during the last thirty years. The ethnologist of today has not only grasped the importance of symbolism in archaic thinking but has seen its intrinsic coherence, its validity, its speculative audacity, its "nobility."

Better still: today we are well on the way to an understanding of one thing of which the nineteenth century had not even a presentiment—that the symbol, the myth and the image are of the very substance of the spiritual life, that they may become disguised, mutilated or degraded, but are never extirpated. It would be well worth while to study the survival of the great myths throughout the nineteenth century: one would then see how they were humbled, minimized, condemned to incessant change of form, and yet survived that hibernation, thanks chiefly to literature. . . .

137. ACTUALIZATION AND INTERPRETATION

Psychological literature, especially that produced by psychoanalysis, will have familiarized the reader with the prolixity of its expositions of individual "case-histories." One volume published in England has seven hundred pages on the "dream mythology" of a single individual! The psychologists are in agreement about the indispensability of exposition *in extenso* of each particular case, and when they resign themselves to its abbreviation, it is almost always with reluctance: their ideal would be to publish complete dossiers. With much greater reason ought one to take the same course when studying a symbolism: we need to present it in general outline, but also with all its subtleties, variants and uncertainties.

The central and the most arduous problem remains, obviously, that of interpretation. In principle, one can always question the validity of a hermeneutic study. By multiple cross references between what is clearly established (texts, rituals and figured monuments) and semi-veiled allusions, we can demonstrate, bit by bit, what this or that symbol "means." But we can also state the problem in another way: do those who are making use of the symbols take all their theoretical implications into account? When, for instance, in studying the implications of the cosmic Tree, we say that the Tree is situated at the "Center of the World," do we mean that all the individuals belonging to societies which know of such Trees are equally aware of the complete symbolism of the "Center"? But the validity of the symbol considered as a form of knowledge does not depend upon any individual's degree of understanding. Texts and figured monuments provide us with abundant proof that for some, at least, of the individuals of an archaic society the symbolism of the "Center" was transparent in its totality; the rest of the society remaining content to "participate" in the symbolism. Moreover, it is not easy to draw the limits of such a participation, for it varies in function with an indefinite number of factors. All we can say is that the *actualization* of a symbol is not automatic; it occurs in relation to the tensions and vicissitudes of the social life, and, finally, with the cosmic rhythms.

138. "RELIGIOUS SYMBOLS"

Man being *homo symbolicus*, and all his activities implying symbolism, every religious fact has necessarily a symbolic character. No assumption could be more certain than that every religious act and every cult object has a meta-empirical purpose. The tree that becomes a cult object is not worshipped as a *tree*, but as a *hierophany*, a manifestation of the sacred. And every religious act, from the moment that it becomes *religious*, is charged with a significance which is, in the final instance, "symbolic," since it refers to supernatural values or forms.

One would therefore be justified in saying that any research undertaken on a religious subject implies the study of religious symbolism. But in the current language of the science of religions, the convention is to confine the term symbol to religious facts of which the symbolism is manifest and explicit. One speaks for example of the wheel as a solar symbol, of the cosmogonic egg as a symbol of the undifferentiated totality, of the serpent as a chthonian, sexual or funerary symbol, etc.

139. WHAT THE SYMBOLS "REVEAL"

The task of the historian of religions remains incomplete if he fails to discover the function of symbolism in general. We know what the theologian, the philosopher and the psychologist have to

SOURCE: *TO*/199.
SOURCE: *TO*/201–8.

say about this problem. Let us now examine the conclusions which the historian of religions reaches when he reflects on his own documents.

The first observation that he is forced to make is that the World "speaks" in symbols, "reveals" itself through them. It is not a question of a utilitarian and objective language. A symbol is not a replica of objective reality. It *reveals* something deeper and more fundamental. Let us try to elucidate the different aspects, the different depths of this revelation.

1. Symbols are capable of revealing a *modality of the real or a condition of the World which is not evident on the plane of immediate experience.* To illustrate the sense in which the symbol expresses a modality of the real inaccessible to human experience, let us take an example: the symbolism of the Waters, which is capable of revealing the preformal, the potential, the chaotic. This is not, of course, a matter of rational cognition, but of apprehension by the active consciousness prior to reflection. It is of such apprehensions that the World is made. Later, by elaborating the significances thus understood, the first reflections on the creation of the World will be set in motion; this is the point of departure of all the cosmologies and ontologies from the Vedas to the Pre-Socratics.

As for the capacity of symbols to reveal an inner pattern of the World, we will refer to what we said earlier about the principal significances of the Cosmic Tree. The Tree reveals the World as a living totality, periodically regenerating itself and, thanks to this regeneration, continually fertile, rich and inexhaustible. Here, too, it is not a question of considered knowledge, but of an immediate comprehension of the "cipher" of the World. The World "speaks" through the medium of the Cosmic Tree, and its "word" is directly understood. The World is apprehended as Life and, for primitive thought, Life is a disguise worn by Being.

A corollary of the preceding observations: religious symbols which touch on the patterns of life reveal a deeper Life, more mysterious than that grasped by everyday experience. They reveal the miraculous inexplicable side of Life, and at the same time the sacramental dimension of human existence. "Deciphered" in the light of religious symbols, human life itself reveals a hidden side: it comes from "elsewhere," from very far away; it is "divine" in the sense that it is the work of Gods or supernatural Beings.

2. This brings us to a second general observation: for primitives, *symbols are always religious*, since they point either to something *real* or to a *World-pattern*. Now, at the archaic levels of culture, the *real*—that is to say the powerful, the significant, the living—is equivalent to the *sacred*. Moreover, the World is a creation of the Gods or of supernatural Beings: to discover a World pattern amounts to revealing a secret or a "ciphered" meaning of the divine work. It is for this reason that archaic religious symbols imply an ontology; a presystematic ontology, of course, the expression of a judgement both of the World and of human existence: judgement which is not formulated in concepts and which cannot always be translated into concepts.

3. An essential characteristic of religious symbolism is its *multivalence*, its capacity *to express simultaneously several meanings the unity between which is not evident on the plane of immediate experience*. The symbolism of the Moon, for example, reveals a connatural unity between the lunar rhythms, temporal becoming, the Waters, the growth of plants, women, death and resurrection, the human destiny, the weaver's craft, etc. In the final analysis, the symbolism of the Moon reveals a correspondence of a "mystical" order between the various levels of cosmic reality and certain modalities of human existence. Let us observe that this correspondence is not indicated by immediate and spontaneous experience, nor by critical reflection. It is the result of a certain mode of "viewing" the World.

Even if we admit that certain of the Moon's functions have been discovered by careful observation of the lunar phases (their relation with rainfall, for instance, and menstruation), it is difficult to imagine that the symbolism could have been built up in its entirety by an act of reason. It requires quite another order of cognition to reveal, for example, the "lunar destiny" of human existence, the fact that man is "measured" by temporal rhythms which are one with the phases of the Moon, that he is consigned to death but that, like the Moon which reappears in the sky after three days of darkness, he also can begin his existence again, and that, in any case, he nourishes the hope of a life beyond the tomb, more certain or better as a consequence of initiation.

4. This capacity of religious symbolism to reveal a multitude of

structurally united meanings has an important consequence: the symbol is capable of *revealing a perspective in which diverse realities can be fitted together or even integrated into a "system."* In other words, a religious symbol allows man to discover a certain unity of the World and at the same time to become aware of his own destiny as an integral part of the World. In the case of lunar symbolism, it is clear in what sense the different meanings of the symbols form a "system." On different registers (cosmological, anthropological, and "spiritual") the lunar rhythm reveals homologous patterns: always it is a matter of modalities of existence subject to the law of Time and cyclic becoming, that is to say of existences destined for a "Life" which carries, in its very structure, death and rebirth. Thanks to the Moon symbolism, the World no longer appears an arbitrary assembly of heterogeneous and divergent realities. The various cosmic levels are mutually related, they are, in a sense, "bound together" by the same lunar rhythm, just as human life is "woven" by the Moon and predestined by the Spinning Goddesses. . . .

5. Perhaps the most important function of religious symbolism—especially important because of the role it will play in later philosophical speculations—is its *capacity for expressing paradoxical situations or certain patterns of ultimate reality that can be expressed in no other way.* One example will suffice: the symbolism of the Symplegades as it can be deciphered in numerous myths, legends and images presenting the paradox of a passage from one mode of existence to another—transfer from this world to another, from Earth to Heaven or Hell, or passage from a profane, purely carnal existence to a spiritual existence, etc. The following are the most frequent images: to pass between two clashing rocks or icebergs, or between two mountains in perpetual movement, or between two jaws, or to penetrate the *vagina dentata* and come out unharmed, or enter a mountain that reveals no opening, etc. One understands the significance of all these images: if the possibility of a "passage" exists, it can only be effectuated "in the spirit"—giving the word all the meanings that it is capable of carrying in archaic societies: a discarnate being, the imaginary world and the world of ideas. One can pass through a Symplegades in so far as one behaves "as a spirit," that is to say shows imagination and intelligence and so

proves oneself capable of detaching oneself from immediate reality. No other symbol of the "difficult passage"—not even the celebrated motif of the bridge filed to the sharpness of a sword-edge, or the razor mentioned in the *Katha Upanishad* (III, 14)—reveals more clearly than the Symplegades that there is a way of being inaccessible to immediate experience, and that this way of being can only be attained by renouncing a crude belief in the impregnability of matter.

One could make similar observations concerning the capacity of symbols to express the contradictory aspects of ultimate reality. Nicolas Cusanus considered the *coincidentia oppositorum* as the most suitable definition of God's nature. . . .[1]

. . . One of the greatest discoveries of the human spirit was naïvely anticipated on the day when, by certain religious symbols, man guessed that oppositions and antagonisms can be fitted and integrated into a unity. From then onwards the negative and sinister aspects of the Cosmos and the Gods not only found a justification but revealed themselves as an integral part of all reality or sacrality.

6. Finally, we must stress the *existential value of religious symbolism*, that is to say the fact that a symbol *always points to a reality or a situation concerning human existence*. It is above all this existential dimension that distinguishes and divides symbols from concepts. Symbols preserve contact with the deep sources of life; they express, one might say, "the spiritual as life experience." This is why symbols have a kind of "numinous" aura: they reveal that the *modalities of the spirit are at the same time manifestations of Life*, and that consequently, they *directly concern human existence*. A religious symbol not only reveals a pattern of reality or a dimension of existence, it brings at the same time a *meaning to human existence*. This is why even symbols concerning ultimate reality also afford existential revelations to the man who deciphers their message.

A religious symbol translates a human situation into cosmological terms, and vice versa; to be more precise, it reveals the unity between human existence and the structure of the Cosmos. Man does not feel himself "isolated" in the Cosmos, he is open to a World

1. See selection 186, "Meanings of the *Coincidentia Oppositorum*." Eds.

which, thanks to the symbol, becomes "familiar." On the other hand the cosmological significances of a symbolism allow him to escape from a subjective situation and recognize the objectivity of his personal experiences.

It follows that the *man who understands a symbol not only "opens himself" to the objective world, but at the same time succeeds in emerging from his personal situation and reaching a comprehension of the universal.* This is to be explained by the fact that symbols "explode" immediate reality as well as particular situations. When some tree or other incarnates the World Tree, or when the spade is assimilated to the phallus and agricultural labor to the act of generation, etc., one may say that the immediate reality of these objects or activities "explodes" beneath the irruptive force of a deeper reality. The same thing takes place in an individual situation, for example that of the neophyte shut in the initiatory hut: the symbolism "explodes" this particular situation by revealing it as exemplary, that is to say endlessly repeatable in many different contexts (for the initiatory hut is approximated to the mother's womb, and also to the belly of a Monster and to Hell, and the darkness symbolizes, as we have seen, cosmic Night, the pre-formal, the foetal state of the World, etc.). *Thanks to the symbol, the individual experience is "awoken" and transmuted into a spiritual act.* To "live" a symbol and correctly decipher its message implies an opening toward the Spirit and finally access to the universal.

◆

WORLD-PATTERNING SYMBOLS

The Sky god, the Earth goddess, the male:female pairing in the primeval sacred marriage; the remarkable "centering" process by which pottery is thrown[1] and by which men everywhere image their own places in the cosmos; the personalized Moon—these are symbols that give pattern to the World, shape it by naming its parts (giving language through which reality is then experienced), and lend it coherence by interrelating the parts and the whole. No one escapes such patterning, though it is easy to forget that reality

---

1. See M. C. Richards, *Centering in Pottery, Poetry, and the Person* (Middletown, 1964).

is socially constructed[2] and to equate reality with a particular perspective upon it.

Selections here range over a wide area of human religious projects: we will read about the process by which human aspects become deity aspects, how biological and natural forces are overlaid with mystical and theological overtones. Perhaps nothing is as threatening as symbols that break and shatter, and the account of the physical destruction of the Achilpas' sacred pole, their symbolic axis of the universe (selection 154), is an amazing account of a concretized symbol in its traverse from birth to death.

140. THE SACREDNESS OF THE SKY

The most popular prayer in the world is addressed to "Our Father who art in heaven." It is possible that man's earliest prayers were addressed to the same heavenly father—it would explain the testimony of an African of the Ewe tribe: "There where the sky is, God is too." The Vienna school of ethnology (particularly in the person of Fr. W. Schmidt, the author of the fullest monograph yet produced on the subject of the origins of the idea of divinity) even claims to have established the existence of a primitive monotheism, basing the proof chiefly on the belief in sky gods among the most primitive human societies. For the moment we will leave on one side this problem of primeval monotheism. What is quite beyond doubt is that there is an almost universal belief in a celestial divine being, who created the universe and guarantees the fecundity of the earth (by pouring rain down upon it). These beings are endowed with infinite foreknowledge and wisdom; moral laws and often tribal ritual as well were established by them during a brief visit to the earth; they watch to see that their laws are obeyed, and lightning strikes all who infringe them.

We shall look at a series of divine figures of the sky, but first it is necessary to grasp the religious significance of the sky as such. There is no need to look into the teachings of myth to see that the

SOURCE: PCR/38–40; cf. Q/34, 45, 48; AR/15–18.
2. See Peter L. Berger and Thomas Luckmann, *The Social Construction of Reality: A Treatise in the Sociology of Knowledge* (Garden City, 1966).

sky itself directly reveals a transcendence, a power and a holiness. Merely contemplating the vault of heaven produces a religious experience in the primitive mind. This does not necessarily imply a "nature-worship" of the sky. To the primitive, nature is never purely "natural." The phrase "contemplating the vault of heaven" really means something when it is applied to primitive man, receptive to the miracles of every day to an extent we find it hard to imagine. Such contemplation is the same as a revelation. The sky shows itself as it really is: infinite, transcendent. The vault of heaven is, more than anything else, "something quite apart" from the tiny thing that is man and his span of life. The symbolism of its transcendence derives from the simple realization of its infinite height. "Most High" becomes quite naturally an attribute of the divinity. The regions above man's reach, the starry places, are invested with the divine majesty of the transcendent, of absolute reality, of everlastingness. Such places are the dwellings of the gods; certain privileged people go there as a result of rites effecting their ascension into heaven; there, according to some religions, go the souls of the dead. The "high" is something inaccessible to man as such; it belongs by right to superhuman powers and beings; when a man ceremonially ascends the steps of a sanctuary, or the ritual ladder leading to the sky he ceases to be a man; the souls of the privileged dead leave their human state behind when they rise into heaven.

All this derives from simply contemplating the sky; but it would be a great mistake to see it as a logical, rational process. The transcendental quality of "height," or the supra-terrestrial, the infinite, is revealed to man all at once, to his intellect as to his soul as a whole. The symbolism is an immediate notion of the whole consciousness, of the man, that is, who realizes himself as a man, who recognizes his place in the universe; these primeval realizations are bound up so organically with his life that the same symbolism determines both the activity of his subconscious and the noblest expressions of his spiritual life. It really is important, therefore, this realization that though the symbolism and religious values of the sky are not deduced logically from a calm and objective observation of the heavens, neither are they exclusively the product of mythical activity and non-rational religious experience. Let me repeat: even before any religious values have been set upon the sky it reveals its transcendence. The sky "symbolizes" transcendence,

power, and changelessness simply by being there. It exists because
it is high, infinite, immovable, powerful.

That the mere fact of being high, of being high up, means being
powerful (in the religious sense), and being as such filled with the
sacred, is shown by the very etymology of some of the gods'
names. To the Iroquois, all that has *orenda* is called *oki*, but the
meaning of the word *oki* seems to be "what is on high"; we even
find a Supreme Being of the sky called Oke. The Sioux express
magico-religious power by the word *wakan*, which is phonetically
extremely close to *wakan*, *wankan*, which means, in the Dakota language, "on high, above"; the sun, the moon, lightning, the wind
possess *wakan*, and this force was personified though imperfectly
in "Wakan," which the missionaries translated as meaning "Lord,"
but who was in fact a Supreme Being of the sky, manifesting himself above all in lightning.

The supreme divinity of the Maoris is called Iho: *iho* means
"raised up, on high." The Akposo negroes have a Supreme God
Uwoluwu; the name means "what is on high, the upper regions."
And one could multiply these examples. We shall see soon that "the
most high," "the shining," "the sky," are notions which have existed more or less explicitly in the terms used by primitive civilizations to express the idea of Godhead. The transcendence of God
is directly revealed in the inaccessibility, infinity, eternity and creative power (rain) of the sky. The whole nature of the sky is an
inexhaustible hierophany. Consequently, anything that happens
among the stars or in the upper areas of the atmosphere—the rhythmic revolution of the stars, chasing clouds, storms, thunderbolts,
meteors, rainbows—is a moment in that hierophany.

When this hierophany became personified, when the divinities *of*
the sky showed themselves, or took the place of the holiness of the
sky as such, is difficult to say precisely. What is quite certain is that
the sky divinities have always been supreme divinities; that their
hierophanies, dramatized in various ways by myth, have remained
for that reason sky hierophanies; and that what one may call the
history of sky divinities is largely a history of notions of "force,"
of "creation," of "laws" and of "sovereignty". . . .

141. THE ANTIQUITY OF SUPREME BEINGS OF THE SKY

We cannot say for certain that devotion to sky beings was the first and only belief that primitive man had, and that all other religious forms appeared later and represent corruptions. Though belief in a supreme sky being is generally to be found among the most archaic of primitive societies (Pygmies, Australians, Fuegians and so on), it is not found amongst them all (there is none, for instance, among the Tasmanians, the Veddas, the Kubu). And it seems to me, in any case, that such a belief would not necessarily exclude all other religious forms. Undoubtedly, from the earliest times man realized the transcendence and omnipotence of the sacred from what he experienced of the sky. The sky needs no aid from mythological imagination or conceptual elaboration to be seen as *the* divine sphere. But innumerable other hierophanies could co-exist with this hierophany of the sky.

One thing we can say with certainty: generally speaking, the sky hierophany and the belief in Supreme Beings of the sky have been superseded by other religious conceptions. Generally speaking, again, it is clear that such beliefs in a Supreme Being of the sky formerly represented the very center of religious life, not a mere sort of subsection on the periphery, as they are among primitives today. The present scant worship of these sky gods indicates purely and simply that the mass of religious practice is given over to other religious forms; in no case does it indicate that such sky gods are the abstract creations of primitive man (or simply of his "priests"), or that he has not had, or been able to have, any real religious relationship with them. Besides, as I have already said, the lack of worship indicates mainly the absence of any religious calendar; occasionally, sporadically, each of these supreme sky beings is honored with prayers, sacrifices and so on. Occasionally they even have a real cult, as witness, for instance, the great ritual feasts of North America in honor of their supreme beings (Tirawa, Chebbeniathan, Awonawilona). Even in Africa, there are quite a number of examples: the night dances in honor of Cagn among the Bushmen, or the regular worship of Uwoluwu (who has priests, places of worship and sacrifices), in honor of Abassi Abumo, the Thunderer, and Abbassi still has a sanctuary in the courtyard of each house among the

SOURCE: *PCR*/54–58.

inhabitants of Calabar, who are the Ibibios' neighbors; there are prayers and sacrifices in honor of Leza; and so on. The Kondes adore their supreme god Mbamba with dances, songs, and prayers: "Mbamba, let our children thrive! May the cattle multiply! May our maize and sweet potatoes flourish! Take pestilence away!"[1] The Wachaggas address their prayers and sacrifices to Ruwa: "Thou Man of Heaven, O Chief, take this head of cattle. We pray thee that thou wouldst lead far past and away the sickness that comes on earth." Pious people offer prayers to Ruwa morning and evening without any sacrifice.[2] Goats are offered to Mulugu, and the Akiku-yus offer numerous sacrifices to Engai of the first-fruits of their harvests and sheep.[3]

An analysis of the various stages of Australian religion shows clearly that the sky divinity held the central place in the most primitive religious life. Originally, Mungangana used to live on earth among men; only later did he withdraw to heaven and leave them. All over Australia one can recognize to some extent the myth of the gradual withdrawal of divine beings. It would in any case be hard to trace the belief in these sky beings back to any earlier belief. It has been said, for instance, that it grew from the cult of the dead, but in South-Eastern Australia (where is one of the oldest of all) there is no cult of the dead.[4] And it is there, where the initiation ceremonies are most in force (that is, in South-East Australia) that we find the sky divinity connected with secret rites. Where, on the other hand, esoterism is gradually disappearing (as is the case with most of the Central Australian tribes—the Arunta and Loritja), the sky divinity (Altjira, Tukura) appears to have lost all religious force and to survive only in the mythological sphere; which means that belief in the sky divinity was undoubtedly once fuller and more intense. From initiation one learns the true theophany, the myth of the tribal genealogy, the corpus of laws, moral and social, in a word, man's place in the cosmos. Initiation is thus an occasion of learning and not merely a ritual of regeneration. Knowledge, the global understanding of the world, the interpretation of the unity of nature, the revelation of the final causes under-

---

1. Sir James Frazer, *The Worship of Nature* (London, 1926), p. 190.
2. *Ibid.*, pp. 212 ff.
3. *Ibid.*, pp. 248 ff.
4. W. Schmidt, *Der Ursprung der Gottesidee* (Münster, 1926), 3: 106.

lying existence, and so on—all these things are possible thanks to contemplation of the sky, the sky hierophany, and the Supreme Divinities of the sky.

However, we should be making a great mistake if we were to see these actions and reflections merely as things of the intellect (as, for instance, Schmidt does). They are, on the contrary, acts of the whole man, who, of course has a certain preoccupation with causality, but has above all—in fact finds himself in the midst of—the problem of existence. All these revelations of a metaphysical nature (the origin of the human race, sacred history of the god and of ancestors, metamorphoses, the meaning of symbols, secret names and so on), made within the framework of initiation ceremonies, are not simply aimed at satisfying the neophyte's thirst for knowledge, but primarily at consolidating his existence as a whole, promoting continuity of life and prosperity and assuring a happier fate after death.

To sum up, then: the most significant thing of all is the presence of sky divinities at the most primitive levels of Australian religion, in the framework of initiation ceremonies. This initiation, as I said, assures the regeneration of the initiate at the same time as revealing to him secrets of a metaphysical nature; it feeds at once life, strength and knowledge. It shows what a close bond there is between the theophany (for in the initiation ritual the true name and nature of the god are revealed), soteriology (for the ceremony of initiation, however elementary it may be, assures the salvation of the neophyte), and metaphysics (for revelation is given about the workings and origin of the universe, the origin of the human race and so on). But at the very heart of this secret ceremony you will find the sky god, the same divinity who originally created the universe and man, and came down to earth to establish culture and the rites of initiation.

That sky gods had, at first, this prerogative of being not only creators and omnipotent, but also all-knowing, supremely "wise," explains why you find them changed in some religions into abstract divine figures, personified concepts used to explain the universe or express its absolute reality. Iho, the sky god of New Zealand and Tahiti, revealed only to those initiated into esoteric priestly learning, is more of a philosophical concept than a real divinity.[5] Other

5. R. Pettazzoni, *Dio* (Rome, 1922), 7: 174.

sky gods—Nzambi of the Bantu peoples, for instance, Sussistinako among the Sia Indians—are asexual: a phenomenon of abstraction which marks the changing of the divinity into a metaphysical principle. Indeed, Awonawilona, among the Zuni Indians, is represented as without any personal characteristics, and may be considered equally well as feminine or as masculine (Lang called it "He-She").

These Supreme Gods of the sky could be transformed into philosophic concepts only because the sky hierophany itself could be transformed into a metaphysical revelation; because, that is, contemplation of the sky by its very nature enabled man to know not only his own precariousness and the transcendence of the divinity, but also the sacred value of knowledge, of spiritual "force." Gazing into the clear blue sky by day or the multitude of stars by night, nowhere could one discern more completely the divine origin and sacred value of knowledge, the omnipotence of him who *sees* and *understands*, of him who "knows" all because he is everywhere, sees everything, makes and governs all things. To the modern mind, of course, such gods, with their vague mythological outlines—Iho and Brahman and the rest—seem rather abstract, and we tend to look on them more as philosophical concepts than as divinities proper. But do not forget that to primitive man, whose invention they were, knowledge and understanding were—and still are—epiphanies of "power," of "sacred force." He who sees and knows all, *is* and *can do* all. Sometimes such a Supreme Being, celestial in origin, becomes the foundation of the universe, author and controller of the rhythms of nature, and tends to become amalgamated either with the principle or metaphysical substance of the universe, or with the Law, with what is eternal and universal among the phenomena of time and change—the Law which the gods themselves cannot do away with. . . .

142. THE EARTH MOTHER

". . . Earth [Gaia], herself, first of all gave birth to a being equal to herself, who could overspread her completely, the starry heaven [Ouranos], who was to present the blessed gods a secure throne

SOURCE: *PCR*/239–40; cf. *FPZ*/37–40.

forever."[1] This primeval pair gave birth to the innumerable family
of gods, Cyclops and other mythical creatures (Cottos, Briareus,
Gyges, "children filled with pride," each with a hundred arms and
fifty heads). The marriage between heaven and earth was the first
hierogamy; the gods soon married too, and men, in their turn, were
to imitate them with the same sacred solemnity with which they
imitated everything done at the dawn of time.

Gaia or Ge was fairly widely worshipped in Greece, but in
time other earth divinities took her place. The etymology suggests
that in her the earth element was present in its most immediate
form (cf. Sanskrit *go*, "earth, place"; Zend *gava*, Gothic, *gawi*,
gauja, "province"). Homer scarcely mentions her; a chthonian divinity—and one belonging pre-eminently to the pre-Hellenic substratum—would be unlikely to find a place in his Olympus. But one
of the Homeric hymns is addressed to her: "It is the earth I sing,
securely enthroned, the mother of all things, venerable ancestress
feeding upon her soil all that exists . . . To thee it belongs to give
life to mortals, and to take it from them . . . Happy the man fa-
voured with thy good will! For him the soil of life is rich with
harvest; in his fields, the flocks thrive, and his house is full of
wealth."[2]

Aeschylus also glorifies her, for it is the earth that "gives birth to
all beings, feeds them, and receives back from them the fertile
seed."[3] We shall see in a moment how genuine and ancient is this
formula of Aeschylus. And there is another very old hymn which,
Pausanias tells us, the Pleiades of Dodona sang: "Zeus was, is and
shall be, O Great Zeus; it is through thy help that the Earth gives
us her fruit. We call her our mother with good reason."[4]

A great many beliefs, myths and rituals have come down to us
which deal with the earth, with its divinities, with the Great Mother.
As the foundation, in a sense, of the universe, the earth is endowed
with manifold religious significance. It was adored because of its
permanence, because all things came from it and all things returned to it. If one studied the history of a single religion, one
might manage to state fairly exactly the function and development

1. Hesiod, *Theogony*, V, 126 ff.
2. *To Earth*, 1 ff.
3. *Choephori*, V, 127–28.
4. X, 12, 10.

of its beliefs about the chthonian epiphanies. But if one is simply dealing with a study of religious forms, the thing becomes impossible; here, as in all our other chapters, we are looking at acts, beliefs and theories belonging to cycles of civilization differing in age, differing in nature. . . .

143. REDISCOVERY OF WOMAN—TANTRISM

Historically, the worship of the Mother Goddess has been a widespread phenomenon. Yet it is still in India that her worship has had the longest and most persistent tradition. In this initial extract Eliade shows the recurrence of this idea as a dynamic rediscovery of feminine values in Hindu culture, as well as the fact that woman-as-religious-symbol reaches its apex in Yogic Tantrism, without losing sight of its roots in a very ancient mythical consciousness of the earth.

. . . We do not know why and under what circumstances it came to designate a great philosophical and religious movement, which, appearing as early as the fourth century of our era, assumed the form of a pan-Indian vogue from the sixth century onward. For it was really a vogue; quite suddenly, tantrism becomes immensely popular, not only among philosophers and theologians, but also among the active practitioners of the religious life (ascetics, yogins, etc.), and its prestige also reaches the "popular" strata. In a comparatively short time, Indian philosophy, mysticism, ritual, ethics, iconography, and even literature are influenced by tantrism. It is a pan-Indian movement, for it is assimilated by all the great Indian religions and by all the "sectarian" schools. . . .

. . . Let us note, however, that, for the first time in the spiritual history of Aryan India, the Great Goddess acquires a predominant position. Early in the second century of our era, two feminine divinities made their way into Buddhism: Prajnaparamita, a "creation" of the metaphysicians and ascetics, an incarnation of Supreme Wisdom, and Tara, the epiphany of the Great Goddess of aboriginal

Source: *Y*/200, 202–3; cf. *MDM*/176–79.

India. In Hinduism the Shakti, the "cosmic force," is raised to the rank of a Divine Mother who sustains not only the universe and all its beings but also the many and various manifestations of the gods. Here we recognize the "religion of the Mother" that in ancient times reigned over an immense Aegeo-Afrasiatic territory and which was always the chief form of devotion among the autochthonous peoples of India. In this sense, the irresistible tantric advance also implies a new victory for the pre-Aryan popular strata.

But we also recognize a sort of religious rediscovery of the mystery of woman, for, as we shall see later, every woman becomes the incarnation of the Shakti. Mystical emotion in the presence of the mystery of generation and fecundity—such it is in part. But it is also recognition of all that is remote, "transcendent," invulnerable in woman; and thus woman comes to symbolize the irreducibility of the sacred and the divine, the inapprehensible essence of the ultimate reality. Woman incarnates both the mystery of creation and the mystery of Being, of everything that *is*, that incomprehensibly becomes and dies and is reborn. The schema of the Samkhya philosophy is prolonged on both the metaphysical and the mythological planes: Spirit, the "male," *purusha*, is the "great impotent one," the motionless, the contemplative; it is Prakriti that works, engenders, nourishes. When a great danger threatens the foundations of the cosmos, the gods appeal to the Shakti to avert it. A well-known myth thus accounts for the birth of the Great Goddess. A monstrous demon, Mahisa, threatened the universe and even the existence of the gods. Brahma and the whole pantheon appealed to Vishnu and Shiva for help. Swollen with rage, all the gods put forth their energies in the form of fire darting from their mouths. The flames joined into a fiery cloud, which finally took the form of a goddess with eighteen arms. And it was this goddess, Shakti, who succeeded in crushing the monster Mahisa and thus saved the world. As Heinrich Zimmer remarks, the gods "had returned their energies to the primeval Shakti, the One Force, the fountain head, whence originally all had stemmed. And the result was now a great renewal of the original state of universal potency."[1]

1. *Myths and Symbols in Indian Art and Civilization*, ed. J. Campbell (New York, 1946), p. 191.

We must never lose sight of this primacy of the Shakti—in the last analysis, of the Divine Woman and Mother—in tantrism and in all the movements deriving from it. It is through this channel that the great underground current of autochthonous and popular spirituality made its way into Hinduism. . . .

144. THE GREAT GODDESS IN INDIA

. . . The coalescence among the Great Goddess (Durga), fertility cults, and popular yoga [is shown by] the *pithas* or places of pilgrimage in honor of the Great Goddess (whatever her name—Devi, Shakti, Durga, Kali, etc.). The tantras and the Puranas speak of four *pithas*, one of them, as we should expect, being Kamarupa. Since each *pitha* represented the actual presence of the Great Goddess, the quaternary symbolism expresses the victory of the cult of Shakti in all India (the *pithas* were distributed among the four cardinal points). But soon the number of *pithas* began to increase, and to show variations; we have lists of seven, eight, forty-two, fifty, and even 108 *pithas* (there is here a relation with the 108 names of the Goddess). A myth whose origin is Brahmanic and Vedic, but which crystallizes, in the sense that interests us, only in the *Mahabharata* (XII, 282–83), explains the multiplicity of *pithas*: Sati, wife of Shiva, dies or kills herself because she has been mistreated by her father, Prajapati. The tantras and Puranas developed the myth: Shiva wanders through the world, dancing and carrying his wife's corpse on his shoulder. To put an end to Shiva's madness, the gods decide to reduce Sati's body to fragments. The operation is described in two variants: according to the first,[1] Brahma, Vishnu, and Shani enter the body by Yoga and divide it into small pieces; the places where the fragments fall become *pithas*. According to the other version, Vishnu pursues Shiva and divides Sati's body with his arrows.[2]

The myth of the dismemberment of the Goddess, though not

SOURCE: *Y*/346–48.
1. *Devibhagavata*, VII, 30; *Kalika Purana*, XVIII, etc.
2. D. C. Sirkar, "The Sākta Pithas," *Journal of the Royal Asiatic Soc. of Bengal* 14 (1948): 1–108, 5 ff.

incorporated into Indian texts until comparatively late, is extremely archaic; in different forms, it is found in southeastern Asia, Oceania, and North and South America, always in connection with the myth of the divinity's self-immolation in order to create edible species of plants. The symbolism of dismemberment also occurs, though in different contexts, in lunar mythologies and in shamanism. In the case of the *pithas*, we have an aboriginal fertility myth incorporated into tantrism; for, as we must not forget, the *pithas* were the outstanding places of pilgrimage for tantrics and Shaktas. Now —and we consider this fact important—the *pithas*, regarded as members of the Great Goddess, were at the same time aniconic altars, which had acquired their rank as holy places from the fact that ascetics and yogins had meditated and obtained *siddhis* there. In other words, the sanctity of the *pithas* was similar to that of the *samadhs* where yogins were buried. Consequently, a *pitha* could equally well be a place containing a member of the Goddess (especially the *yoni*) or a place where an ascetic had gained his "yogic perfection" (*siddha pitha*) . . . Here we have an illuminating example of the many complex coalescences and syntheses brought about and encouraged by yogic tantrism. An archaic myth is incorporated both into Yoga and into the popular devotion to the Great Goddess of fertility. The place consecrated by the yogic conquest of deliverance later becomes sacred because it is reputed to contain a member of the Great Goddess. Durga, as Shakti and wife of Shiva, becomes the goddess of yogins and ascetics, at the same time remaining, for the rest of the population, the Great Goddess of vegetation and fertility.

145. THE PRIMEVAL PAIR: SKY AND EARTH

The divine couple, Heaven and Earth, presented by Hesiod, are one of the *leitmotiven*[1] of universal mythology. In many mythologies in which the sky plays the part of supreme divinity, the earth is represented as his companion, and . . . the sky has a place almost everywhere in primitive religious life. Let us recall some examples of this. The Maoris call the Sky Rangi and the earth Papa;

Source: *PCR*/240–42; cf. *PCR*/300–306, *SP*/141–44.
1. *Leitmotiven*: leading motifs. Eds.

at the beginning, like Ouranos and Gaia, they were joined in a close embrace. The children born of this infinite union—Tumata-nenga, Tanemahuta and others—who longed for the light and groped around in the darkness, decided to separate from their parents. And so, one day, they cut the cords binding heaven to earth and pushed their father higher and higher until Rangi was thrust up into the air and light appeared in the world.

The creation motif of a primeval pair, Heaven and Earth, occurs in all the civilizations of Oceania, from Indonesia to Micronesia. You find it in Borneo, among the Minehassa, in the northern Celebes (where Luminuut, the goddess of earth, is the chief divinity); among the Toradja of the central Celebes (I-lai and I-ndora), in innumerable other Indonesian islands, and so on. In some places one also meets the motif of the sky and earth separated by force; at Tahiti, for instance, it is believed that this was effected by a plant which raised the sky up by growing. This motif is quite widespread in other areas of civilization too. We find the primeval couple, heaven and earth, in Africa; for instance, the Nzambi and Nzambi-Mpungu of the Bawili tribe, in the Gabon, Olorun and Oduna ("the black") among the Yoruba, the divine couple of the Ewe, and of the Akwapim, and so on. Among the Kumana, an agricultural tribe of southern Africa, the marriage between sky and earth takes on the same sense of cosmic fertility as it has in the hymns of the Pleiades of Dodona: "The Earth is our mother, the Sky is our father. The Sky fertilizes the Earth with rain, the Earth produces grains and grass." And as we shall see, this formula covers a large part of the beliefs concerning agriculture. The divine couple also figure in the mythologies of the Americas. In southern California, the Sky is called Tukmit and the Earth Tamaiovit; among the Navahos we find Yadilqil Hastqin (sky man) and his wife Nihosdzan Esdza (earth woman); among the Pawnees, in north America, with the Sioux, the Hurons (one of the main tribes of Iroquois), the Hopi, the Zuni, in the West Indies, and elsewhere we find the same cosmic duality. In the mythologies of the East, it plays an equally important part in the creation of the universe. The "queen of the lands" (the goddess Arinna) and her husband U or Im, the god of storm, are the Hittite version, the goddess of earth and the god of sky are the Chinese; Izanagi and Izanami the Japanese; and so on. Among the Germanic peoples, Frigga, the wife of Tyr, and later of Othin, is in essence a goddess of earth. And it is merely a chance of grammar that the Egyptians had a goddess, Nut, to represent the sky (the word for sky was feminine), and a god, Geb, for the earth.[2]

146. EARTH MOTHER: THEOPHANY OF THE SOIL

In all the mythological and ritual patterns we have examined, the earth is primarily honored for its endless capacity to bear fruit. That is why, with time, the Earth-Mother imperceptibly turned into the Corn Mother. But the theophany of the soil never totally disappeared from the picture of "Mothers," or earth divinities. To give but one example, we can perceive attributes that were originally those of the Earth-Mother in all the female figures of the Greek religion—Nemesis, the Furies, Themis. And Aeschylus[1] prays first to the Earth, then to Themis. It is true that Ge or Gaia was eventually replaced by Demeter, but the Hellenes never lost the consciousness of the bond between the goddess of cereals and the Earth-Mother. Euripides,[2] speaking of Demeter, says: "She is the Earth. . . . Call her what you will!"

Agricultural divinities took the place of the primitive divinities of the soil, but this substitution did not involve the abolition of all the primeval rites. Underlying the "form" of the agricultural Great Goddesses, we can still detect the presence of the "mistress of the place," the Earth-Mother. But the newer divinities are clearer in feature, more dynamic in their religious structure. Their history starts to involve emotion—they *live* the drama of birth, fertility and death. The turning of the Earth-Mother into the Great Goddess of agriculture is the turning of simple existence into living drama.

Source: *PCR*/261–62; cf. *SP*/138–47, and selection 105, on the Earth Mother motif.

2. As stated at the beginning of this volume, we have been forced to suppress most of the bibliographic references in Eliade's writings. This selection will give the reader some idea of this reduction: in the original version, section 85 of *PCR*, from which part is reprinted here, contains sixteen footnote references, and the division of *PCR* in which it appears concludes with two solid pages of additional readings. Eds.
1. *Eumenides*, 1.
2. *Bacchae*, 274.

From the cosmic hierogamy of heaven and earth to the least of the practices that bear witness to the holiness of the soil, the same central intuition comes in as a constantly repeated *leitmotiv*: the earth produces living forms, it is a womb which never wearies of procreating. In every kind of phenomenon to which the epiphany of the soil has given rise—whether a "sacred presence," a still formless divinity, a clearly defined divine figure, or merely a "custom" that results from some confused memory of subterranean powers—everywhere we can discern the activity of motherhood, of an inexhaustible power of creation. This creation may be of a monstrous kind, as in Hesiod's myth of Gaia. But the monsters of the *Theogony* merely illustrate the endless creative resources of the Earth. In some cases the sex of this earth divinity, this universal procreatrix—does not even have to be defined. A great many earth divinities, and some divinities of fertility, are bisexual. In such cases the divinity contains all the forces of creation—and this formula of polarity, of the coexistence of opposites, was to be taken up again in the loftiest of later speculation. All divinities tend to become *everything* to their believers, to take the place of all other religious figures, to rule over every sphere of the cosmos. And few divinities have ever had as much right or power to become *everything* as had the earth. But the ascent of the Earth-Mother to the position of the supreme, if not unique, divinity, was arrested both by her hierogamy with the sky and by the appearance of the divinities of agriculture. And traces of this tremendous story are preserved in the bisexuality of certain of the earth divinities. But the Earth-Mother never entirely lost her primitive prerogatives of being "mistress of the place," source of all living forms, keeper of children, and womb where the dead were laid to rest, where they were reborn to return eventually to life, thanks to the holiness of Mother Earth.

147. ZEUS, JUPITER, YAHWEH

The only sky gods of rain and fertility who managed to preserve their autonomy, despite unions with innumerable Great Goddesses, are those who developed along the lines of sovereignty; who held on to their scepters, as well as their thunders and fecundating powers, and thus remained the guarantors of the order of the universe, guardians of the norms, and personifications of Law. Zeus and Jupiter are two such gods. Naturally, these two ruling figures had personalities closely fashioned according to the peculiar leaning of the Greek and Roman mind towards the notions of norm and law. But rationalizations of this sort are only possible because based upon a religious and mythical intuition of the rhythms of nature, with their harmony and agelessness. T'ien, too, with his tendency to be revealed as a hierophany of Law and cosmic rhythm, is a good example of the sovereignty of the sky. We shall grasp these aspects better when we come to study the religious patterns of the sovereign and of sovereignty.

The "evolution" of the supreme God of the Hebrews is to be found on a plane that is in some ways parallel. Yahweh's personality and religious history are far too complex to be summed up in a few lines. Let me say, however, that his celestial and atmospheric hierophanies very early became the center of those religious experiences which made later revelations possible. Yahweh displayed his power by means of storms; thunder is his voice and lightning is called Yahweh's "fire," or his "arrows."[1] The Lord of Israel declares his presence: ". . . thunders began to be heard and lightning to flash, and a very thick cloud to cover the mount"[2] while he was transmitting the Law to Moses. "And all Mount Sinai was on a smoke: because the Lord was come down upon it in fire."[3] Deborah recalled with holy dread how at the Lord's footstep "the earth trembled and the heavens dropped water."[4] Yahweh warns Elias of his approach by "a great and strong wind . . . overthrowing the mountains, and breaking the rocks in pieces: the Lord is not in the wind. And after the wind an earthquake: the Lord is not in the earthquake. And after the earthquake a fire: the Lord is not in the fire. And after the fire a whistling of a gentle air."[5] The fire of the Lord descends on the holocausts of Elias[6] when the prophet prays

1. Cf. Ps. 17, etc.
2. Exod. 19:16.
3. *Ibid.*, 18:18.
4. Judges 5:4.
5. I Kings 19:11–12.
6. I Kings 18:38.

that he will show himself and confound the priests of Ba'al. The burning bush in the story of Moses, and the pillar of fire and cloud which leads the Israelites through the desert are epiphanies of Yahweh. And Yahweh's covenant with the descendants of Noe after his escape from the Flood is expressed by a rainbow: "I will set my bow in the clouds, and it shall be the sign of a covenant between me, and between the earth."[7]

These hierophanies of sky and weather, unlike those of other storm gods, manifest above all the "power" of Yahweh. "God is high in his strength: and none is like him among the law-givers."[8] "In his hands he hideth the light, and commandeth it to come again. He showeth his friend concerning it. . . . At this my heart trembleth and is moved out of its place. Hear ye attentively the terror of his voice, and the sound that cometh out of his mouth. He beholdeth under all the heavens: and his light is upon the ends of the earth. After it a noise shall roar: he shall thunder with the voice of his majesty . . ."[9] The Lord is the true and only Master of the cosmos. He can make all things, annihilate all things. His "power" is absolute, which is why his freedom knows no bounds. Uncontested sovereign, he measures his mercy or his anger as he will: and this absolute liberty the Lord enjoys is the most effective revelation of his absolute transcendence and autonomy; for by nothing can the Lord be "bound"—nothing constrains him, not even good actions or obedience to his laws.

This notion of God's "power" as the only absolute reality is the jumping-off point for all later mystical thought and speculation on the freedom of man, and his possibility of achieving salvation by obedience to the Law and rigorous moral conduct. No one is "innocent" before God. Yahweh made a "covenant" with his people, but his sovereignty meant that it was quite possible for him to annul it at any moment. That he did not was due not to the "covenant" itself—for nothing can "bind" God—but to his infinite goodness. Throughout the religious history of Israel, Yahweh shows himself a sky god and storm god, creator and omnipotent, absolute sovereign and "Lord of Hosts," support of the kings of Da-

7. Gen. 9:13.
8. Job 36:22.
9. Job 36:32–37:4.

vid's line, author of all the norms and laws that make it possible for life on earth to go on. The "Law," in every form, finds its basis and justification in a revelation from Yahweh. But unlike other supreme gods, who cannot contravene their own laws (Zeus could not save Sarpedon from death),[10] Yahweh maintains his absolute freedom.

148. THE WORLD AT HAND AS MICROCOSM

In archaic and traditional societies, the surrounding world is conceived as a microcosm. At the limits of this closed world begins the domain of the unknown, of the formless. On this side there is ordered—because inhabited and organized—space; on the other, outside this familiar space, there is the unknown and dangerous region of the demons, the ghosts, the dead and of foreigners—in a word, chaos or death or night. This image of an inhabited microcosm, surrounded by desert regions regarded as a chaos or a kingdom of the dead, has survived even in highly evolved civilizations such as those of China, Mesopotamia, and Egypt. Indeed, a good many texts liken the enemies who are attacking national territory to ghosts, demons or the powers of chaos. Thus the adversaries of the Pharaoh were looked upon as "sons of ruin, wolves, dogs," etc. The Pharaoh was likened to the God Re, victor over the dragon Apophis, whilst his enemies were identified with that same mythical dragon. Because they attack, and endanger the equilibrium and the very life of the city (or of any other inhabited and organized territory), enemies are assimilated to demonic powers, trying to reincorporate the microcosm into the state of chaos; that is, to suppress it. The destruction of an established order, the abolition of an archetypal image, was equivalent to a regression into chaos, into the preformal, undifferentiated state that preceded the cosmogony. Let us note that the same images are still invoked in our own days when people want to formulate the dangers that menace a certain type of civilization: there is much talk of "chaos," of "disorder," of the "dark ages" into which "our world" is subsiding. All these expressions, it is felt, signify the abolition of an order, of a Cosmos, of a

SOURCE: *IS*/37–41; cf. *SP*/22, 36–47, 57.
10. *Iliad*, XVI, 477 ff.

structure, and the re-immersion in a state that is fluid, amorphous, in the end chaotic.

The conception of the enemy as a demonic being, a veritable incarnation of the powers of evil, has also survived until our days. The psychoanalysis of these mythic images that still animate the modern world will perhaps show us the extent to which we project our own destructive desires upon the "enemy." But that is a problem beyond our competence. What we wish to bring to light is that, for the archaic world in general, the enemies threatening the microcosm were dangerous, not in their capacity as human beings but because they were incarnating the hostile and destructive powers. It is very probable that the defenses of inhabited areas and cities began by being magical defenses; for these defenses—ditches, labyrinths, ramparts, etc.—were set up to prevent the incursions of evil spirits rather than attacks from human beings. Even fairly late in history, in the Middle Ages for instance, the walls of cities were ritually consecrated as a defense against the Devil, sickness and death. Moreover, the archaic symbolism finds no difficulty in assimilating the human enemy to the Devil or to Death. After all, the result of their attacks, whether demonic or military, is always the same: ruin, disintegration, and death.

Every microcosm, every inhabited region, has what may be called a "Center"; that is to say, a place that is sacred above all. It is there, in that Center, that the sacred manifests itself in its totality, either in the form of elementary hierophanies—as it does among the "primitives" (in the totemic centers, for example, the caves where the *tchuringas* are buried, etc.)—or else in the more evolved form of the direct epiphanies of the gods, as in the traditional civilizations. But we must not envisage this symbolism of the Center with the geometrical implications that it has to a Western scientific mind. For each one of these microcosms there may be several "centers." As we shall see before long, all the Oriental civilizations—Mesopotamia, India, China, etc.—recognized an unlimited number of "Centers." Moreover, each one of these "Centers" was considered and even literally called the "Center of the World." The place in question being a "sacred space," consecrated by a hierophany, or ritually constructed, and not a profane, homogeneous, geometrical space, the plurality of "Centers of the Earth" within a single inhabited region presented no difficulty. What we have here is a sacred, mythic geography, the only kind effectually *real*, as opposed to profane geography, the latter being "objective" and, as it were, abstract and nonessential—the theoretical construction of a space and a world that we do not live in, and therefore do not *know*.

In mythical geography, sacred space is the essentially *real space*, for, as it has lately been shown, in the archaic world the myth alone is real. It tells of manifestations of the only indubitable reality—the *sacred*. It is in such space that one has direct contact with the sacred—whether this be materialized in certain objects (*tchuringas*, representations of the divinity, etc.) or manifested in the hierocosmic symbols (the Pillar of the World, the Cosmic Tree, etc.). In cultures that have the conception of three cosmic regions—those of Heaven, Earth and Hell—the "center" constitutes the point of intersection of those regions. It is here that the breakthrough on to another plane is possible and, at the same time, communication between the three regions. We have reason to believe that this image of three cosmic levels is quite archaic; we meet with it, for instance, among the Semang pygmies of the Malay peninsula: at the center of their world there stands an enormous rock, Batu-Ribn, and beneath it is Hell. From the Batu-Ribn a treetrunk formerly reached up towards the sky.[1] Hell, the center of the earth and the "door" of heaven are all to be found, then, upon the same axis, and it is along this axis that the passage from one cosmic region to another is effected. We might hesitate to believe in the authenticity of this cosmological theory among the Semang pygmies, were we not bound to admit that the same theory already existed in outline in prehistoric times. The Semang say that the trunk of a tree *formerly* connected the summit of the Cosmic Mountain, the Center of the World, with Heaven. This is an allusion to a mythic theme of extremely wide diffusion: formerly, communication with Heaven and relations with the divinity were easy and natural"; until, in consequence of a ritual fault, these communications were broken off, and the gods withdrew to still higher heavens. Only medicine men, shamans, priests, and heroes, or the sovereign rulers were now able to re-establish communication with Heaven, and that only in a temporary way and for their own use. . . .

1. P. Schebesta, *Les Pygmeés*, French trans. (Paris, 1940), pp. 156 ff.

149. THE SYMBOLISM OF THE CENTER

. . . The architectonic symbolism of the Center may be formulated as follows:

1. The Sacred Mountain—where heaven and earth meet—is situated at the center of the world.

2. Every temple or palace—and, by extension, every sacred city or royal residence—is a Sacred Mountain, thus becoming a Center.

3. Being an *axis mundi*, the sacred city or temple is regarded as the meeting point of heaven, earth, and hell.

A few examples will illustrate each of these symbols:

1. According to Indian beliefs, Mount Meru rises at the center of the world, and above it shines the polestar. The Ural-Altaic peoples also know of a central mountain, Sumeru, to whose summit the polestar is fixed. Iranian beliefs hold that the sacred mountain Haraberezaiti (Elburz) is situated at the center of the earth and is linked with heaven. The Buddhist population of Laos, north of Siam, know of Mount Zinnalo, at the center of the world. In the *Edda*, Himinbjorg, as its name indicates, is a "celestial mountain"; it is here that the rainbow (Bifrost) reaches the dome of the sky. Similar beliefs are found among the Finns, the Japanese, and other peoples. We are reminded that for the Semangs of the Malay Peninsula an immense rock, Batu-Ribn, rises at the center of the world; above it is hell. In past times, a tree trunk on Batu-Ribn rose into the sky. Hell, the center of the earth, and the "gate" of the sky are, then, situated on the same axis, and it is along this axis that passage from one cosmic region to another was effected. We should hesitate to credit the authenticity of this cosmological theory among the Semang pygmies if we did not have evidence that the same theory already existed in outline during the prehistoric period.[1] According to Mesopotamian beliefs, a central mountain joins heaven and earth; it is the Mount of the Land,[2] the connection between territories. Properly speaking, the ziggurat was a cosmic mountain, i.e., a symbolic image of the cosmos, the seven stories

---

SOURCE: *CH*/12–17; cf. *IS*/42–43, 52–54; *SP*/38–40; *PCR*/99–102, 372–79.

1. Cf., for example, W. Gaerte, "Kosmische Vorstellungen im Bilde prähistorischer Zeit: Erdberg, Himmelsberg, Erdnabel und Weltströme," *Anthropos* 9 (Salzburg, 1914): 956–79.

2. Alfred Jeremias, *Handbuch der altorientalischen Geisteskultur*, 2d ed., (Berlin, 1929), p. 130.

representing the seven planetary heavens (as at Borsippa) or having the colors of the world (as at Ur).

Mount Tabor, in Palestine, could mean *tabbur*, i.e., navel, *omphalos*. Mount Gerizim, in the center of Palestine, was undoubtedly invested with the prestige of the Center for it is called "navel of the earth" (*tabbur eres*; cf. Judges 9:37: ". . . See there come people down by the middle [Heb., navel] of the land . . ."). A tradition preserved by Peter Comestor relates that at the summer solstice the sun casts no shadow on the "Fountain of Jacob" (near Gerizim). And indeed, Peter continues, "sunt qui dicunt locum illum esse umbilicum terrae nostrae habitabilis." Palestine, being the highest country—because it was near to the summit of the cosmic mountain—was not covered by the Deluge. A rabbinic text says: "The land of Israel was not submerged by the deluge." For Christians, Golgotha was situated at the center of the world, since it was the summit of the cosmic mountain and at the same time the place where Adam had been created and buried. Thus the blood of the Saviour falls upon Adam's skull, buried precisely at the foot of the Cross, and redeems him. The belief that Golgotha is situated at the center of the world is preserved in the folklore of the Eastern Christians.

2. The names of the Babylonian temples and sacred towers themselves testify to their assimilation to the cosmic mountain: "Mount of the House," "House of the Mount of All Lands," "Mount of Tempests," "Link Between Heaven and Earth." A cylinder from the period of King Gudea says that "The bed-chamber [of the god] which he built was [like] the cosmic mountain . . ."[3] Every Oriental city was situated at the center of the world. Babylon was a *Bab-ilani*, a "gate of the gods," for it was there that the gods descended to earth. In the capital of the Chinese sovereign, the gnomon must cast no shadow at noon on the day of the summer solstice. Such a capital is, in effect, at the center of the universe, close to the miraculous tree (*kien-mu*), at the meeting place of the three cosmic zones: heaven, earth, and hell. The Javanese temple of Borobudur is itself an image of the cosmos, and is built like an artificial mountain (as were the ziggurats). Ascending it, the pilgrim

3. W. F. Albright, "The Mouth of the Rivers," *The American Journal of Semitic Languages and Literatures* 35 (Chicago, 1919): 173.

approaches the center of the world, and, on the highest terrace, breaks from one plane to another, transcending profane, heterogeneous space and entering a "pure region." Cities and sacred places are assimilated to the summits of cosmic mountains. This is why Jerusalem and Zion were not submerged by the Deluge. According to Islamic tradition, the highest point on earth is the Kaaba, because "the polestar proves that . . . it lies over against the center of heaven."

3. Finally, because of its situation at the center of the cosmos, the temple or the sacred city is always the meeting point of the three cosmic regions: heaven, earth, and hell. *Dur-an-ki*, "Bond of Heaven and Earth," was the name given to the sanctuaries of Nippur and Larsa, and doubtless to that of Sippara. Babylon had many names, among them "House of the Base of Heaven and Earth," "Bond of Heaven and Earth." But it is always Babylon that is the scene of the connection between the earth and the lower regions, for the city had been built upon *bab apsi*, the "Gate of the Apsu"—*apsu* designating the waters of chaos before the Creation. We find the same tradition among the Hebrews. The rock of Jerusalem reached deep into the subterranean waters (*tehom*). The Mishnah says that the Temple is situated exactly above the *tehom* (Hebrew equivalent of *apsu*). And just as in Babylon there was the "gate of the *apsu*," the rock of the Temple in Jerusalem contained the "mouth of the *tehom*." We find similar conceptions in the Indo-European world. Among the Romans, for example, the *mundus*— that is, the trench dug around the place where a city was to be founded—constitutes the point where the lower regions and the terrestrial world meet. "When the *mundus* is open it is as if the gates of the gloomy infernal gods were open," says Varro (cited by Macrobius, *Saturnalia*, I, 16, 18). The Italic temple was the zone where the upper (divine), terrestrial, and subterranean worlds intersected.

The summit of the cosmic mountain is not only the highest point of the earth; it is also the earth's navel, the point at which the Creation began. There are even instances in which cosmological traditions explain the symbolism of the Center in terms which might well have been borrowed from embryology. "The Holy One created the world like an embryo. As the embryo proceeds from the navel onwards, so God began to create the world from its navel onwards and from there it was spread out in different directions." The *Yoma* affirms: "The world was created beginning from Zion." In the *Rig Veda* (for example X, 149), the universe is conceived as spreading from a central point. The creation of man, which answers to the cosmogony, likewise took place at a central point, at the center of the world. According to Mesopotamian tradition, man was formed at the "navel of the earth" in *uzu* (flesh), *sar* (bond), *ki* (place, earth), where *Dur-an-ki*, the "Bond of Heaven and Earth," is also situated. Ormazd creates the primordial ox Evagdath, and the primordial man, Gajomard, at the center of the earth. Paradise, where Adam was created from clay, is, of course, situated at the center of the cosmos. Paradise was the navel of the Earth and, according to a Syrian tradition, was established on a mountain higher than all others. According to the Syrian *Book of the Cave of Treasures*, Adam was created at the center of the earth, at the same spot where the Cross of Christ was later to be set up. The same traditions have been preserved by Judaism. The Jewish apocalypse and a midrash state that Adam was formed in Jerusalem. Adam being buried at the very spot where he was created, i.e., at the center of the world, on Golgotha, the blood of the Savior—as we have seen —will redeem him too.

The symbolism of the Center is considerably more complex, but the few aspects to which we have referred will suffice for our purpose. We may add that the same symbolism survived in the Western world down to the threshold of modern times. The very ancient conception of the temple as the *imago mundi*, the idea that the sanctuary reproduces the universe in its essence, passed into the religious architecture of Christian Europe: the basilica of the first centuries of our era, like the medieval cathedral, symbolically reproduces the Celestial Jerusalem. As to the symbolism of the mountain, of the Ascension, and of the "Quest for the Center," they are clearly attested in medieval literature, and appear, though only by allusion, in certain literary works of recent centuries.

150. MANDALAS AND MYTHS IN HEALING

One detail in the healing ritual of the Bhils is of particular interest. The magician "purifies" the space beside the patient's bed and draws a *mandol* with corn flour. At the center of the design he puts the house of Isvor and Bhagwân, together with their figures. This drawing is preserved until the patient is completely cured.[1] The term "*mandol*" itself testifies to an Indian origin. This is, of course, the *mandala*, a complex design that plays a large part in Indo-Tibetan tantric rites. But the *mandala* is primarily an *imago mundi*; it represents the Cosmos in miniature and, at the same time, the pantheon. Its construction is equivalent to a magical re-creation of the world. Hence when the Bhil magician draws a *mandol* at the patient's bedside he is repeating the cosmogony, even if the ritual songs that he sings do not expressly refer to the cosmogonic myth. The operation certainly has a therapeutic purpose. Made symbolically contemporary with the Creation of the World, the patient is immersed in the primordial fullness of life; he is penetrated by the gigantic forces that, *in illo tempore*, made the Creation possible.

In this connection it is of interest to note that, among the Navahos, the cosmogonic myth, followed by the myth of the emergence of the first men from the bosom of the Earth, is seldom recited except on the occasion of a cure or during the initiation of a shaman. "All the ceremonies center around a patient, Hatrali (one sung over), who may be sick or merely sick in mind, i.e., frightened by a dream, or who may be needing only a ceremony, in order to learn it in the course of being initiated into full power of officiating in that chant—for a Medicine Man cannot give a healing ceremony until he has the ceremony given over him."[2] The ceremony also includes executing complex sand paintings, which symbolize the various stages of Creation and the mythical history of the gods, the ancestors, and mankind. These drawings (which strangely resemble the Indo-Tibetan *mandala*) successively re-enact the events which took place in mythical times. As he hears the cosmogonic

Source: *MR*/24–26; cf. *IS*/44–54; *PCR*/372–73.

1. L. Jungblut, "Magic Songs of the Bhils of Jhabura State," *Internationales Archiv für Ethnographie* 43 (1943): 5.

2. Hasteen Klah, *Navajo Creation Myth: The Story of the Emergence* (Santa Fé, 1942), p. 19. Cf. also *ibid.*, pp. 25 ff., 32 ff.

myth and then the origin myths recited and contemplates the sand paintings, the patient is projected out of profane time into the fullness of primordial Time; he is carried "back" to the origin of the World and is thus present at the cosmogony.

151. SACRED STONE; OMPHALOS

The stone upon which Jacob slept was not only the "House of God"; it was also the place where, by means of the angels' ladder, communication took place between heaven and earth. The bethel was, therefore, a center of the world, like the Ka'aba of Mecca or Mount Sinai, like all the temples, palaces, and "centers" consecrated by ritual. Its being a "ladder" uniting heaven and earth derived from a theophany which took place at that spot; God, manifesting himself to Jacob on the bethel, was also indicating the place where he could come to earth, the point at which the transcendent might enter the immanent. As we shall see later, ladders of this kind are not necessarily placed in a definite, concrete geographical spot; the "center of the world" can be consecrated by ritual in inumerable points of the globe without the authenticity of one invalidating the rest.[1]

For the moment I will simply note a few beliefs about the *omphalos* ("navel") of which Pausanias says:[2] "What the inhabitants of Delphi call *omphalos* is of white stone, and thought to be at the center of the earth; and Pindar, in one of his odes, confirms this notion." Much has been written on the subject. Rohde and J. H. Harrison think that the *omphalos* originally represented the stone placed on the tomb; Varro[3] mentions a tradition that the *omphalos* was the tomb of the sacred serpent of Delphi, Python: *quem Pythonis aiunt tumulum*. Roscher, who devotes three monographs to this question, declares that the *omphalos* was from the first believed to be the "center of the earth." Nilsson[4] is not satisfied

SOURCE: *PCR*/231–33.

1. On ladders and the motif of "ascent," see selections 98–100. Eds.
2. X, 16, 2.
3. *De Lingua Latina*, VII, 17.
4. M. P. Nilsson, *Geschichte der griechischen Religion* (Munich, 1941), 1: 189.

with either interpretation, and believes the conception of the burial stone and of the "center of the world" both came after, and took the place of a more "primitive" belief.

But, actually, both interpretations are "primitive," and they are not mutually exclusive. A tomb, seen as a point of contact between the world of the dead, of the living, and of the gods, can also be a "center," an "*omphalos* of the earth." To the Romans, for instance, the *mundus* represented the communicating point of the three spheres; "when the *mundus* is open, open too is the gate of the unhappy gods of the underworld," writes Varro.[5] The *mundus* is not, of course, a tomb, but the symbolism of it will give us a clearer understanding of the similar function fulfilled by the *omphalos*: that it first originated with burial does not contradict the fact of its being a "center." The place where communication could be made between the world of the dead and that of the gods of the underworld was consecrated as a connecting link between the different levels of the universe, and such a place could only be situated in a "center." . . .

When Apollo superseded the ancient earth religion of Delphi, he took over the *omphalos* and its privileges. Pursued by the Furies, Orestes was purified by Apollo beside the *omphalos*, the supremely sacred spot, in the "center" where the three cosmic zones are linked, in the "navel" which guarantees by its symbolism a new birth and a reintegrated conscience. The manifold significance of the "center stone" is even better preserved in Celtic traditions. Lia Fail, "the stone of Fail" (the name is doubtful; Fail might mean Ireland), starts singing when anyone worthy of being king sits on it; in ordeals, if the accused is innocent, he becomes white when he gets on to it; when a woman who is doomed to remain sterile comes near, the stone exudes blood; when if the woman will become a mother, it exudes milk. Lia Fail is a theophany of the soil divinity, the only divinity to recognize his master (the High King of Ireland), the only one who controls the economy of fertility, and guarantees ordeals. There are also, of course, later phallic variants of these Celtic *omphaloi*; fertility, above all, is an attribute of the "center," and emblems of it are often sexual. That the Celts saw the religious (and implicitly the political) significance of the center is

5. Quoted by Macrobius, *Saturn.*, I, 16, 18.

evidenced by such words as *medinemetum, mediolanum*[6] which exist even today in French place names. Bearing in mind what we learn from Lia Fail and some of the traditions preserved in France, we have good reason to identify these "centers" with omphalic stones. In the village of Amancy (district of La Roche), for instance, there can be found—proof positive of the "center"—a "Middle-of-the-World Stone." . . .

152. THE COSMIC MOUNTAIN

. . . The Tatars of the Altai imagine Bai Ügän in the middle of the sky, seated on a golden mountain. The Abakan Tatars call it "The Iron Mountain"; the Mongols, the Buryat, the Kalmyk know it under the names of Sumbur, Sumur, or Sumer, which clearly show Indian influence (= Mount Meru). The Mongols and the Kalmyk picture it with three or four storeys; the Siberian Tatars, with seven; in his mystical journey the Yakut shaman, too, climbs a mountain with seven storeys. Its summit is in the Pole Star, in the "Navel of the Sky." The Buryat say that the Pole Star is fastened to its summit.

The idea of a Cosmic Mountain as Center of the World is not necessarily of Oriental origin, for, as we have seen, the symbolism of the "Center" seems to have preceded the rise of the paleo-Oriental civilizations. But the ancient traditions of the peoples of Central and North Asia—who doubtless knew the image of a "Center of the World" and of the Cosmic Axis—were modified by the continual influx of Oriental religious ideas, whether Mesopotamian in origin (and disseminated through Iran) or Indian (disseminated through Lamaism). . . .

* * *

We have shown . . . how frequent and essential this symbolism of the "Center" is both in the archaic ("primitive") cultures and in all the great civilizations of the East. To summarize very briefly: palaces, royal cities, and even simple houses were believed to stand

Source: *S*/266, 269; cf. *IS*/42–43; *SP*/38–40; *PCR*/99–102, 374–79.
6. Cf. Caesar, *De Bello Gallico*, VI, 13: *media regio*.

at the "Center of the World," on the summit of the Cosmic Mountain. We have already seen the deeper meaning of this symbolism; it is at the "Center" that the breakthrough in plane, that is, communication with the sky, becomes possible.

It is such a Cosmic Mountain that the future shaman climbs in dream during his initiatory illness and that he later visits on his ecstatic journeys. Ascending a mountain always signifies a journey to the "Center of the World." As we have seen, this "Center" is made present in many ways, even in the structure of the human dwelling place—but it is only the shamans and the heroes who *actually scale* the Cosmic Mountain, just as it is primarily the shaman who, climbing his ritual tree, is really climbing a World Tree and thus reaches the summit of the universe, in the highest sky. For the symbolism of the World Tree is complementary to that of the Central Mountain. Sometimes the two symbols coincide; usually they complete each other. But both are merely more developed mythical formulations of the Cosmic Axis (World Pillar, etc.).

153. THE COSMIC TREE

. . . There exist innumerable variants of the symbolism of the Cosmic Tree. A certain number of these variants can be considered as coming from only a few centers of diffusion. One can even admit the possibility that *all* the variants of the Cosmic Tree come in the last analysis from one single center of diffusion. In this case, we might be permitted to hope that one day the *history* of the symbolism of the Cosmic Tree may be reconstructed, by pinning down the center of origin, the paths of diffusion, and the different values with which this symbol has been endowed during its migrations. Were such a historical monograph possible, it would render a great service to the science of religions. But the problem of the symbolism of the Cosmic Tree as such would not thereby be resolved. Quite another problem remains to be dealt with. What is the meaning of this symbol? What does it *reveal*, what does it *show* as a religious symbol? Each type or variety of this symbol reveals with a particular intensity or clarity *certain* aspects of the sym-

SOURCE: *MRS*/93–94; cf. *PCR*/265–69, 168–76, 316 ff.; *IS*/44–47, 161 ff.; *SP*/147–50; *TO*/196–99; *MDM*/20–21, 63; *S*/125–26, 259–65, 273 ff.

bolism of the Cosmic Tree, leaving other aspects unemphasized. There are examples where the Cosmic Tree reveals itself chiefly as the *imago mundi*, and in other examples it presents itself as the *axis mundi*, as a pole that supports the Sky, binds together the three cosmic zones (Heaven, Earth, and Hell), and at the same time makes communication possible between Earth and Heaven. Still other variants emphasize the function of the periodic regeneration of the universe, or the role of the Cosmic Tree as the Center of the World or its creative potentialities, etc.

We have studied the symbolism of the Cosmic Tree in several of our previous works, and need not restate the problem here in its entirety. Suffice it to say that it is impossible to understand the meaning of the Cosmic Tree by considering only one or some of its variants. It is only by the analysis of a considerable number of examples that the structure of a symbol can be completely deciphered. Moreover one can understand the meaning of a certain type of Cosmic Tree only after having studied the most important types and varieties. Only after an elucidation of the specific meanings of the Cosmic Tree in Mesopotamia or in ancient India can one understand the symbolism of Yggdrasil or the Cosmic Trees of Central Asia and of Siberia. In the science of religions, as elsewhere, comparisons are made in order to find both parallels and distinctions.

But there is still more. Only after taking account of all the variants do the differences of their meanings fall into relief. It is because the symbol of the Indonesian Cosmic Tree does not coincide with that of the Altaic Cosmic Tree that the first reveals all its importance for the science of religion. Thus the question is posed: Is there, in either instance, some innovation, obscuration of meaning, or a loss of the original meaning? Since we know what the Cosmic Tree means in Mesopotamia, in India, or in Siberia, the question arises: Because of what religio-historical circumstances, or by what interior reason, does the same symbol in Indonesia reveal a different meaning? Diffusion as such does not solve the problem. For even if one could demonstrate that the symbol had been diffused from a single center, one could still not give the reason why certain cultures have retained certain primary meanings, whereas others have forgotten, rejected, modified, or enriched them. One can come to understand the process of enrichment only by disengaging the structure of the symbol. It is because the Cosmic Tree symbolizes the mystery of a world in perpetual regeneration that it can symbolize, at the same time or successively, the pillar of the world and the cradle of the human race, the cosmic *renovatio* and the lunar rhythms, the Center of the World and the path by which one can pass from Earth to Heaven, etc. Each one of these new valorizations is possible because from the beginning the symbol of the Cosmic Tree reveals itself as a "cipher" of the world grasped as a living reality, sacred and inexhaustible. . . .

154. THE BROKEN CENTER

One of the African tribes whose religion Eliade studies in Australian Religions *is the Achilpa. This story involves Numbakulla, whose name means "always existing" or "out of nothing," and who made mountains, rivers and other plants and animals. He also created the ancestral Achilpa, and taught them various ceremonies.*

Now, Numbakulla had planted a pole called *kauwa-auwa* in the middle of a sacred ground. (A representation of this pole, made from the trunk of a young gum tree, is erected on the ceremonial ground during the long series of initiation rites known as the Engwura.) After anointing it with blood, he began to climb it. He told the first Achilpa Ancestor to follow him; but the blood made the pole too slippery, and the man slid down. "Numbakulla went on alone, drew up the pole after him and was never seen again."[1]

This pole is charged with important symbolism and plays a central role in ritual. The fact that Numbakulla disappeared into the sky after climbing it suggests that the *kauwa-auwa* is somehow an *axis mundi* which unites heaven and earth. Elsewhere, and particularly in the Oriental cultures and the areas under their influence, the *axis mundi* (conceived as a pillar, a tree, a mountain, etc.) actually constitutes a "center of the world." This implies, among other things, that it is a consecrated place from which all orientation takes

SOURCE: *AR*/51–53; cf. *SP*/32–36, 53.
    1. B. Spencer and F. J. Gillen, *The Arunta* (London, 1927), 1: 355 ff., especially 360.

place. In other words, the "center" imparts structure to the surrounding amorphous space. Both the Achilpa myth and the actual ceremonial use of the pole illustrate very well this double function of communication with heaven and means of orientation. The myth relates in seemingly endless detail the wanderings of the first Achilpa Ancestors after the disappearance of Numbakulla. They traveled continuously, in small groups, carrying out ceremonies, circumcising the young men, occasionally leaving one of them behind. When these mythical groups performed the Engwura rituals, the *kauwa-auwa* "was always erected and made to lean in the direction in which they intended to travel."[2] In other words, the sacred pole helped them to chart the unknown space into which they were preparing to adventure.

One day an accident befell one of these mythical groups: while pulling up the *kauwa-auwa*, which was very deeply implanted, the old chief broke it just above the ground. They carried the broken pole until they met another group. They were so tired and sad that they did not even try to erect their own *kauwa-auwa* "but, lying down together, died where they lay. A large hill, covered with big stones, arose to mark the spot."[3] Seldom do we find a more pathetic avowal that man cannot live without a "sacred center" which permits him both to "cosmicize" space and to communicate with the transhuman world of heaven. So long as they had their *kauwa-auwa*, the Achilpa Ancestors were never lost in the surrounding "chaos." Moreover, the sacred pole was for them the proof par excellence of Numbakulla's existence and activity. . . .

155. "OUR WORLD" AS CENTER

From all that has been said, it follows that the true world is always in the middle, at the Center, for it is here that there is a break in plane and hence communication among the three cosmic zones. . . .

To us, it seems an inescapable conclusion that *the religious man*

Source: *SP*/42–44.

2. *Ibid.*, p. 382.

3. *Ibid.*, p. 388.

sought to live as near as possible to the Center of the World. He knew that his country lay at the midpoint of the earth; he knew too that his city constituted the navel of the universe, and, above all, that the temple or the palace were veritably Centers of the World. But he also wanted his own house to be at the Center and to be an *imago mundi.* And, in fact . . . , houses are held to be at the Center of the World and, on the microcosmic scale, to reproduce the universe. In other words, the man of traditional societies could only live in a space opening upward, where the break in plane was symbolically assured and hence communication with the *other world,* the transcendental world, was ritually possible. Of course the sanctuary—the Center par excellence—was there, close to him, in the city, and he could be sure of communicating with the world of the gods simply by entering the temple. But he felt the need to live at the Center *always*—like the Achilpa, who, as we saw, always carried the sacred pole, the *axis mundi,* with them, so that they should never be far from the Center and should remain in communication with the supraterrestrial world. In short, whatever the dimensions of the space with which he is familiar and in which he regards himself as situated—his country, his city, his village, his house—religious man feels the need always to exist in a total and organized world, in a cosmos. . . .

156. EARTH, WOMAN, FERTILITY

No one doubts that agriculture was discovered by women. Man was almost always in pursuit of game, or pasturing his flocks. Woman, on the other hand, with her keen, though circumscribed, powers of observation, was in a position to watch the natural phenomena of seeds falling and growing, and to try and reproduce those phenomena artificially. And then too, because she was linked up with the other centers of cosmic fertility—Earth and the Moon— woman also became endowed with the prerogative of being able to influence and distribute fertility. That is the reason for the dominant role played by women when agriculture was in its infancy—

SOURCE: *PCR*/257–58.

particularly when this skill was still the province of women—and which in some civilizations she still plays. Thus, in Uganda, a barren woman is thought to be a danger to the garden, and her husband can seek a divorce simply on economic grounds. We find the same belief in the danger to farming of female sterility in the Bhantu tribe, in the Indies. In Nicobar it is thought that the harvest will be richer if the seed is sown by a pregnant woman. In southern Italy, it is thought that everything undertaken by a pregnant woman will be a success, and that everything she sows will grow as the foetus grows. In Borneo ". . . the women play the principal part in the rites and actual operations of the *padi* culture; the men only being called in to clear the ground and to assist in some of the later stages. The women select and keep the seed grain, and they are the repositories of most of the lore connected with it. It seems to be felt that they have a natural affinity to the fruitful grain, which they speak of as becoming pregnant. Women sometimes sleep out in the *padi* fields while the crop is growing, probably for the purpose of increasing their own fertility, or that of the *padi*; but they are very reticent on this matter."[1]

The Orinoco Indians left the task of sowing maize and planting roots to their women; for "as women knew how to conceive seed and bear children, so the seeds and roots planted by them bore fruit far more abundantly than if they had been planted by male hands."[2] At Nias, a palm tree planted by a woman has more sap than one planted by a man. The same beliefs are to be found in Africa, among the Ewe. In South America, among the Jibaros, for instance, it is believed "that women exercise a special, mysterious influence on the growth of cultivated plants."[3] This solidarity of woman with fertile furrows was preserved even after farming became a masculine skill, and the plough took the place of the primitive spade. This solidarity accounts for a great many rites and beliefs which we shall examine when we come to look at the various rituals of agriculture.

1. Hose and MacDougall, *Pagan Tribes of Borneo*, pp. i, iii, quoted by Lévy-Bruhl, *L'Expérience mystique* (Paris, 1938), p. 254.

2. Sir James G. Frazer, *Spirits of the Corn and of the Wild* (London, 1912), 1: 124.

3. Rafael Karsten, quoted by Lévy-Bruhl, *L'Expérience mystique*, p. 255.

157. WOMAN AND FURROW

The identification of woman with the ploughed earth can be found in a great many civilizations and was preserved in European folklore. "I am the earth," declares the beloved in an Egyptian love song. The *Videvdat* compares fallow land to a woman with no children, and in fairy tales, the barren queen bewails herself: "I am like a field on which nothing grows."[1] On the other hand, a twelfth-century hymn glorifies the Virgin Mary as *terra non arabilis quae fructum parturiit*. Ba'al was called "the spouse of the fields."[2] And it was a common thing among all Semitic peoples to identify woman with the soil.[3] In Islamic writings, woman is called "field," "vine with grapes," etc. Thus the Koran:[4] "Your wives are to you as fields." The Hindus identified the furrow with the vulva (*yoni*), seeds with *semen virile*.[5] "This woman is come as a living soil: sow seed in her, ye men!"[6] The Laws of Manu also teach that "woman may be looked upon as a field, and the male as the seed."[7] Narada makes this comment: "Woman is the field, and man the dispenser of the seed."[8] A Finnish proverb says that "maidens have their field in their own body."[9]

Obviously, to identify woman with a furrow implies an identification of phallus with spade, of tilling with the act of generation. Such anthropotelluric comparisons could only come in civilizations which understood both agriculture and the true causes of conception. In certain Australasian languages, the word *lak* means both phallus and spade. Przyluski has suggested that a similar Australasian term is at the root of the Sanskrit words *langula* (tail, spade) and *lingam* (male generative organ). The phallus-plough identification has even been represented pictorially. The origins of this representa-

SOURCE: *PCR*/259–60.

1. W. Van der Leeuw, *Religion in Essence and Manifestation* (London, 1938), p. 96.
2. Robertson Smith, *Religion of the Semites* (London, 1923 ed.), pp. 108, 536 ff.
3. *Ibid.*, p. 537.
4. II, 223.
5. *Shatapatha-Brahmana*, VII, 2, 2, 5.
6. *AV*, XIV, 2, 14.
7. ix, 33.
8. Cf. Pisani, "La Donna et la terra," *Anthropos* (1942–45): 37–40 *passim*.
9. B. Nyberg, *Kind und Erde* (Helsinki, 1931), p. 232, n. 83.

tion are much older: a drawing of a plough of the Kassite period shows joined to it symbols of the generative act. Primitive intuitions of this sort take a long time to disappear not only from the spoken tongue, but even from the vocabulary of serious writers. Rabelais used the expression "the member we call the husbandman of nature."[10]

And finally, for examples of the identification of agricultural labour with the act of generation, consider the myth of the birth of Sita, the heroine of *Ramayana*. Her father Janaka (the name means "progenitor") found her in his field while he was ploughing, and called her Sita, "furrow."[11] An Assyrian text brings to us the prayer addressed to a god whose plough has fertilized the earth."[12]

Even today, a lot of primitive peoples still use magic amulets representing the generative organs to make the earth fruitful. The Australian aboriginals practise a most curious fecundation ritual: armed with arrows which they carry in phallic fashion, they dance round a ditch shaped like the female generative organ; and conclude by planting sticks in the ground. It must be remembered what a close connection there is between woman and sexuality on one hand and tilling and the fertility of the soil on the other. Thus, there is one custom whereby naked maidens must mark out the first furrows with the plough, a custom which calls to mind the archetypal union of the goddess Demeter with Jason at the beginning of spring, in a freshly sown furrow.[13] All these ceremonies and legends will yield up their meaning when we come to study the structure of agricultural cults.

158. THE STRUCTURE OF CHTHONIAN HIEROPHANIES[1]

. . . Before there were myths to tell any stories about the earth, the mere *existence* of the soil was seen as significant in the religious sphere. The earth, to the primitive religious consciousness, was

Source: *PCR*/242–45.
10. *Gargantua*, II, 1.
11. *Ramayana*, 66.
12. Quoted by S. Langdon, *Semitic Mythology* (Boston, 1931), p. 99.
13. *Odyssey*, V, 125.
1. Chthonian: of the earth; hierophany: a manifestation of the sacred. Eds.

something immediately experienced and accepted; its size, its so-
lidity, its variety of landscape and of vegetation, formed a live and
active cosmic unity. The first realization of the religious significance of the earth was "indistinct"; in other words, it did not lo-
calize sacredness in the earth as such, but jumbled together as a
whole all the hierophanies in nature as it lay around—earth, stones,
trees, water, shadows, everything. The primary intuition of the
earth as a religious "form" might be formularized thus: "The cosmos—repository of a wealth of sacred forces." We saw the notion
of seeds, latencies and rebirth in the various meanings—religious,
magical or mythological—given to water, but the primal intuition
of the Earth shows it as the *foundation* of every expression of existence. All that *is* on earth, is united with everything else, and all
make up one great whole.

The cosmic structure of these elemental intuitions makes it almost impossible for us to discern the element of earth as such. Men
lived in their surroundings as a whole, and it is very hard to distinguish, in such intuitions, what belongs properly to the earth
from what is merely *manifested* through the earth: mountains, for-
ests, water, vegetation. Only one thing can be said with certainty
of these primary institutions: . . . that is, that they appear as *forms*,
that they reveal realities, that they must, of necessity, obtrude themselves, that they strike the mind. The earth, with all that it supports
and contains, has been seen from the first as an inexhaustible fount
of existences, and of existences that reveal themselves directly to
man.

What makes it quite certain that the hierophany of the earth was
cosmic in form before being truly chthonian (which it became only
with the appearance of agriculture), is the history of the beliefs as
to the origin of children. Before the physiological causes of conception were known, men thought that maternity resulted from
the direct insertion of the child into a woman's womb. We are in
no way concerned here with the question of whether what entered
the woman's womb was thought to be already a foetus—which
up till then had lived its life in caves, crevices, wells, trees and such
—or whether they thought it merely a seed, or even the "soul of
an ancestor," or what they thought it was. What we are concerned
with is the idea that children were not conceived by their father,

but at some more or less advanced stage of development, they were placed in their mother's womb as a result of a contact between her and some object or animal in the country round about.

Although this problem belongs more to ethnology than to the history of religion properly so called, it may here help us to clarify the matter in hand. Man has no part in creation. The father was father to his children only in the legal sense, not the biological. Men were related to each other through their mothers only, and that relationship was precarious enough. But they were related to their natural surroundings far more closely than any modern, profane mind can conceive. They were literally, and in no mere allegorical sense, "the people of the land." Either they were brought by water animals (fish, frogs, crocodiles, swans or some such), or they grew among rocks, in chasms or in caves, before being thrust by magic into their mother's womb; or before birth, they began life in water, in crystals, in stones, in trees; or they live—in an obscure, prehuman form as "souls" of "child-ancestors"—in one of the nearby cosmic zones. Thus, to mention only a few examples, the Armenians thought the earth was the "maternal womb, whence men came forth."[2] The Peruvians believed that they were descended from mountains and stones.[3] Other peoples placed the origins of children in caves, crevices, springs and so on. Even today there are people in Europe who believe children "come" from pools, springs, rivers, trees and so on. What is significant about these superstitions is the cosmic form the "earth" takes; it can be identified with the whole surrounding area, with the microcosm, not merely with the earth as such. "The earth" here, means all that surrounds man, the whole "place"—with its mountains, its waters and its vegetation.

The human father merely *legitimizes* such children by a ritual which has all the marks of adoption. They belong, first of all, to the "place," to the surrounding microcosm. The mother has only received them; she has "welcomed" them, and at the most, perfected their human form. It is easy to understand, from this, that the feeling of solidarity with the surrounding microcosm, with the

2. A. Dieterich, *Mutter Erde* (Berlin, 1925), p. 14.
3. B. Nyberg, *Kind und Erde* (Helsinki, 1931), p. 62.

"place," was a prevailing one with man at this stage of his mental development—or, rather, for man where he envisaged human life in this fashion. We might say in a sense that *man was not yet born*, that he did not yet realize that he belonged wholly to the biological species he represented. It might be better to consider that at this stage his life was in a prenatal phase: man still continued to share, directly, in a life that was not his own, in a "cosmicomaternal" life. He had, we might say, a "phylogenetic" experience of being, which he only partly understood; he felt himself to have emerged from two or three "wombs" at the same time.

It is not hard to realize that a background of this sort involved man in a certain number of specific attitudes regarding both the cosmos and his fellow-men. The precariousness of human paternity was balanced by the solidarity existing between man and various protective forces or substances in nature. But, on the other hand, this solidarity with "place" could hardly inspire man to feel himself a creator in the biological order. The father, legitimizing his children, who had either come to him from some source in nature or were "the souls of ancestors," did not really have any children at all, but simply new members for his family, fresh tools for his work or his protection. The bond between him and his offspring was not really procreative. His biological life ended with himself and could never be passed on through other beings—though the Indo-Europeans came later to offer an interpretation of the feeling men have of family continuity, which was basically that the body is passed on directly (the parents creating the body, or "substance" of the child) while the soul descends indirectly from ancestors (the souls of ancestors were incarnate in the new-born).

The earth, then, was, in the earliest of religious experiences or mythical intuitions, "the whole place" in which man found himself. A large number of the words for earth have etymologies which manifest impressions of space—"place," "wide," "province" (cf. *prithivi*, "the wide"), or primary impressions of sense, "firm," "what stays," "black," and so on. Any religious evaluation of the earth simply as such can only have occurred later on—in the pastoral cycle and, above all, in the agricultural cycle, to talk in terms of ethnology. Up till then, what one would call the "divinities of the earth" were really "divinities of the place"—in the sense of the cosmic surroundings.

159. CHTHONIAN MATERNITY

One of the first theophanies of the earth as such, and particularly of the earth as soil, was its "motherhood," its inexhaustible power of fruitfulness. Before becoming a mother goddess, or divinity of fertility, the earth presented itself to men as a Mother, *Tellus Mater*. The later growth of agricultural cults, forming a gradually clearer and clearer notion of a Great Goddess of vegetation and harvesting, finally destroyed all trace of the Earth-Mother. In Greece, the place of Gaia was taken by Demeter. However, certain ancient ethnological documents reveal relics of the old worship of the Earth-Mother. Smohalla, an Indian prophet of the Umatilla tribe, forbade his followers to dig the earth, for, he said, it is a sin to wound or cut, tear or scratch our common mother by the labours of farming. And he defended his anti-agricultural attitude by saying: "You ask me to plough the ground? Shall I take a knife and tear my mother's bosom? Then when I die she will not take me to her bosom to rest. You ask me to dig for stone? Shall I dig under her skin for her bones? Then when I die I cannot enter her body to be born again. You ask me to cut grass and make hay and sell it, and be rich like white men! But how dare I cut off my mother's hair?"[1]

Such a mystical devotion to the Earth-Mother is not an isolated instance. The members of a primitive Dravidian tribe of central India, the Baiga, carried on a nomadic agriculture, sowing only in the ashes left when part of the jungle had burnt away. And they went to such trouble because they thought it a sin to tear their mother's bosom with a plough.[2] In the same way some Altaic and Finno-Ugrian peoples thought it a terrible sin to pluck the grass, because it hurt the earth as much as it would hurt a man to pluck out his hair or his beard. The Votyaks, whose custom was to place their offerings in a ditch, were careful never to do it in the autumn, as that was the time when the Earth was asleep. The Cheremisses often thought the earth was ill, and at such times would avoid sitting on it. And there are many other indications that beliefs about

Source: *PCR*/245–46.

1. James Mooney, "The Ghost-Dance Religion and the Sioux Outbreak of 1890," *Annual Report of the Bureau of American Ethnology* (Washington, 1896), 14: 721.

2. Sir James G. Frazer, *Adonis, Attis, Osiris* 1 (London, 1936): 89.

Mother Earth persisted, even though sporadically, among both agricultural and nonagricultural peoples. Earth religion, even if it is not, as some scholars believe, the oldest of man's religions, is one that dies hard. Once established in an agricultural framework, thousands of years may go by without its altering. In some cases there is no break in the continuity from prehistoric times to the present. The "dead man's cake," for instance (*coliva* in Rumanian), was known by the same name in ancient Greece, which had it as a heritage from prehistoric, pre-Hellenic times. . . .

160. MAN'S DESCENT FROM THE EARTH

Saint Augustine,[1] following Varro, mentions the name of a Latin goddess, Levana, who raised children from out of the earth: *levat de terra*. Dieterich notes, in connection with this fact, the customs, still current in the Abbruzzi, of placing babies upon the earth as soon as they are washed and swaddled.[2] The same ritual took place among the Scandinavians, the Germans, the Parsees, the Japanese, and other races. The child was picked up by its father (*de terra tollere*), who thus expressed his recognition of it.[3] Dieterich interprets this rite as a way of dedicating the child to the earth, *Tellus Mater*, which is its true mother. Goldmann objects that the placing of a baby (or an ill or dying person) on the ground does not necessarily imply any descent from the earth, nor even any consecration to the Earth-Mother, but is simply intended to make a contact with the magic powers in the soil.[4] Others are of the opinion that this rite is meant to procure the child a soul, which comes to it from *Tellus Mater*.

We are obviously faced with two different interpretations, but they contradict each other only on the surface; both follow from the same primordial conception: that of the earth as the source at once of force, of "souls," of fecundity—the fecundity of the Earth-

Source: *PCR*/247–48.
1. *De civ. dei*, iv, 11.
2. Dieterich, *Mutter Erde* (Berlin, 1925), p. 7.
3. B. Nyberg, *Kind und Erde* (Helsinki, 1931), p. 31.
4. E. Goldmann, "Cartam levare," *Mitteilungen des Instituts f. oester. Geschichtsforschungen* 35 (1914): 1 ff.

Mother. Lying on the ground (*humi positio*) is a custom found frequently and among a great many peoples; among the Gurions of the Caucasus, and in some parts of China, women lie on the ground as soon as the pains of childbirth begin, so that they will be on the ground when their child is born;[5] the Maori women in New Zealand have their children beside a stream, in the bushes; in a lot of African tribes, it is usual for women to give birth in forest, sitting on the ground; we find the same ritual in Australia, in Northern India, among the Indians of North America, Paraguay and Brazil. Samter notes (p. 6) that this custom had been abandoned by the Greeks and Romans by historical times, but it certainly existed at one time; some statues of the goddesses of birth (Eilithyia, Damia, Auxeia) represent them kneeling in the exact position of a woman having a child straight on the ground. In the Middle Ages in Germany, among the Japanese, in certain Jewish communities, in the Caucasus, in Hungary, Rumania, Scandinavia, Iceland, and elsewhere, the same ritual can be found. The expression "to sit on the ground" in Egyptian, was used in demotic writings to mean "giving birth."

The basic meaning of this extremely widespread ritual was undoubtedly the maternity of the earth. . . .

161. THE MARRIAGE OF EARTH AND SKY

Let me say at once that the Earth-Mother and her human representative, woman, though they play a dominant part in this ritual pattern, do not play it alone. There is room not only for the earth or woman, but also for the man and the god. Fertility is preceded by a hierogamy. An old Anglo-Saxon charm used when the land was barren gives a perfect picture of the trust farming societies placed in that hierogamy: "Hail, Earth, Mother of men, be fertile in the god's embrace, be filled with fruit for man's use."[1] At Eleusis, the priest pronounced the ancient agricultural formula "Make it to rain!—Mayest thou bear fruit!," looking first to the sky,

Source: *PCR*/257.

5. E. Samter, *Geburt, Hochzeit und Tot* (Berlin, 1911), pp. 5 ff.

1. Quoted in Krappe, *Études de mythologie et de folklore germaniques* (Paris, 1928), p. 62.

then to the earth. It is probable that this sacred marriage between heaven and earth was the primeval model both of the fertility of the land and of human marriage. A text from the *Atharva Veda*,[2] for instance, compares the bride and bridegroom to earth and heaven.

162. "KING" AND "QUEEN"

. . . In some places the coming of the May is an occasion for all sorts of competitions, choosing the sturdiest pair (to be "king" and "queen"), ritual wrestling, etc. All such tests, whatever their original meaning, came to be aimed at stimulating the energies of nature. The day usually starts with a race to the Maypole, or a competition among the young men and boys to see who can climb it the quickest. I will give a few examples only: in Saxony the ceremony took place on May 1, or Whitsunday, and consisted first in bringing young trees from the forest (*majum quaerere*) to decorate the houses, then in setting up one tree, the May, solemnly in the center of the village. Its branches were cut off, except perhaps a few of the topmost ones which were laden with gifts (sausages, eggs, cakes). Then young men competed, in some regions, to see who could most quickly climb to the top, in others, who could run quickest to where the Maypole stood. Sometimes there was a race on horseback. The winner was borne shoulder-high and given honours. At one time he was presented with a red cloth by the prettiest girls.

163. SEXUALITY AND VEGETATION

In some places (in France, England, and Bohemia, for instance), it was the custom to choose a May Queen. But most of the folk traditions of Europe retain the primeval pair under one name or another: king and queen, master and mistress, betrothed couple, lovers (as in Sicily and Sardinia). It is unquestionably a watered-down version of the old image of a young couple spurring on the

Source: *PCR*/313.
Source: *PCR*/314–16; cf. *PCR*/356–59.
2. XIV, 2, 71.

creative forces of nature by mating ritually on ploughed land to re-enact the cosmic hierogamy of Sky and Earth. This couple would always lead the procession carrying the Maypole from farm to farm collecting gifts. They were often looked upon thereafter as married. In other cultural patterns and frameworks the ceremonial pair lost their original meaning (of a sacred marriage), and became part of a whole ritual orgy. And in some cases it is hard to see exactly how far a given rite is expressing an erotic symbolism and how far simply a symbolism of earth and agriculture. Life is a single thing; the various levels of cosmic life fit together (moon-woman-earth; sky-rain-man; etc.) and even cut across each other at certain central points (all the cosmological attributes of the moon, night, water, earth, seeds, birth, regeneration, resurrection and so on are present, virtually at least, in woman, and can be actualized and increased by feminine rituals or hierogamies). We must therefore constantly direct our attention to this totality of units which in one sense gives rise to all the rituals and in another results from them. Vegetation cults, above all, must be interpreted in the light of the original bio-cosmological conception which gave rise to them. That they appear so various is often merely an illusion of modern vision; basically they flow from one primitive ontological intuition (that the *real* is not only what *is* indefinitely the same, but also what *becomes* in organic but cyclic forms), and converge towards one object—that of assuring the regeneration of the powers of nature by one means or another.

Thus, in certain islands of the Amboina group, for instance, when the clove plantations seem poor, the men go to them during the night with nothing on, and try to fertilize the trees, crying "Cloves!" Among the Bagandas of central Africa, any woman who gives birth to twins shows by that proof of her fertility that she is a center of life and can fertilize the banana trees; if a banana leaf is placed between her legs and pushed away by her husband during intercourse, it gains such extraordinary powers that the farmers from neighboring villages will try to get hold of it and are ready to pay a lot for it. In both cases, we have an application of human sexuality to vegetative life; an application that is grotesque, overconcrete, and limited to individual objects (certain trees, certain women)—not projected by magic over the whole pattern, over life as a whole.

These exceptional cases confirm the principle implied in the sacred marriage, in the springtime union of young couples on
ploughed land, in the races and competitions used to stimulate the
forces of plant life during certain festivals of spring and summer,
in the May King and Queen, and so on. In all of them we perceive
the desire to spur on the circuit of bio-cosmic energy, and particularly vegetative energy, on a vast scale. As we have seen, it is not
always a question of man's stimulating vegetation with ceremonial
and hierogamy; often it is human fertility which is stimulated by
plant life (as for instance with the marriage of trees in India; fertility coming through fruits and seeds, through the shadow of a tree
and so on). It is the same closed circuit of the substance of life
springing up from every cosmic level, but being concentrated and
thrust into certain centres (woman, vegetation, animals) according to man's needs. This circulation of the substance of life and
sacred powers among the various bio-cosmic levels, a circulation
directed by man for his own immediate gain, was later to be used
as the best way of attaining immortality or the "salvation" of the
soul (cf. the Greco-Oriental mysteries).

164. THE MOON AND FERTILITY

The fertility of animals, as well as that of plants, is subject to
the moon. The relationship between the moon and fecundity occasionally becomes somewhat complicated owing to the appearance
of new religious "forms"—like the Earth-Mother, and the various
agricultural divinities. However, there is one aspect of the moon
that remains permanently evident, however many religious syntheses
have gone towards making up these new "forms"; and that is the
prerogative of fertility, of recurring creation, of inexhaustible life.
The horns of oxen, for instance, which are used to characterize the
great divinities of fecundity, are an emblem of the divine *Magna
Mater*. Wherever they are to be found in Neolithic cultures, either
in iconography, or as part of idols in the form of oxen, they de-
note the presence of the Great Goddess of fertility. And a horn is
always the image of the new moon: "Clearly the ox's horn became

SOURCE: PCR/163–67; cf. PCR/159–61; SP/129–36.

a symbol of the moon because it brings to mind a crescent; therefore both horns together represent two crescents, or the complete career of the moon."[1] And also in the iconography of the prehistoric Chinese cultures of Kansu and Yang-kao you will often find symbols of the moon and symbols of fertility together—stylized horns are framed by a pattern of lightning-flashes (signifying the rain and the moon) and lozenges (which are a symbol of femininity).[2]

Certain animals become symbols or even "presences" of the moon because their shape or their behaviour is reminiscent of the moon's. So with the snail which goes in and out of its shell; the bear, which disappears in midwinter and reappears in the spring; the frog because it swells up, submerges itself, and later returns to the surface of the water; the dog, because it can be seen in the moon, or because it is supposed in some myths to be the ancestor of the race; the snake, because it appears and disappears, and because it has as many coils as the moon has days (this legend is also preserved in Greek tradition);[3] or because it is "the husband of all women," or because it sloughs its skin (that is to say, is periodically reborn, is "immortal"), and so on. The symbolism of the snake is somewhat confusing, but all the symbols are directed to the same central idea: it is immortal because it is continually reborn, and therefore it is a moon "force," and as such can bestow fecundity, knowledge (that is, prophecy) and even immortality. There are innumerable myths telling the disastrous story of how the serpent stole the immortality given to man by his god. But they are all later variants on a primitive myth in which the serpent (or a sea monster) guarded the sacred spring and the spring of immortality (the Tree of Life, the Fountain of Youth, the Golden Apples).

I can only mention here a few of the myths and symbols connected with the serpent, and only those which indicate its character of a lunar animal. In the first place, its connection with women and with fecundity: the moon is the source of all fertility, and also governs the menstrual cycle. It is personified as "the master of women." A great many peoples used to think—and some think it to this day

---

1. Hentze, *Mythes et symboles lunaires* (Antwerp, 1932), p. 96.
2. Cf. Hentze, *Mythes*, figs. 74–82.
3. Aristotle, *Hist. Animal.*, II, 12; Pliny, *Hist. Nat.*, XI, 82.

—that the moon, in the form of a man, or a serpent, copulates with their women. That is why, among the Eskimos for instance, unmarried girls will not look at the moon for fear of becoming pregnant. The Australians believe that the moon comes down to earth in the form of a sort of Don Juan, makes women pregnant and then deserts them. This myth is still current in India.

Since the serpent is an epiphany of the moon, it fulfills the same function. Even today it is said in the Abruzzi that the serpent copulates with all women. The Greeks and Romans also believed it. Alexander the Great's mother, Olympia, played with snakes.[4] The famous Aratus of Sicyon was said to be a son of Aesculapius because, according to Pausanias,[5] his mother had conceived him of a serpent. Suetonius[6] and Dio Cassius[7] tell how the mother of Augustus conceived from the embrace of a serpent in Apollo's temple. A similar legend was current about the elder Scipio. In Germany, France, Portugal and elsewhere, women used to be afraid that a snake would slip into their mouths when they were asleep, and they would become pregnant, particularly during menstruation. In India, when women wanted to have children, they adored a cobra. All over the East it was believed that woman's first sexual contact was with a snake, at puberty or during menstruation. The Komati tribe in the Mysore province of India use snakes made of stone in a rite to bring about the fertility of the women. Claudius Aelianus[8] declares that the Hebrews believed that snakes mated with unmarried girls; and we also find this belief in Japan. A Persian tradition says that after the first woman had been seduced by the serpent, she immediately began to menstruate. And it was said by the rabbis that menstruation was the result of Eve's relations with the serpent in the Garden of Eden. In Abyssinia it was thought that girls were in danger of being raped by snakes until they were married. One Algerian story tells how a snake escaped when no one was looking and raped all the unmarried girls in a house. Similar traditions are to be found among the Mandi Hottentots of East Africa, in Sierra Leone and elsewhere.

4. Plutarch, *Vita. Alex.*, II.
5. II, 10, 3.
6. *Divus Augustus*, 94.
7. 55, 1.
8. *Nat. Animal.*, VI, 17.

Certainly the menstrual cycle helps to explain the spread of the belief that the moon is the first mate of all women. The Papoos thought menstruation was a proof that women and girls were connected with the moon, but in their iconography (sculptures on wood) they pictured reptiles emerging from their genital organs, which confirms that snakes and the moon are identified. Among the Chiriguanoes, various fumigations and purifications are performed after a woman's first menstrual period, and after that the women of the house drive away every snake they come upon, as responsible for this evil. A great many tribes look upon the snake as the cause of the menstrual cycle. Its phallic character, which Crawley was one of the first ethnologists to demonstrate,[9] far from excluding its connection with the moon, only confirms it. A great deal of the iconographical documentation which remains—both of the Neolithic civilizations of Asia (such as the idol of the Panchan culture, at Kansu, and the sculptured gold of Ngan-Yang) and of the Amerindian civilizations (such as the bronze discs of Calchaqui)—show the double imagery of the snake decorated with lozenges (symbolizing the vulva). The two together undoubtedly have an erotic meaning, but the coexistence of the snake (phallus) and lozenges also expresses an idea of dualism and reintegration which is a supremely lunar notion, for we find that same motif in the lunar imagery of "rain," of "light and darkness," and the rest.

165. THE MOON, WOMAN, AND SNAKES

The moon then can also be personified as reptile and masculine, but such personifications (which often break away from the original pattern and follow a path of their own in myth and legend), are still fundamentally based on the notion of the moon as source of living reality, and basis of all fertility and periodic regeneration. Snakes are thought of as producing children; in Guatemala, for instance, in the Urabunna tribe of central Australia (who believe themselves to be descended from two snakes which traveled about the world and left *maiaurli*, or "the souls of children" wher-

Source: PCR/167–69.
9. *The Mystic Rose*, ed. Besterman (London, 1927), 7: 23 ff.; 2: 17, 133.

ever they stopped), among the Togos in Africa (a giant snake dwells in a pool near the town of Klewe, and receiving children from the hands of the supreme god Namu, brings them into the town before their birth). In India, from Buddhist times (cf. the Jatakas), snakes were held to be the givers of all fertility (water, treasures). . . . Some of the Nagpur paintings[1] depict the mating of women with cobras. A mass of beliefs in present day India evince the beneficent and fertilizing power of snakes: they prevent women from being sterile and ensure that they will have a large number of children.

There are a great many different woman-snake relationships, but none of them can be fully explained by any purely erotic symbolism. The snake has a variety of meanings, and I think we must hold its "regeneration" to be one of the most important. The snake is an animal that "changes." Gressman[2] tried to see in Eve a primitive Phoenician goddess of the underworld, personified by a snake.[3] The Mediterranean deities are represented with snakes in their hands (the Arcadian Artemis, Hecate, Persephone and so on), or with snakes for hair (the Gorgon, Erinyes and others). And there are some central European superstitions to the effect that if, when a woman is under the moon's influence (that is, when she is menstruating), you pull out some of her hair and bury it, the hairs will turn into snakes.

One Breton legend says that the hair of a witch turns into snakes. This cannot therefore happen to ordinary women, except when under the influence of the moon, when sharing in the magic power of "change." There is a great deal of ethnological evidence to show that witchcraft is a thing bestowed by the moon (either directly, or through the intermediary of snakes). To the Chinese, for instance, snakes are at the bottom of all magic power, while the Hebrew and Arabic words for magic come from words that mean "snakes." Because snakes are "lunar"—that is, eternal—and live underground, embodying (among many other things) the souls of the dead, they know all secrets, are the source of all wisdom, and can foresee the

---

1. J. H. Rivett-Carnac, *Rough Notes on the Snake-symbol in India* (Calcutta, 1879).
2. "Mythische Reste in der Paradieserzählung," *Archiv für Religionswissenschaft*, x, 345–67.
3. Particularly pp. 359 ff.

future. Anyone, therefore, who eats a snake becomes conversant with the language of animals, and particularly of birds (a symbol which can also have a metaphysical meaning: access to the transcendent reality); this is a belief held by a tremendous number of races, and it was accepted even by the learned of antiquity.

The same central symbolism of fertility and regeneration governed by the moon, and bestowed by the moon itself or by forms the same in substance (*magna mater, terra mater*) explains the presence of snakes in the imagery and rites of the Great Goddesses of universal fertility. As an attribute of the Great Goddess, the snake keeps its lunar character (of periodic regeneration) in addition to a telluric one. At one stage the moon was identified with the earth and itself considered the origin of all living forms. Some races even believe that the earth and the moon are formed of the same substance. The Great Goddesses share as much in the sacred nature of the moon as in that of the earth. And because these goddesses are also funeral goddesses (the dead disappear into the ground or into the moon to be reborn and reappear under new forms), the snake becomes very specially the animal of death and burial, embodying the souls of the dead, the ancestor of the tribe, etc. And this symbolism of regeneration also explains the presence of snakes in initiation ceremonies.

166. COSMO-BIOLOGY AND MYSTICAL PHYSIOLOGY

These assimilations do not simply serve a function of classification. They are obtained by an attempt to integrate man and the universe fully into the same divine rhythm. Their meaning is primarily magic and redemptive; by taking to himself the powers that lie hidden in "letters" and "sounds," man places himself in various central points of cosmic energy and thus effects complete harmony between himself and all that is. "Letters" and "sounds" do the work of images, making it possible, by contemplation or by magic, to pass from one cosmic level to another. To give only one example: in India, when a man is going to make a divine image, he must first meditate, and his meditation will include, among others, the follow-

SOURCE: *PCR*/178–81.

ing exercise (in which the moon, mystical physiology, the written symbol and the sound value together form a pattern of consummate subtlety): "Conceiving in his own heart the moon's orb as developed from the primal sound [*prathamasvara-parinatam*, i.e., evolved from the letter 'A'], let him visualize therein a beautiful blue lotus, within its filaments the moon's unspotted orb, and thereon the yellow seed-syllable *Tam*. . . ."[1]

Clearly, man's integration into the cosmos can only take place if he can bring himself into harmony with the two astral rhythms, "unifying" the sun and moon in his living body. The "unification" of the two centers of sacred and natural energy aims—in this technique of mystical physiology—at reintegrating them in the primal undifferentiated unity, as it was when not yet broken up by the act that created the universe; and this "unification" realizes a transcendence of the cosmos. In one Tantric text,[2] an exercise in mystical physiology seeks to change "vowels and consonants into bracelets, the sun and moon into rings." The Tantric and Hathayoga schools developed to a very high degree these complex analogies between the sun, the moon and various "mystical" centers or arteries, divinities, blood and *semen virile*, etc. The point of these analogies is first of all to unite man with the rhythms and energies of the cosmos, and then to unify the rhythms, fuse the centers and finally effect that leap into the transcendent which is made possible when all "forms" disappear and the primal unity is re-established. A technique like this is of course the polished product of a long mystical tradition, but we find the rudimentary groundwork of it as often among primitive peoples as in the syncretist periods of the Mediterranean religions (the moon influences the left eye and the sun the right: the moon and the sun in funeral monuments as a symbol of eternity; and so on).

By its mode of being, the moon "binds" together a whole mass of realities and destinies. The rhythms of the moon weave together harmonies, symmetries, analogies and participations which make up an endless "fabric," a "net" of invisible threads, which "binds" together at once mankind, rain, vegetation, fertility, health, animals, death, regeneration, after-life, and more. That is why the

---

1. *Kimcit-Vistara-Tara-Sadhana*, no. 98 of *Sadhanamala*.
2. Carya 11, *Krishnapada*.

moon is seen in so many traditions personified by a divinity, or acting through a lunar animal, "weaving" the cosmic veil, or the destinies of men. It was lunar goddesses who either invented the profession of weaving (like the Egyptian divinity Neith), or were famous for their ability to weave (Athene punished Arachne, for daring to rival her, by turning her into a spider),[3] or wove a garment of cosmic proportions (like Proserpine and Harmonia), and so on. It was believed in medieval Europe that Holda was patroness of weavers, and we see beyond this figure to the chthonian and lunar nature of the divinities of fertility and death.

We are obviously dealing here with extremely complex forms in which myths, ceremonials and symbols from different religious structures are crystallized, and they have not always come directly from the intuition of the moon as the measure of cosmic rhythms and the support of life and death. On the other hand, we find in them the syntheses of the moon and Mother Earth with all that they imply (the ambivalence of good and evil, death, fertility, destiny). Similarly, you cannot always limit every mythological intuition of a cosmic "net" to the moon. In Indian thought, for instance, the universe was "woven" by the air[4] just as breath (*prana*) "wove" human life. Corresponding to the five winds that divide the Cosmos and yet preserve its unity, there are five breaths (*pranas*) "weaving" human life into a whole (the identity of breath and wind can be found as early as in Vedic writings). What we have got in these traditions is the primitive conception of the living whole—whether cosmic or microcosmic—in which the different parts are held together by a breathing force (wind or breath) that "weaves" them together.

167. LUNAR METAPHYSICS

We must try to get a general picture of all these lunar hierophanies. What do they reveal? How far do they fit together and complement each other, how far do they make up a "theory"— that is, express a succession of "truths" which, taken together,

Source: PCR/182–85.
3. Ovid, *Metamorphoses*, VI, 1 ff.
4. *Brihadaranyaka Upanishad*, III, 7, 2.

could constitute a system? The hierophanies of the moon that we have noted may be grouped round the following themes: (*a*) fertility (waters, vegetation, women; mythological "ancestor"); (*b*) periodic regeneration (the symbolism of the serpent and all the lunar animals; "the new man" who has survived a watery catastrophe caused by the moon; the death and resurrection of initiations; etc.); (*c*) time and destiny (the moon "measures," or "weaves" destinies, "binds" together diverse cosmic levels and heterogeneous realities); (*d*) change, marked by the opposition of light and darkness (full moon—new moon; the "world above" and the "underworld"; brothers who are enemies, good and evil), or by the balance between being and nonbeing, the virtual and the actual (the symbolism of hidden things: dusky night, darkness, death, seeds and larvae). In all these themes the dominant idea is one of *rhythm* carried out by a succession of contraries, of "becoming" through the succession of opposing modalities (being and nonbeing; forms and hidden essences; life and death; etc.). It is a becoming, I need hardly add, that cannot take place without drama or *pathos*; the sublunar world is not only the world of change but also the world of suffering and of "history." Nothing that happens in this world under the moon can be "eternal," for its law is the law of becoming, and no change is final; every change is merely part of a cyclic pattern.

The phases of the moon give us, if not the historical origin, at least the mythological and symbolic illustration of all dualisms. "The underworld, the world of darkness, is typified by the waning moon (horns = crescents, the sign of the double volute = two crescents facing the opposite way, placed one on top of the other and fastened together = lunar change, a decrepit and bony old man). The higher world, the world of life and of growing light, is typified by a tiger (the monster of darkness and of the new moon) letting humanity, represented by a child, escape its jaws (the child being the ancestor of the tribe, likened to the new moon, the 'Light that returns')."[1] These images come from the cultural area of primitive China, but light and darkness symbols were complementary there; the owl, a symbol of darkness, is to be found beside the pheasant, symbol of light. The cicada, too, is at once related to the

1. C. Hentze, *Objets rituels* (Antwerp, 1938), p. 55.

demon of darkness and to the demon of light. At every cosmic level a "dark" period is followed by a "light," pure, regenerate period. The symbolism of emerging from the "darkness" can be found in initiation rituals as well as in the mythology of death, and the life of plants (buried seed, the "darkness" from which the "new plant" [*neophyte*] arises), and in the whole conception of "historical" cycles. The "dark ages," *kali yuga*, is to be followed, after a complete break-up of the cosmos (*mahapralaya*), by a new, regenerate era. The same idea is to be found in all the traditions that tell of cosmic historic cycles, and though it does not seem to have first entered the human mind with the discovery of the moon's phases, it is undoubtedly illustrated perfectly by their rhythm.

It is in this sense that we can talk of the positive value of periods of shadow, times of large-scale decadence and disintegration; they gain a suprahistorical significance, though in fact it is just at such times that "history" is most fully accomplished, for then the balance of things is precarious, human conditions infinitely varied, new developments are encouraged by the disintegration of the laws and of all the old framework. Such dark periods are a sort of darkness, of universal night. And as such, just as death represents a positive value in itself, so do they; it is the same symbolism as that of larvae in the dark, of hibernation, of seeds bursting apart in the earth so that a new form can appear.

It might be said that the moon shows man his true human condition; that in a sense man looks at himself, and finds himself anew in the life of the moon. That is why the symbolism and mythology of the moon have an element of *pathos* and at the same time of consolation, for the moon governs both death and fertility, both drama and initiation. Though the modality of the moon is supremely one of change, of rhythm, it is equally one of periodic returning; and this pattern of existence is disturbing and consoling at the same time—for though the manifestations of life are so frail that they can suddenly disappear altogether, they are restored in the "eternal returning" regulated by the moon. Such is the law of the whole sublunary universe. But that law, which is at once harsh and merciful, can be abolished, and in some cases one may "transcend" this periodic becoming and achieve a mode of existence that is absolute. . . . In certain Tantric techniques, an attempt is made to "unify" the moon and the sun, to get beyond the opposition between things, to be reintegrated in the primeval unity. This myth of reintegration is to be found almost everywhere in the history of religion in an infinity of variations—and fundamentally it is an expression of the thirst to abolish dualisms, endless returnings and fragmentary existences. It existed at the most primitive stages, which indicates that man, from the time when he first realized his position in the universe, desired passionately and tried to achieve concretely (i.e., by religion and by magic together) a passing beyond his human status ("reflected" so exactly by the moon's). . . . Myths of this nature mark man's first attempt to get beyond his "lunar mode of being."

168. COSMIC SYMBOLISM

We can pick out one characteristic that all these folk ceremonies have in common: they celebrate a cosmic event (spring or summer) by using some symbol of vegetation. A tree, flower or animal is displayed; a tree is ceremonially decorated and carried in procession, or if not a tree, then a piece of wood, a man dressed in leaves, or some effigy; there are sometimes contests, fights, or scenes acted out relating to a death or a resurrection. For a moment, the life of the whole human group is concentrated into a tree or some effigy of vegetation, some symbol intended to represent and consecrate the thing that is happening to the universe: spring. It is as if the human group were incapable of expressing its joy and assisting in the arrival of spring on a larger scale (objectively speaking), on any scale embracing all nature. Man's joy, and his cooperation in effecting the final victory of vegetal life, are restricted to a microcosm: a branch, a tree, an effigy, a person in fancy dress. The presence of nature is indicated by a single object (or symbol). It is no pantheist adoration of nature or sense of being at one with it, but a feeling induced by the presence of the symbol (branch, tree or whatever it may be), and stimulated by the performing of the rite (processions, contests, fights, and the rest). This ceremonial is based on a comprehensive notion of the sacredness of all living force as expressed at every level of life, growing, wearing itself out and being regularly regenerated. This "bio-cosmic sacredness" is personified

SOURCE: *PCR*/321–22.

in many different forms, changing, it would seem, to suit mood or circumstance. A spirit of vegetation appears from time to time in a mythical creation, lives, becomes widespread, and finally vanishes. What remains, what is basic and lasting, is the "power" of vegetation, which can be felt and manipulated equally well in a branch, an effigy or a mythological figure. But it would be wrong to see a more authentic religious significance in a ceremony built round a mythical person (such, for instance, as Kostrubonko) than in a ceremony in which there is only a *sign* (branch, or maypole, or some such). These are differences which, it must be realized, flow simply from differences in the mythological creativity of the various societies, or even from a chance of history. In neither case do they matter very much. In all of them we find the same basic idea and the same inclination to celebrate in a microcosm what is happening in the whole cosmos, to celebrate it symbolically.

◆

Symbols for Transitions in Life

Some symbols and symbolic themes reappear with remarkable frequency, and among these are the labyrinth, spinning, and various initiatory motifs. The symbols discussed in this section have to do with the transitions in life-situation and status: death, conflict, and reaction to duality and polarity.

The Earth Goddess appears again, now in her role as guardian of the passage into death or into heaven; other "bridge" symbols appear also, and we see that such images as spinning, ropes, and nets can have much greater symbolic depth than contemporary persons might suppose. The role of initiation is stressed again in the last of this section: death and its transcendence, and the polarities of Life:Death or Good:Evil are heightened for the initiate, who learns how to live with the tensions (the *unification* of opposites is discussed in selection 186).

169. LABYRINTHS

. . . Clearly, if the galleries of mines and the mouths of rivers were likened to the *vagina* of the Earth-Mother, the same symbolism applied *a fortiori* to grottoes and caverns. And we know that caverns had a religious significance in the paleolithic period. In prehistoric times the cavern, often resembling, or ritually transformed into, a labyrinth, was at once a theatre of initiation and a place where the dead were buried. The labyrinth, in its turn, was homologized with the body of the Earth-Mother. To penetrate into a labyrinth or a cavern was the equivalent of a mystical return to the Mother—an end pursued in the rites of initiation as well as in funeral obsequies. . . . Troy was felt to be like the Earth, that is, like a Goddess: the inviolability of the ancient cities was homologized with the virginity of the protective divinity. All these symbols, overlapping and complementing one another, attest the perennial sway of the primordial image of the Earth-Woman.

170. LABYRINTH AND TOOTHED VAGINA

. . . In the funerary mythology of Malekula, a terrifying female figure, named Temes or Le-hev-hev, awaits the dead man's soul at the mouth of a cave or beside a rock. Before her, drawn on the ground, is a labyrinthine design; and when the dead man comes near, the woman obliterates half of the design. If the dead man already knows the labyrinthine design—that is, if he has been initiated—he finds the road easily; if he does not, the woman devours him. As the work of Deacon and Layard has shown, the numerous labyrinthine designs drawn on the ground in Malekula are intended to teach the road to the abode of the dead.[1] In other words, the labyrinth plays the role of a post-mortem initiatory ordeal; it falls in the category of the obstacles that the dead person—or, in other contexts, the Hero—must confront in his journey through the beyond. What I should like to emphasize here is that the labyrinth is presented as a "dangerous passage" into the bowels of Mother

SOURCE: *RSI*/62–63, 66; cf. *RSI*/51–53.

1. A. B. Deacon, "Geometrical Drawings from Malekula and Other Islands of the New Hebrides," *Journal of the Royal Anthropological Institute* 66 (1934): 132 ff.; and *Malekula: A Vanishing People of the New Hebrides* (London, 1934), especially pp. 552 ff.; J. Layard, "Totenfahrt auf Malekula," *Eranos-Jahrbuch* 4 (1937): 242–91, and *Stone Men of Malekula* (London, 1942), pp. 340 ff., 649 ff.

Earth, a passage in which the soul runs the risk of being devoured by a female monster. Malekula gives us other mythical figures of the threatening and dangerous female principle; for example, the Crab Woman with two immense claws, or a giant clam (*Tridacna deresa*), which, when it is open, resembles the female sexual organ. These terrifying images of aggressive female sexuality and devouring motherhood bring out still more clearly the initiatory character of descent into the body of the chthonian Great Mother. For Hentze[2] was able to show that a number of South American iconographic motifs represent the mouth of Mother Earth as a *vagina dentata*. The theme of the *vagina dentata* is quite complex, and I do not intend to treat it here. But it is important to note that the ambivalence of the chthonian Great Mother is sometimes expressed, mythically and iconographically, by identifying her mouth with the *vagina dentata*. In initiatory myths and sagas, the Hero's passage through a giantess' belly and his emergence through her mouth are equivalent to a new birth. But the passage is infinitely dangerous.

. . . The *vagina dentata* can represent not only passage into Mother Earth, but also the door of Heaven. In a North American tale, this door is alternatively made of the "two halves of the eagle's beak" or of the *vagina dentata* of the Daughter of the King of Heaven. . . .

171. THE BRIDGE AND THE "DIFFICULT PASSAGE"

Shamans, like the dead, must cross a bridge in the course of their journey to the underworld. Like death, ecstasy implies a "mutation," to which myth gives plastic expression by a "perilous passage." We have seen a considerable number of examples. As we intend to return to this subject in a special work, we shall confine ourselves here to a few brief remarks. The symbolism of the funerary bridge is universally disseminated and extends far beyond the bounds of shamanic ideology and mythology. This symbolism is linked, on the one hand, with the myth of a bridge (or tree, vine, etc.) that once connected earth and heaven and by means of which

SOURCE: *S*/482–86.
2. C. Hentze, *Tod, Auferstehung, Weltordnung* (Zurich, 1955), pp. 79 ff., 90 ff.

human beings effortlessly communicated with the gods; on the other hand, it is related to the initiatory symbolism of the "strait gate" or of a "paradoxical passage," which we shall illustrate by a few examples. We here have a mythological complex whose principal constituents would appear to be the following: (a) *in illo tempore*, in the paradisal time of humanity, a bridge connected earth with heaven and people passed from one to the other without encountering any obstacles, because there was not yet *death*; (b) once the *easy* communications between earth and heaven were broken off, people could not cross the bridge except "in spirit," that is, either as dead or in ecstasy; (c) this crossing is difficult; in other words, it is sown with obstacles and not all souls succeed in traversing it; demons and monsters seeking to devour the soul must be faced, or the bridge becomes as narrow as a razoredge when the wicked try to cross it, and so on; only the "good," and especially the *initiates*, cross the bridge easily (these latter in some measure know the road, for they have undergone ritual death and resurrection); (d) certain privileged persons nevertheless succeed in passing over it during their lifetime, be it in ecstasy, like the shamans, or "by force," like certain heroes, or, finally, "paradoxically," through "wisdom" or initiation (we shall return to the "paradox" in a moment).

The important point here is that numerous rites are conceived of as symbolically "building" a "bridge" or a "ladder," and as accomplishing this by the sheer power of the rite itself. This idea is documented, for example, in the symbolism of the Brahmanic sacrifice.[1] We saw that the cord connecting the ceremonial birches set up for the shamanic séance is called the "bridge" and symbolizes the shaman's ascent to the heavens. In some Japanese initiations the candidates are made to construct a "bridge" upon seven arrows and with seven boards. This rite is comparable to the ladders of knives climbed by candidates during their initiation as shamans and, in general, to initiatory ascension rites. The meaning of all these "dangerous passage" rites is this: communication between earth and heaven is established, in an effort to restore the "communicability" that was the law *in illo tempore*. From one point

1. Cf. *Taittiriya Samhita*, VI, 5, 3, 3; VI, 5, 4, 2; VII, 5, 8, 5; etc.

of view, all these initiation rites pursue the reconstruction of a "passage" to the beyond and hence abolition of the break between planes that is typical of the human condition after the "fall."

The vitality of this bridge symbolism is further demonstrated by the part that it plays in Christian and Islamic apocalypses as well as in the initiatory traditions of the western Middle Ages. The Vision of St. Paul describes a bridge "narrow as a hair" connecting our world with paradise. The same image is found in the Arabic writers and mystics: the bridge is "narrower than a hair," and connects earth with the astral spheres and paradise; just as in Christian tradition, sinners cannot cross it and are cast into hell. Arabic terminology clearly brings out the nature of the bridge or the "path" as "difficult of access." Medieval legends tell of a "bridge under water" and of a "sword-bridge," which the hero (Lancelot) must cross barefoot and bare-handed; it is "sharper than a scythe" and it is crossed "with great pain and agony." The initiatory character of crossing the sword-bridge is also confirmed by another fact: before he starts over it, Lancelot sees two lions on the further bank, but when he is there he sees only a lizard; successfully undergoing the initiatory ordeal in itself makes the "danger" disappear. In Finnish tradition, Väinämöinen and the shamans who journey to the other world (Tuonela) in trance must cross a bridge made of swords and knives.

The "narrow passage" or "dangerous passage" is a common motif in both funerary and initiatory mythologies (we have seen how closely they may be connected, sometimes to the point of coalescence). In New Zealand the deceased must pass through a very narrow space between two demons that try to capture him; if he is "light" he gets through, but if he is "heavy" he falls and becomes the demons' prey. "Lightness" or "swiftness"—as in the myth of passing very quickly through the jaws of a monster—is always a symbolic formula for "intelligence," "wisdom," "transcendence," and, in the last analysis, for initiation. "A sharpened edge of a razor, hard to traverse, / A difficult path is this—poets declare!" says the *Katha Upanishad*.[2] This formula illuminates the initiatory nature of metaphysical knowledge. "Strait is the gate and

2. III, 14 (trans. R. E. Hume, p. 353).

narrow is the way which leadeth unto life, and few there be that find it."[3]

And indeed the symbolism of the "strait gate" and the "dangerous bridge" is bound up with the symbolism of what we have called the "paradoxical passage" because it sometimes proves to be an impossibility or a situation from which there is no escape. It will be remembered that candidate shamans or the heroes of certain myths sometimes find themselves in apparently desperate situations. They must go "where night and day meet," or find a gate in a wall, or go up to the sky through a passage that opens but for an instant, pass between two constantly moving millstones, two rocks that clash together, through the jaws of a monster, and the like. As Coomaraswamy rightly saw, all these mythical images express the need to transcend opposites, to abolish the polarity typical of the human condition, in order to attain to ultimate reality.[4] . . . In the myths the "paradoxical" passage emphatically testifies that he who succeeds in accomplishing it has transcended the human condition; he is a shaman, a hero, or a "spirit," and indeed this "paradoxical" passage can be accomplished only by one who is "spirit."

These few examples throw light on the function of the myths, rites, and symbols of "passage" in shamanic techniques and ideologies. By crossing, in ecstasy, the "dangerous" bridge that connects the two worlds and that only the dead can attempt, the shaman proves that he is spirit, is no longer a human being, and at the same time attempts to restore the "communicability" that existed *in illo tempore* between this world and heaven. For what the shaman can do today *in ecstasy* could, at the dawn of time, be done by all human beings *in concreto*; they went up to heaven and came down again without recourse to trance. Temporarily and for a limited number of persons—the shamans—ecstasy re-establishes the primordial condition of all mankind. In this respect, the mystical experience of the "primitives" is a return to origins, a reversion to the mystical age of the lost paradise. For the shaman in ecstasy, the bridge or the tree, the vine, the cord, and so on—which, *in illo tempore*, connected earth with heaven—once again, for the space of an instant, becomes a present reality.

3. Matt. 7: 14.
4. A. K. Coomaraswamy, "Symplegades," in *Studies and Essays . . . George Sarton . . . 1914*, ed. A.M.F. Montague (New York, 1946), pp. 463–88, 486.

172. INITIATORY SYMBOLISM OF THE SYMPLEGADES

. . . The representation of the beyond as the bowels of Mother Earth or the belly of a gigantic monster is only one among the very many images that figure the Other World as a place that can be reached only with the utmost difficulty. The "clashing rocks," the "dancing reeds," the gates in the shape of jaws, the "two razor-edged restless mountains," the "two clashing icebergs," the "active door," the "revolving barrier," the door made of the two halves of the eagle's beak, and many more—all these are images used in myths and sagas to suggest the insurmountable difficulties of passage to the Other World. (The Symplegades were two rocks at the entrance to the Black Sea that clashed together intermittently, but remained apart when Jason and the Argonauts passed through in the *Argo*.) Let us note that these images emphasize not only the danger of the passage—as in the myths of entering a giantess' or a sea monster's body—but especially the impossibility of imagining that the passage could be made by a being of flesh and blood. The Symplegades show us the paradoxical nature of passage into the beyond, or, more precisely, of transfer from this world to a world that is transcendent. For although originally the Other World is the world after death, it finally comes to mean any transcendent state, that is, any mode of being inaccessible to fleshly man and reserved for "spirits" or for man as a spiritual entity.

The paradox of this passage is sometimes expressed in spatial as well as in temporal terms. According to the *Jaiminiya Upanishad Brahmana* (I, 5, 5; I, 35, 7–9; IV, 15, 2–5), the gate of the world of heavenly Light is to be found "where Sky and Earth embrace" and the "Ends of the year" are united.[1] In other words no human being can go there except "in the spirit." All these mythical images and folklore motifs of the dangerous passage and the paradoxical transfer express the necessity for a change in mode of being to make it possible to attain to the world of spirit. As A. K. Coomaraswamy well put it: "What the formula states literally is that whoever would transfer from this to the Otherworld, or return, must do so through the undimensioned and timeless 'interval' that divides related but

SOURCE: *RSI*/64–66; cf. *TO*/205–6.
1. A. K. Coomaraswamy, "Symplegades," in *Studies and Essays . . . George Sarton . . . 1914*, ed. A. M. F. Montague (New York, 1946), pp. 463–88, 470.

contrary forces, between which, if one is to pass at all, it must be 'instantly.' "[2]

Coomaraswamy's interpretation is already a metaphysical exegesis of the symbolism of the Symplegades; it presupposes becoming conscious of the necessity for abolishing contraries; and, as we know, gaining such a consciousness is amply documented in Indian speculation and in mystical literature. But the interest of the Symplegades lies above all in the fact that they constitute a sort of prehistory of mysticism and metaphysics. In short, all these images express the following paradox: to enter the beyond, to attain to a transcendent mode of being, one must acquire the condition of "spirit." It is for this reason that the Symplegades form part of an initiatory scenario. They fall in the class of the ordeals that the Hero—or the dead man's soul—must face in order to enter the Other World.

As we saw, the Other World constantly enlarges its frontiers; it signifies not only the land of the dead but also any enchanted and miraculous realm, and, by extension, the divine world and the transcendent plane. The *vagina dentata* can represent not only passage into Mother Earth, but also the door of Heaven. In a North American tale, this door is alternatively made of the "two halves of the eagle's beak" or of the *vagina dentata* of the Daughter of the King of Heaven. This is but one more demonstration that mythical imagination and philosophical speculation have made particularly good use of the initiatory structure of the Symplegades. The Symplegades become in some sort "guardians of the threshold," homologizable with the monsters and griffins that guard a treasure hidden at the bottom of the sea, or a miraculous fountain from which flows the Water of Youth, or a garden in the midst of which stands the Tree of Life. It is as difficult to enter the Garden of the Hesperides as it is to pass between the clashing rocks or to enter a monster's belly. Each of these exploits constitutes a preeminently initiatory ordeal. He who emerges from such an ordeal victorious is qualified to share in a superhuman condition—he is a Hero, omniscient, immortal.

2. *Ibid.*, p. 486.

173. SPINNING, WEAVING, AND SEXUALITY

. . . The symbolism of [spinning and weaving] is highly significant; in the final phases of culture we find them raised to the rank of a principle explaining the world. The moon "spins" Time, and "weaves" human lives. The Goddesses of Destiny are spinners. We detect an occult connection between the conception of the periodical creations of the world (a conception derived from a lunar mythology) and the ideas of Time and of Destiny, on the one hand, and, on the other, nocturnal work, women's work, which has to be performed far from the light of the sun and almost in secret. In some cultures, after the seclusion of the girls is ended they continue to meet in some old woman's house to spin together. Spinning is a perilous craft, and hence can be carried on only in special houses and then only during particular periods and until certain hours. In some parts of the world spinning has been given up, and even completely forgotten, because of its magical peril. Similar beliefs still persist today in Europe (e.g., the Germanic fairies Perchta, Holda, Frau Holle). In some places—Japan, for example—we still find the mythological memory of a permanent tension, and even conflict, between the groups of young spinning girls and the men's secret societies. At night the men and their Gods attack the spinning girls and destroy not only their work but also their shuttles and weaving apparatus.

There is a mystical connection between female initiations, spinning, and sexuality. Even in developed societies, girls enjoy a certain prenuptial freedom, and their meetings with boys take place in the house where they gather to spin. The custom was still alive in Russia at the beginning of the twentieth century. It is surprising that in cultures where virginity is highly prized, meetings between young men and girls are not only tolerated but encouraged by their parents. We have here not a case of dissolute manners but a great secret—the revelation of female sacrality; the experience touches the springs of life and fertility. Prenuptial freedoms for girls are not erotic in nature, but ritual; they constitute fragments of a forgotten mystery, not profane festivities. In the Ukraine, during certain holy periods, and especially on the occasion of mar-

Source: *RSI*/45–46; cf. *PCR*/181–82.

riages, girls and women behave in a manner that is almost orgiastic. This complete reversal of behavior—from modesty to exhibition-ism—indicates a ritual goal, which concerns the entire community. It is a case of the religious need for periodical abolition of the norms that govern profane life—in other words, of the need to suspend the law that lies like a dead weight on customs, and to re-create the state of absolute spontaneity. The fact that cases of such ritual behavior have been preserved down to the twentieth century among peoples long since Christianized proves, I believe, that we are here dealing with an extremely archaic religious experience, a basic experience of woman's soul. . . .

174. COSMIC ROPES AND TISSUES OF BREATH

In Indian cosmological and physiological speculations, there is abundant use of images of the cord and the thread. Briefly one might say that their role is to implement *all living unity*, both cosmic and human. These primordial images serve at once to reveal the structure of the Universe and to describe the specific situation of man. Images of the rope and the thread succeed in suggesting what philosophy will afterwards make more explicit: that all things ex-isting are, by their nature, produced, "projected" or "woven" by a superior principle, and that all existence in Time implies an "artic-ulation" or "web." It is important, however, to distinguish be-tween several parallel themes:

1. The cosmic cords (that is to say, the winds) hold the Universe together, just as breath holds together and articulates the body of a man. The identity between breath (*pranas*) and the Winds is already stated in the *Atharva Veda* (XI, 4, 15). The organs are held to-gether by the breath, that is to say, in the final instance by the *at-man*: "I know the stretched thread on which these living beings are woven; I know the thread of the thread and also the great *brahman*" (*Atharva Veda*, X, 8, 38). This thread (*sutra*) is the *at-man*, and in the *Brihadaranyaka Upanishad*, II, 7, 1, the doctrine of *sutratman* is clearly formulated: "Do you know, Kapya, the thread by which this world and the other world and all beings are bound

Source: *TO*/170–73; cf. selection 35 above.

together? . . . He who knows the thread, the ruler within, he knows *brahman*, he knows the worlds, he knows the gods, he knows *atman*, he knows all things."

2. When, at the end of the world, the ropes of the winds are cut (*vrashcanam vatar-ajjunam*), the Universe will fall apart (*Maitri Upanishad*, I, 4). And since "it is by the air, as by a thread, that this world and the other world and all beings are strung together . . . they say of a dead man that his limbs have become unstrung— (*vyasramsisatasyan gani*), for it is the Air (the breath) that binds them like a thread" (*Brihadaranyaka Upanishad*, III, 7, 2).

Let us add that similar ideas are to be found in China. Chuang tze (III, 4) affirms that "the ancients describe death as the loosening of the cord on which God had hung Life."

3. The Sun binds the worlds to itself by means of a thread. As the *Shatapatha Brahmana* repeats many times, "the Sun binds (*samavayata*) these worlds together by a thread. Now, this thread is the same as the wind" (*vayuh*, VIII, 7, 3, 10; see also VII, 3, 2, 13). "The Sun is the connecting link, since these worlds are attached to the Sun by the four points of the compass" (*Shatapatha Brahmana*, VI, 7, I, 17). The Sun is "well-meshed," because it sews together "the days and the nights" (*ibid.*, IX, 4, 1, 8). This allusion to the joining of the days and the nights is closely connected with the Vedic image of the two sisters—Night and Dawn—who "like two weavers working in happy agreement weave the taut thread together" (*Rig Veda*, II, 3, 6) weaving the web of time.

4. Since it binds the World to itself by a thread, the Sun is the Cosmic Weaver, and is very often compared to a spider. "The weaver of the cloth is certainly he who shines down there, for he moves across the worlds as if across a cloth" (*Shatapatha Brahmana*, XIV, 2, 2, 22). A sacrificial *gatha* cited in the *Kausitaki Brahmana*, XIX, 3, speaks of the Sun (= the Year) as a spider. Several Upanishads use the image of the spider and its web, suiting it in each case to the religious orientation proper to itself. Sometimes it is the *atman* that is compared to a spider, sometimes the "imperishable" (*akshara*), sometimes God. "As a spider comes out with its thread . . . so from the *atman* issue all breaths, all worlds, all gods, all beings (*Brihadaranyaka Upanishad*, II 1, 20; see *Maitri Upanishad*, VI, 32). "Just as a spider draws out and draws back (*srjate grhnate*, lit. 'pours out and dries up') . . . so all is born in this world

from the imperishable (*aksarat*)" (*Mundaka Upanishad*, I, 1, 7). In a theistic Upanishad like the *Shvetasvatara*, it is the "only God who, like the spider, envelops himself with threads drawn from primordial Matter" (*pradhana*, VI, 10).

5. Finally, a number of post-Vedic texts identify the Cosmic Weaver with *atman* or Brahman, or even with a personal God like Krishna in the *Bhagavad-Gita*. When, in a famous passage of the *Brihadaranyaka Upanishad* (III, 6, 1), Gargi asks the question: "Yajnavalkya, if the Waters are a web on which all is woven, on what web are the Waters themselves woven?" Yajnavalkya replies "On the air." The air in its turn, explains Yajnavalkya, is woven on the Worlds of the Sky, and these are woven on the worlds of the Gandharvas, and they on the Worlds of the Sun, and so on to the Worlds of Brahma. But when Gargi asks: "And the worlds of Brahma, on what web they woven?" Yajnavalkya refuses to reply. "Do not ask too much, O Gargi, or your head will fall off. You are asking too much about a deity beyond whom there is no more to ask!" But in the following verses (III, 7, 1ff.) Yajnavalkya states that it is the "inner ruler" (*antaryaninam*) who is the true Ground of the Universe. And this inner ruler is the *sutratman*, the *atman* imagined as a thread.

In the *Bhagavad-Gita* it is God who "weaves" the World. Krishna proclaims himself the Supreme Person "by whom this Universe is woven" (*yena sarvam idam tatam*, VIII, 22). "All this is woven by me" (*maya tatam idam sarvam*, IX, 4). And, after the blinding theophany of Lesson XI, Arjuna cries: "All is the Primordial God, the Ancient Spirit . . . by you all has been woven" (*tvaya tatam vishvam*, XI, 38).

175. POLARITY AND COMPLEMENTARITY

Dualistic symbols are common in religious systems, and they may be expanded into a four- or threefold system. Selections 175–180 show concretizations of such polar ideologies, especially as they shape initiatory symbolism.

Source: *Q*/138–41.

The conceptions related to our themes are probably more nuanced and better articulated into a general system than one can infer from some of our older sources. When a qualified fieldworker takes the trouble to report not only behavior and rituals but also the significance that they have for the aborigines, a whole world of meaning and values is revealed to us. I shall cite as an example the usage made by the Kogi from Sierra Nevada of the ideas of polarity and complementarity in their explanation of the world, society, and the individual. The tribe is divided between the "people from above" and the "people from below," and the village, as well as the cultic hut, is separated into two halves. The world is equally divided into two sections, determined by the sun's course. Furthermore, there are many other polar and antagonistic couples: male/female, right hand/left hand, warm/cold, light/darkness, etc. These pairs are associated with certain categories of animals and plants, with colors, winds, diseases, and, likewise, with the concepts of good and evil.

The dualistic symbolism is evident in all magico-religious practices. However, the contraries coexist in every individual as well as in certain tribal deities. The Kogi believe that the function and the permanence of a principle of good (identified in an exemplary way with the right direction) are determined by the simultaneous existence of a principle of evil (the left). The good exists only because the evil is active; if the evil would disappear, the good would equally cease to be. A conception dear to Goethe, but known also in other cultures: one must commit sins, thus proclaiming the active influence of evil. According to the Kogi, the central problem of the human condition is precisely how to bring these two contraries to equilibrium and yet maintain them as complementary forces. The fundamental concept is *yulúka*, a term that can be translated "being in agreement," "being equal," "being identified." Knowing how to balance the creative and destructive energies, "being in agreement," is the guiding principle of human behavior.

This scheme of complementary oppositions is integrated in its turn into a quadripartite system of the universe: to the four cardinal directions correspond other series of concepts, mythical personages, animals, plants, colors, and activities. The antagonism reappears in the quadripartite general system (for example, red and white, "light colors," correspond to South and East, and are opposed to the "evil side," formed by the "dark colors" of North and West). The quadripartite structure informs both macrocosmos and microcosmos. The world is sustained by four mythical giants; Sierra Nevada is divided into four zones; the villages built on a traditional plan have four points of entrance where there are four sacred sites for offerings. Finally, the cultic house has four hearths around which the members of the four principal clans take their places. (But here again there reappears the antagonistic bipartition: the "right side"—red—is reserved for "those who know less," while on the "left side"—light blue—sit "those who know more," for the latter are more often confronted with the negative forces of the universe.)

The four cardinal directions are completed by the "central point," which plays an important role in the life of the Kogi. It is the Center of the World, the Sierra Nevada, whose replica is the center of the cultic house where the principal offerings are buried; there, the priest (*máma*) sits down when he wants to "speak with the gods."

Finally, this schema is developed in a tridimensional system with seven guiding marks: North, South, East, West, Zenith, Nadir, and Center. The last three constitute the cosmic axis that traverses and sustains the world, which is conceived of as an egg. As Reichel-Dolmatoff points out, it is the cosmic egg that introduces the dynamic element, namely the concept of the nine stages. The world, and man as well, have been created by the Universal Mother. She has nine daughters, each one representing a certain quality of arable soil: black, red, clayish, sandy, etc. These arable soils constitute as many layers inside the cosmic egg, and also symbolize a scale of values. Men live on the fifth earth—the black soil—which is the one in the Center. The great pyramid-like hills of Sierra Nevada are imagined to be "worlds" or "houses" of a similar structure. Likewise, the principal cultic houses are their microcosmic replicas; consequently, they are situated at the "Center of the World."

The associations do not stop here. The cosmic egg is interpreted as the uterus of the Universal Mother, in which mankind lives. The earth is equally a uterus, as is Sierra Nevada and each cultic house, home, and tomb. The caves and crevices of the earth represent the orifices of the mother. The roofs of the cultic houses symbolize the sexual organ of the Mother; they are the "doors" which give access to the higher levels. During the funeral ritual the deceased returns to the uterus; the priest lifts the corpse nine times to indicate that the dead goes again, but backwards, through the nine months of gestation. But the tomb itself represents the cosmos and the funerary ritual is an act of "cosmicization."

I have insisted on this example because it admirably illustrates the function of polarity in the thinking of an archaic people. As we have seen, the binary division of space is generalized to the entire universe. The pairs of opposites are at the same time complementaries. The principle of polarity seems to be the fundamental law of nature and life, as well as the justification for ethics. For the Kogi, human perfection does not consist in "doing good," but in securing the equilibrium of the two antagonistic forces of good and evil. On the cosmic level, this interior equilibrium corresponds to the "central point," the Center of the World. This point is to be found at the intersection of the four cardinal directions and the vertical Zenith-Nadir axis, in the middle of the cosmic egg, which is identical with the uterus of the Universal Mother. Thus the different systems of polarities express the structures of the world and of life, as well as man's specific mode of being. Human existence is understood and assumed as a "recapitulation" of the universe; conversely, the cosmic life is rendered intelligible and significative by being grasped as a "cipher."

I do not intend to add other South American examples. I think I have, on the one hand, sufficiently emphasized the variety of spiritual creations occasioned by the effort of "reading" nature and human existence through the cipher of polarity, and, on the other hand, shown that the particular expressions of what have sometimes been called binary and dualistic conceptions disclose their profound significance only if they are integrated in the all-encompassing system of which they are a part.

We encounter a similar, though more complex, situation among the North American tribes. There also one finds the bipartition of the village and the world, and the resulting cosmological system (the four directions, the Zenith-Nadir axis, the "Center," etc.), as well as various mythological and ritual expressions of religious polarities, antagonisms, and dualisms. Of course, such conceptions are neither universally nor uniformly distributed. A number of North American ethnic groups know but a rudimentary bipartite cosmology, and many other tribes ignore the "dualistic" conceptions though they utilize systems of classification of a binary type. Now, it is precisely this problem which is of interest, namely, the diverse religious valorizations, in various cultural contexts, of the basic theme of polarity and dualism.

176. DUALISM AND ANTAGONISM

. . . It is true that a certain type of dualism seems to be the systematic elaboration of agricultural societies, but the most radical dualism is found among the Californian tribes which ignore agriculture. Sociogenesis, like any other "genesis," cannot explain the functions of an existential symbolism. For instance, the bipartition of the inhabited territory and of the village, together with the antagonism between two polar principles, is attested among many tribes, and yet their mythologies and religions do not present a dualist structure. These tribes have simply applied the territorial bipartition as an immediate datum of experience, but their mythological and religious creativity express itself on other planes of reference.

As for the tribes which have actually faced the enigma of polarity and have tried to resolve it, we recall the surprising variety of solutions that have been proposed. There is, among the central Algonkians, the *personal* antagonism between the Culture Hero and the inferior Powers, which explains the origin of death and the installation of the initiation hut. But such antagonism was not inevitable: it is the result of an accident (the murder of Mänäbush's brother). In regard to the initiation cabin, we have seen that it existed already among some other Algonkian tribes, namely the Ojibwa. They claim to have received the hut from the Great God, and its symbolism expresses the cosmic polarities as well as their integration. Among the maize cultivators, the dualism receives totally different expressions. With the Zuni, dualism is weak in mythology while it dominates the ritual and the liturgical calendar; among the Iroquois, on the contrary, both mythology and cult are articulated in such a rigorous dualism that one is even reminded of the classical Iranian type. Finally, among the Californians the antago-

Source: Q/158–59.

nism between God and his adversary, Coyote, open the way to a "mythologization" of the human condition, comparable to—and yet different from—that effectuated by the Greeks.

177. COMPETITIONS AND CONTESTS

Ancient India permits us to grasp in process the passage from a mythico-ritual scenario to a paleotheology that will later inspire different metaphysical speculations. Moreover, India illustrates better than any other culture the resumption on multiple levels, and the creative reinterpretation, of an archaic and well-diffused theme. The Indian documents help one to understand that a fundamental symbol, pursuing the revelation of a profound dimension of human existence, is always "open." In other words, India admirably illustrates that such a symbol may inaugurate what could be called a *chain-symbolization of all experiences laying bare man's situation in the universe*, thus influencing a sort of presystematic reflection and articulating its first results. Of course, it is impossible to recall here all the important creations of Indian genius. I shall begin with an example of ritual valorization of the motif of antagonism between two polar principles. I shall quote afterwards a few examples of elaboration and creative reinterpretation of this familiar motif on the planes of mythology and metaphysics.

The vedic mythology is dominated by the theme of the exemplary combat between Indra and the dragon Vritra. I have insisted elsewhere on the cosmogonic structure of the myth. Releasing the waters imprisoned by Vritra in the mountains, Indra saves the world; symbolically, he creates it anew. In other variants of the myth, the decapitation and dismemberment of Vritra express the passage from virtuality to the actuality of creation, for the Snake is a symbol of the nonmanifest. The exemplary myth *par excellence*, this combat between Indra and Vritra furnishes the model for other forms of creation and many types of activities. "He verily slays Vritra who is a victor in the battle," says a vedic hymn.[1] Kui-

SOURCE: Q/163–66; cf. PCR/319–21; Q/141–44.
1. *Maitrayani-Samhita*, *II*, 13, quoted by F. B. J. Kuiper, "The Ancient Aryan Verbal Contest," *Indo-Iranian Journal* 4 (1960): 251.

per has recently pointed out two series of convergent facts. First, he has shown that the verbal contests in vedic India reiterate the primordial struggle against the forces of resistance. . . . The poet compares himself to Indra: "I am a slayer of my rivals, unhurt and uninjured like Indra" (*Rig Veda*, X, 166, 2). The oratorical contest, the competition between poets, represents a creative act and consequently a renovation of life. Second, Kuiper has shown that there are reasons to believe that the mythico-ritual scenario centered on the combat between Indra and Vritra constituted, in fact, the New Year festival. All forms of contest and combat—chariot courses, struggles between two groups, etc.—were considered likely to stimulate the creative forces during the winter ritual. Benveniste has rendered the Avestan term *vyaxana* as "oratorical contest" having a "military quality" that secures the victory.[2]

Thus, it seems that there existed a rather archaic Indo-Iranian conception which exalted the renovating and creative virtues of the verbal contest. Moreover, this view was not exclusively Indo-Iranian. Violent verbal confrontations are attested, for example, among the Eskimos, the Kwakiutl, and the ancient Germans. As Sierksma has recently pointed out, verbal contests were highly esteemed in Tibet.[3] The public debates of the Tibetan monks, whose aggressiveness and cruelty were not only verbal, are well known. Though the disputes bear upon problems of Buddhist philosophy and follow, at least in part, the rules established by the great Indian Buddhist doctors, especially Asanga, the passion with which the public controversy is carried out seems to be characteristic of the Tibetans. Moreover, Rolf Stein has shown that in Tibet the verbal contest falls among other forms of competition, such as horse races, athletic games, wrestling, competition in archery, cow milking, and beauty contests.[4] On the occasion of the New Year, the most important competition besides the horse races took place between the members or representatives of different clans, who recited the cosmogonic myth and exalted the tribal ancestors. The essential theme of the New Year mythico-ritual scenario was the

2. Quoted in *ibid.*, p. 247.
3. F. Sierksma, "*Rtsod-pa*: The Monacal Disputations in Tibet," *Indo-Iranian Journal* 8 (1964): 130–52, especially 142 ff.
4. R. A. Stein, *Recherches sur l'épopée et le barde au Tibet* (Paris, 1959), p. 441.

combat between the Sky God and the demons, represented by two mountains. As in similar scenarios, the god's victory assured the victory of new life in the following year. As for the oratorical contests, they were, according to Stein, part of

an ensemble of competitions which, on the social plane, exalt the prestige, and on the religious plane fasten the social group to its habitat. The gods are present at the spectacle and laugh in common with men. The contest of enigmas and the recitation of tales, like the Epic of Gesar, have an effect on the crops and cattle. Gods and men being reunited at the occasion of the great festivals, the social oppositions are reaffirmed and appeased at the same time. And the group, connected again with its past (origin of the world and of the ancestors) and with its habitat (ancestors—sacred mountains) feels invigorated.[5]

Rolf Stein has also indicated the Iranian influences in the Tibetan New Year festival.[6] But this does not mean that the entire scenario has been borrowed. Most probably, Iranian influences have reinforced certain indigenous elements already in existence. The New Year scenario was certainly archaic, since it disappeared quite early in India.

178. INITIATORY RENEWAL

. . . Initiation lies at the core of any genuine human life. And this is true for two reasons. The first is that any genuine human life implies profound crises, ordeals, suffering, loss and reconquest of self, "death and resurrection." The second is that, whatever degree of fulfillment it may have brought him, at a certain moment every man sees his life as a failure. This vision does not arise from a moral judgment made on his past, but from an obscure feeling that he has missed his vocation; that he has betrayed the best that was in him. In such moments of total crisis, only one hope seems to offer any issue—the hope of beginning life over again. This means, in short, that the man undergoing such a crisis dreams of new, regenerated life, fully realized and significant. This is something other and far

SOURCE: *RSI*/135–36; cf. *IS*/151–59; *MDM*/207–9; *FC*/153–54.
5. *Ibid.*, pp. 440–41.
6. *Ibid.*, pp. 390–91, etc. Cf. Sierksma, "Rtsod-pa," pp. 146 ff.

more than the obscure desire of every human soul to renew itself periodically, as the cosmos is renewed. The hope and dream of these moments of total crisis are to obtain a definitive and total *renovatio*, a renewal capable of transmuting life. Such a renewal is the result of every genuine religious conversion.

But genuine and definitive conversions are comparatively rare in modern societies. To us, this makes it all the more significant that even nonreligious men sometimes, in the depths of their being, feel the desire for this kind of spiritual transformation, which, in other cultures, constitutes the very goal of initiation. It does not fall to us to determine to what extent traditional initiations fulfilled their promises. The important fact is that they proclaimed their intention, and professed to possess the means, of transmuting human life. The nostalgia for an initiatory renewal which sporadically arises from the inmost depths of modern nonreligious man hence seems to us highly significant. It would appear to represent the modern formulation of man's eternal longing to find a positive meaning in death, to accept death as a transition rite to a higher mode of being. If we can say that initiation constitutes a specific dimension of human existence, this is true above all because it is only in initiation that death is given a positive value. Death prepares the new, purely spiritual birth, access to a mode of being not subject to the destroying action of Time.

179. ALCHEMY: LIVING MATTER AND INITIATION

It is sufficient for our purpose to single out very briefly certain alchemistic symbolisms and operations and to demonstrate their solidarity with the primitive symbolisms and techniques linked with the processes of matter. In our view, one of the principal sources of alchemy is to be sought in those conceptions dealing with the Earth-Mother, with ores and metals, and, above all, with the *experience* of primitive man engaged in mining, fusion and smithcraft. The "conquest of matter" began very early, perhaps in the palaeolithic age, that is, as soon as man had succeeded in making

SOURCE: *FC*/142–46, 148–52; cf. *Y*/278–84; *FC*/192–99; *S*/145–48, 165–68.

tools from silex and using fire to change the states of matter. In any case certain techniques—mainly agriculture and pottery—were fully developed during the neolithic age. Now these techniques were at the same time mysteries, for, on the one hand, they implied the sacredness of the cosmos and, on the other, were transmitted by initiation (the "craft-secrets"). Tilling, or the firing of clay, like, somewhat later, mining and metallurgy, put primitive man into a universe steeped in sacredness. . . .

Not that man in primitive society was still "buried in Nature," powerless to free himself from the innumerable "mystic" participations in Nature, totally incapable of logical thought or utilitarian labour in the modern sense of the word. Everything we know of our contemporary "primitives" shows up the weakness of these arbitrary judgements. But it is clear that a thinking dominated by cosmological symbolism created an experience of the world vastly different from that accessible to modern man. To symbolic thinking the world is not only "alive" but also "open": an object is never simply itself (as is the case with modern consciousness), it is also a sign of, or a repository for, something else. To take one example, the tilled field is something more than a patch of earth, it is also the body of the Earth-Mother: the spade is a phallus while still remaining an agricultural tool; ploughing is at once a "mechanical" labour (carried out with man-made tools) and a sexual union prescribed for the hierogamous fertilization of the Earth-Mother.

There is an abundance of testimony in the works on metallurgy and the craft of the goldsmith in the ancient Orient to show that men of primitive cultures were able to gain knowledge of, and mastery over, matter. . . . It is certain that the smelters, smiths and master-goldsmiths of oriental antiquity could calculate quantities and control physico-chemical processes of smelting and alloyage. For all that, we must recognize that for them it was not solely a metallurgical or chemical operation, a technique or science in the strict sense of the word. . . . However advanced the desanctification of the cosmos was at that time, the trades still retained their ritual character, though the hierurgical[1] context is not necessarily indicated in the prescriptions.

1. Hierurgical: priestly use in rituals. Eds.

The fact remains that historical documents allow us to distinguish three periods in the beginnings of Greco-Egyptian alchemy:

1. the period of technical prescriptions;

2. the philosophical period, probably ushered in by Bolos de Mendes (second century B.C.), and manifesting itself in the *Physika Kai Mystika* attributed to Democritus; and, finally,

3. The period of alchemistic writings proper, that of the apocryphas, of Zosimos (third–fourth centuries A.D.) and the commentators (fourth to seventh centuries)....

If, therefore, alchemy could not be born from the desire to counterfeit gold (gold assay had been known for at least twelve centuries), nor from a Greek scientific technique . . . it was probably the old conception of the Earth-Mother, bearer of embryo-ores, which crystallized faith in artificial transmutation (that is, operated in a laboratory). It was the encounter with the symbolisms, myths and techniques of the miners, smelters and smiths which probably gave rise to the first alchemical operations. But above all it was the experimental discovery of the *living* Substance, such as it was felt by the artisans, which must have played the decisive role. Indeed, it is the conception of a *complex and dramatic Life of Matter* which constitutes the originality of alchemy as opposed to classical Greek science. One is entitled to suppose that the *experience* of *dramatic life* was made possible by the knowledge of Greco-oriental mysteries.

It is known that the essence of initiation into the Mysteries consisted of participation in the passion, death and resurrection of a God. We are ignorant of the modalities of this participation but one can conjecture that the sufferings, death and resurrection of the God, already known to the neophyte as a myth or as authentic history, were communicated to him during initiations, in an "experimental" manner. The meaning and finality of the Mysteries were the transmutation of man. By experience of initiatory death and resurrection, the initiate changed his mode of being (he became "immortal"). . . .

Let us note that Zosimos's description recalls not only the dismemberment of Dionysius and other "dying Gods" of the Mysteries (whose passion is, on a certain plane, closely allied with the different moments of the vegetal cycle, especially with the tortures, death and resurrection of the Spirit of Corn), but that it presents striking analogies with the initiation visions of the shamans and, in general, with the fundamental pattern of all primitive initiations. It is known that every initiation comprises a series of ritual tests symbolizing the death and resurrection of the neophyte. In the shamanic initiations, these ordeals, although undergone "in the second state," are of an extreme cruelty. The future shaman is present, in a dream, at his own dismemberment, decapitation and death. If one takes account of the universality of the initiation pattern and the close parallelism between workers in metals, smiths and shamans; if one reflects that the ancient Mediterranean guilds of metallurgists and smiths very probably had at their disposal mysteries which were peculiar to them, one finally realizes that Zosimos's vision has its place in that spiritual universe which the preceding pages have attempted to interpret and define. And now one is in a position to measure the extent of the alchemists' innovation: *they projected on to Matter the initiatory function of suffering.* Thanks to the alchemical operations, corresponding to the tortures, death and resurrection of the initiate, the substance is transmuted, that is, attains a transcendental mode of being: it becomes gold. Gold, we repeat, is the symbol of immortality. In Egypt the flesh of the Gods was believed to be of gold. By becoming God, the flesh of Pharaoh also became gold. Alchemical transmutation is therefore equivalent to the perfecting of matter or, in Christian terminology, to its redemption.

We have seen that ores and metals were regarded as living organisms: one spoke in terms of their gestation growth, birth and even marriage. . . . The alchemists adopted and gave a new significance to these primitive beliefs. The alchemical combination of sulphur and mercury is always expressed in terms of "marriage." But this marriage is also a mystical union between two cosmological principles. Herein lies the novelty of the alchemical perspective: the life of Matter is no longer designated in terms of "vital" hierophanies as it was in the outlook of primitive man; it has acquired a spiritual dimension; in other words, by taking on the initiatory significance of drama and suffering, matter also takes on the destiny of the spirit. The "initiation tests" which, on the spiritual plane, culminate in freedom, illumination and immortality, culminate on the material plane, in transmutation, in the Philosopher's Stone.

180. THE INITIATORY SIGNIFICANCE OF SUFFERING

What can be the meaning of [initiatory] tortures? The first European observers used to speak of the innate cruelty of the natives. However, that is not the explanation: the natives are no more cruel than the civilized. But for every traditional society, suffering has a ritual value, for the torture is believed to be inflicted by superhuman beings and its purpose is the spiritual transmutation of the victim. The torture is, in itself, an expression of initiatory death. To be tortured means that one is cut into pieces by the demon-masters of initiation, that one is put to death by dismemberment. We may recall how St. Anthony was tortured by devils; he was lifted into the air, smothered under the earth; the devils gashed his flesh, dislocated his limbs and cut him to pieces. Christian tradition calls these tortures "the temptation of St. Anthony"—and that is true to the degree that the temptation is homologized with the initiatory ordeal. In confronting all these ordeals victoriously—that is, in resisting all the "temptations"—the monk Anthony becomes holy. That is to say that he has "killed" the profane man that he was, and has come to life again as another, a regenerated man, a saint. But in a non-Christian perspective, this also means that the demons have succeeded in their aim, which was just that of "killing" the profane man and enabling him to regenerate himself. In identifying the forces of evil with the devils Christianity has deprived them of any positive function in the economy of salvation: but before Christianity the demons were, among others, masters of initiation. They seized the neophytes, tortured them, subjected them to a great number of ordeals, and finally killed them so that they could be born again, regenerated both in body and soul. It is significant that they discharge the same initiatory function in the temptation of St. Anthony; for, after all, it was their tortures and "temptations" that provided opportunity for St. Anthony to attain to sainthood.

These reflections are not a digression from our subject. What we want to emphasise is this: that the initiatory tortures of the Mandan were not inspired by an innate cruelty in the American-Indian nature; that they were of a ritual significance, namely, that of being cut to pieces by the demons of initiation. This religious evaluation

SOURCE: *MDM*/207–9.

of suffering is confirmed by other facts: certain grave illnesses, psycho-mental maladies above all, are regarded by the primitives as "demonic possession," in the sense that the sufferer has been chosen by divine beings to become a shaman and a mystic: it follows that he is in process of being initiated—that is, tortured, cut to pieces and "killed" by "demons." We have recorded elsewhere a number of examples of such initiatory maladies suffered by future shamans. Our conclusion, therefore, must be as follows: that sufferings, both physical and psychic, are homologous with the tortures that are inseparable from initiation; illness was esteemed among primitives as the sign of a supernatural election; and was therefore regarded as an initiatory ordeal. One had to "die" to something to be able to be reborn; that is, to be cured: one died to what one was before, died to the profane condition; the man who was effecting this cure was another, a newborn man—in this case, a shaman, a mystic.

At different levels and in various contexts we find the same initiatory schema comprising ordeals, tortures, ritual putting-to-death, and symbolic resurrection. We have now identified this scenario of spiritual regeneration both in the initiations effected at puberty, which are obligatory for all members of the clan, and in the secret associations of the men, which create a "closed circle" within the clan. But we observe, furthermore, that individual mythical vocations, as well as the initiatory illnesses of future shamans, comprise the same scenario of sufferings, torture, death and resurrection; and all this compels us to conclude that the mystery of spiritual regeneration consists of an archetypal process which is realized on different planes in many ways; it is effected whenever the need is to surpass one mode of being and to enter upon another, higher mode; or, more precisely, whenever it is a question of spiritual transmutation.

◆

Symbols Concerning Paradise

Beyond the actual life-transitions, role changes, and adjustments to sex/social/professional status, man seeks—according to Eliade—the sacred. And now "the sacred" appears not only as the World revealing its sacredness in power and force, but as perfection, as the paradise that symbolizes transcending the limitations of the human condition. Both the mystic and the shaman act out an experiencing of Paradise Now, but as a motif Paradise has often appeared as a goal of *social* striving—as in the first century or so of American social thought.

Dissatisfaction with the presently limited stage of man's existence can also lead to stress on experiencing the Beyond and the Now simultaneously, embodying the ultimate opposites within his own self. He becomes, for example, the *jivan mukta* of India, the man liberated toward time and eternity while living in (but not constrained by) the everyday world. It is the polyvalence of the divine that is expressed in such symbols as the Chinese *yin* and *yang*, and it is the experiencing of this polyvalence as at the same time (and paradoxically as) a *unity*, that occurs both in archaic and ultramodern theologies (cf. the recent "death of god" theologies)—representing a religious sensitivity of the utmost sophistication.

181. "NOSTALGIA FOR PARADISE"

In short, all the symbolisms and equations we have looked at prove that, however different sacred space may be from profane, man cannot live except in this sort of sacred space. And when there is no hierophany to reveal it to him, he constructs it for himself according to the laws of cosmology and geomancy. Thus, although the "center" is conceived as being "somewhere" where only the few who are initiated can hope to enter, yet every house is, none the less, thought of as being built at this same center of the world. We may say that one group of traditions evinces man's desire to place himself at the "center of the world" without any effort, while another stresses the difficulty, and therefore the merit, of attaining it. I do not at the moment want to determine the history of each of these traditions. The fact that the first—according to which it is easy to construct a center in every man's house—can be found almost everywhere induces us, if not to decide at once that it is the more primitive, at least to see it as significant, as characteristic of mankind as a whole. It shows up very clearly a specific condition of man in the cosmos—what we may call "the nostalgia for Paradise." I mean by this the desire to be always, effortlessly, at the

Source: *PCR*/382–83; cf. *Y*/219–27.

heart of the world, of reality, of the sacred, and, briefly, to transcend, by natural means, the human condition and regain a divine state of affairs: what a Christian would call the state of man before the Fall. . . .

182. PARADISE SYMBOLISM

. . . The most representative mystical experience of the archaic societies, that of shamanism, betrays the *Nostalgia for Paradise*, the desire to recover the state of freedom and beatitude before "the Fall," the will to restore communication between Earth and Heaven; in a word, to abolish all the changes made in the very structure of the Cosmos and in the human mode of being by that primordial disruption. The shaman's ecstasy restores a great deal of the paradisiac condition: it renews the friendship with the animals; by his *flight* or ascension, the shaman reconnects Earth with Heaven; up there, in Heaven, he once more meets the God of Heaven face to face and speaks directly to him, as man sometimes did *in illo tempore*.

Now, an analogous situation can be studied in the latest and most highly elaborated mysticism of all: that of Christianity. Christianity is ruled by the longing for Paradise. "Praying toward the East reconnects us with the paradisiac themes . . . To turn toward the East appears to be an expression of the nostalgia for Paradise."[1] The same paradisiac symbolism is attested in the rites of baptism: "instead of Adam, falling under the domination of Satan and being expelled from Paradise, the catechumen appears as though set free by the New Adam from the power of Satan and re-admitted into Paradise."[2] "Christianity thus seems to be the realization of Paradise. The Christ is the Tree of Life (Ambrose, *De Isaac*, 5, 43) or the fountain of Paradise" (Ambrose, *De Paradiso*, III, 272, 10). But this realization of Paradise takes place in three successive phases. Baptism is the entry into Paradise (Cyril of Jerusalem, *Procatech.*, P.G. XXXIII, 375A); the mystical life is a deeper entry into Para-

SOURCE: *MDM*/66–68; cf. *FPZ*/IV–H; *IS*/166 ff.; *Q*/Ch. VI.
1. Jean Daniélou, S.J., *Bible et Liturgie* (Paris, 1951), p. 46.
2. *Ibid.*, p. 47.

dise (Ambrose, *De Paradiso*, I, 1); and finally, death introduces the martyrs into Paradise (*Passio Perpet.* I, P.L. III, 28A). It is remarkable indeed to have found the paradisiac language applied to all these aspects of the Christian life.[3]

Naturally, it is mysticism that best exemplifies the restoration of the life of Paradise. The first syndrome of that restoration is the recovery of dominion over the animals. As we know, in the beginning Adam was enjoined to provide the animals with names (*Genesis* 2:19); for to name the animals was equivalent to ruling over them. St. Thomas explains Adam's power over the nonrational creation, as follows: "The soul, by its commandment, rules over the sensitive powers, such as the appetites of anger and concupiscence, which, in a manner, are obedient to reason. *Whence*, in the state of innocence, man by his commandment ruled over the other animals."[4] But "the fact of giving names or changing them plays a similarly important part in eschatological pronouncements . . . the messianic kingdom brings about a moral conversion of humanity, and even a transformation of the animals . . . which characterizes the world fresh from the hand of God."[5] And, in the mystical state, the animals are sometimes obedient to the saints, as they were to Adam. "The tales about the ancient fathers of monasticism show them—and this is not a rare happening—being obeyed by wild animals which they feed just like domestic animals."[6] St. Francis of Assisi does what the desert Fathers did before him. Friendship with the wild animals, and their spontaneous acceptance of man's authority, are manifest signs of the recovery of a paradisiac situation.

183. THE SHAMAN'S CRIES OF LONGING

. . . All too often the Occidental allows himself to be impressed by the *manifestation* of an ideology, when he is ignorant of the one thing it is important above all others to know: the ideology itself,

SOURCE: *MDM*/72.

3. Jean Daniélou, S.J., *Sacramentum futuri* (Paris, 1950), p. 16.
4. Dom Anselme Stolz, *Théologie de la Mystique*, French trans., 2d ed. (Chevertogne, 1947), p. 104.
5. J. Daniélou, S.J., *Sacramentum futuri*, p. 6.
6. Stolz, *Théologie*, p. 31.

that is, the myths. But the manifestations depend, in the first place, upon local fashions and cultural styles, and these may or may not be immediately accessible. One then judges according to the impression: a ceremony is *beautiful*, a certain dance is *sinister*, a rite of initiation is *savage* or an *aberration*. Yet if one takes the trouble to understand the ideology that underlies all these manifestations, if we study the myths and the symbols that condition them, we can free ourselves from the subjectivity of impressions and obtain a more objective view. Sometimes an understanding of the ideology is enough to re-establish the "normality" of a kind of behavior. To recall just one example: the imitation of the animals' cries. For more than a century it was thought that the strange cries of the shaman were a proof of his mental disequilibrium. But they were signs of something very different: of the nostalgia for Paradise which had haunted Isaiah and Virgil, which had nourished the saintliness of the Fathers of the Church, and that blossomed anew, victorious, in the life of St. Francis of Assisi.

184. THE AMERICAN PARADISE

. . . Certain pioneers already saw Paradise in the various regions of America. Traveling along the coast of New England in 1614, John Smith compared it to Eden: "heaven and earth never agreed better to frame a place for man's habitation . . . we chanced in a lande, even as God made it." George Alsop presents Maryland as the only place seeming to be the "Earthly Paradise." Its trees, its plants, its fruits, its flowers, he wrote, speak in "Hieroglyphicks of our Adamitical or Primitive situation." Another writer discovered the "future Eden" in Georgia—a region located on the same latitude as Palestine: "That promis'd *Canaan*, which was pointed out by God's own choice, to bless the Labours of a favorite People." For Edward Johnson, Massachusetts was the place "where the Lord will create a new Heaven and a new Earth." Likewise, the Boston Puritan, John Cotton, informed those preparing to set sail from England for Massachusetts that they were granted a privilege of

Source: Q/94–95.

Heaven, thanks to "the grand charter given to *Adam* and his posterity in Paradise."[1]

But this reflects just one aspect of the millenarist experience of the pioneers. For many new immigrants, the New World represented a desert haunted by demonic beings. This, however, did not diminish their eschatological exaltation, for they were told in sermons that the present miseries were but a moral and spiritual trial before arriving at the Earthly Paradise that had been promised to them. The pioneers considered themselves in the situation of the Israelites after the crossing of the Red Sea, just as, in their eyes, their condition in England and Europe had been a sort of Egyptian bondage. After the terrible trial of the desert, they would enter Canaan. As Cotton Mather wrote, "The Wilderness through which we are passing to the Promised Land is all over filled with Fiery flying serpents."[2]

But, later on, a new idea was born; the New Jerusalem would be in part produced by work. Jonathan Edwards (1703–58) thought that through work New England would be transformed into a sort of "Paradise on Earth." We see how the millenarianism of the pioneers gradually ends in the idea of progress. In the first stage, a relationship was established between paradise and the earthly possibilities presenting themselves in the New World. During the next stage, the eschatological tension was reduced by the omission of the period of decadence and misery that was supposed to precede the "Last Days," and by arriving finally at the idea of a progressive and uninterrupted amelioration.

But before the American idea of progress crystallized, the millenarianism of the pioneers underwent other transformations. The first important crisis in this Puritan eschatology was provoked by the struggle among the European powers for the colonial empire. Rome and the Catholic nations were identified with the Antichrist, on whose destruction the coming of the future Kingdom depended.

At one particular time, English colonial literature was dominated by a single theme: the invasion of America by the Antichrist, who threatened to ruin the hope for the glorious triumph of Christ. For

1. Texts quoted in C. L. Sanford, *The Quest for Paradise* (Urbana, 1961), pp. 83–85.
2. *Ibid.*, p. 87.

John Winthrop, the first duty of New England was to "raise a rampart against the kingdom of the Antichrist that the Jesuits are in the process of establishing in these regions." Other authors affirmed that the New World was a true Paradise before the arrival of the Catholics.

Obviously, the rivalry among the European powers for the domination of the transatlantic empires was in large measure economic in character, but it was exacerbated by an almost Manichean eschatology: everything seemed to be reduced to a conflict between Good and Evil. Colonial authors spoke of the threat that the French and the Spanish posed for the English colonies as a "new Babylonian captivity" or "an Egyptian bondage." The French and the Spanish were tyrants, slaves of the Antichrist. Catholic Europe was presented as a fallen world, a Hell, by contrast with the Paradise of the New World. The saying was "Heaven or Europe," meaning "Heaven or Hell." The trials of the pioneers in the desert of America had as their principal goal the redemption of man from the carnal sins of the pagan Old World.

185. THE RELIGIOUS ORIGINS OF THE "AMERICAN WAY OF LIFE"

. . . Eschatological millenarianism and the expectation of the Earthly Paradise were subjected in the end to a radical secularization. The myth of progress and the cult of novelty and youth are among the most noteworthy consequences. However, even in drastically secularized form, one detects the religious enthusiasm and the eschatological expectations inspiring the ancestors. For, in short, both the first colonists and the later European immigrants journeyed to America as *the country where they might be born anew*, that is, begin a new life. The "novelty" which still fascinates Americans today is a desire with religious underpinnings. In "novelty" one hopes for a "renaissance"; one seeks a new life.

New England, *New* York, *New* Haven—all these names express not only the nostalgia for the native land left behind, but above all the hope that in these lands and these new cities life will know

SOURCE: Q/97–99.

new dimensions. And not only life: everything in this continent that was considered an earthly paradise must be greater, more beautiful, stronger. In New England, described as resembling the Garden of Eden, partridges were supposedly so big that they could no longer fly, and the turkeys as fat as lambs.[1] This American flair for the grandiose, likewise religious in origin, is shared even more by the most lucid minds.

The hope of being born again to a new life—and the expectation of a future not only better, but beatific—may also be seen in the American cult of youth. According to Charles L. Sanford, since the era of industrialization, Americans have more and more sought their lost innocence in their children. The same author believes that the exaltation of things new, which followed the pioneers to the Far West, fortified individualism over authority, but also contributed to the American irreverence toward history and tradition.[2]

We shall end here these few considerations of the metamorphosis of the millenarist eschatology of the pioneers. We have seen how, in setting out in search of the Earthly Paradise across the ocean, the first explorers were conscious of playing an important role in the history of salvation; how America, after being identified with the Earthly Paradise, became the privileged place where the Puritans were to perfect the Reformation, which supposedly had failed in Europe; and how the immigrants believed that they had escaped from the Hell of Europe and expected a new birth in the New World. We have likewise seen to what extent modern America is the result of these messianic hopes, this confidence in the possibility of reaching paradise here on earth, this faith in youth and in the simplicity of the mind and soul.

One might continue the analysis and show how the long resistance of American elites to the industrialization of the country, and their exaltation of the virtues of agriculture, may be explained by the same nostalgia for the Earthly Paradise. Even when urbanization and industrialization had triumphed everywhere, the favorite images and clichés used by the pioneers retained their prestige. In order to prove that urbanization and industrialization did not necessarily imply (as in Europe!) vice, poverty, and the dissolution of

1. Texts quoted in C. L. Sanford, *Quest for Paradise* (Urbana, 1961), p. 111.
2. Cf. *ibid.*, pp. 112 ff.

mores, owners of factories multiplied their philanthropic activities, constructing churches, schools, and hospitals. At all costs, it had to be made plain that, far from threatening spiritual and religious values, science, technology and industry guaranteed their triumph. A book appearing in 1842 was entitled *The Paradise within the Reach of All Men, by Power of Nature and Machinery*. And one might detect the nostalgia for Paradise, the desire to find again that "Nature" of their ancestors, in the contemporary tendency to leave the metropolis and seek refuge in suburbia—luxurious and peaceful neighborhoods arranged with utmost care in paradisiacal landscapes.

But our concern here is not to present an analysis of the metamorphosis of the American millenarist ideal. What must be emphasized, as other authors have, is that the certainty of the eschatological mission, and especially of attaining once again the perfection of early Christianity and restoring Paradise to earth, is not likely to be forgotten easily. It is very probable that the behavior of the average American today, as well as the political and cultural ideology of the United States, still reflects the consequences of the Puritan certitude of having been called to restore the Earthly Paradise.

186. MEANINGS OF THE *COINCIDENTIA OPPOSITORUM*

What is revealed to us by all the myths and symbols, all the rites and mystical techniques, the legends and beliefs that imply more or less clearly the *coincidentia oppositorum*, the reunion of opposites, the totalization of fragments? First of all, man's deep dissatisfaction with his actual situation, with what is called the human condition. Man feels himself torn and separate. He often finds it difficult properly to explain to himself the nature of this separation for sometimes he feels himself to be cut off from "something" *powerful*, "something" utterly *other* than himself, and at other times from an indefinable, timeless "state," of which he has no precise memory, but which he does however remember in the depths of his being: a primordial state which he enjoyed before Time, before History. This separation has taken the form of a fissure, both in

Source: *TO*/122–24; cf. *IS*/12–20; *Z*/Ch. 3; *Y*/226–73; *TO*/82–91, 98–100, 108–17; *PCR*/419–25; *Q*/168–70.

himself and in the World. It was the "fall," not necessarily in the Judaeo-Christian meaning of the term, but a fall nevertheless since it implies a fatal disaster for the human race and at the same time an ontological change in the structure of the World. From a certain point of view one may say that many beliefs implying the *coincidentia oppositorum* reveal a nostalgia for a lost Paradise, a nostalgia for a paradoxical state in which the contraries exist side by side without conflict, and the multiplications form aspects of a mysterious Unity.

Ultimately, it is the wish to recover this lost unity that has caused man to think of the opposites as complementary aspects of a single reality. It is as a result of such existential experiences, caused by the need to transcend the opposites, that the first theological and philosophical speculations were elaborated. Before they became the main philosophical concepts, the One, the Unity, the Totality were desires revealed in myths and beliefs and expressed in rites and mystical techniques. On the level of presystematic thought, the mystery of totality embodies man's endeavor to reach a perspective in which the contraries are abolished, the Spirit of Evil reveals itself as a stimulant of Good, and Demons appear as the night aspect of the Gods. The fact that these archaic themes and motifs still survive in folklore and continually arise in the worlds of dream and imagination proves that the mystery of totality forms an integral part of the human drama. It recurs under various aspects and at all levels of cultural life—in mystical philosophy and theology, in the mythologies and folklore of the world, in modern men's dreams and fantasies and in artistic creation.[1]

---

1. Nevertheless, it is important to state that all expressions of the *coincidentia oppositorum* are not equivalent. We have observed on many occasions that by transcending the opposites one does not always attain the same mode of being. There is every possible difference, for instance, between spiritual androgynization and the "confusion of the sexes" obtained by orgy; between regression to the formless and "spooky" and the recovery of "paradisaical" spontaneity and freedom. The element common to all the rites, myths and symbols which we have just recalled lies in this: that all seek to come out of a particular situation in order to abolish a given system of conditions and reach a mode of "total" being. But, according to the cultural context, this "totality" may be either a primordial indistinction (as in "orgy" or "chaos"), or the situation of a *jivan mukta*, or the liberty and blessedness of one who has reached the Kingdom in his own soul. We should need much more space than we have reserved for this essay to discover, in the case of each example we

It is not by chance that Goethe searched throughout his life for the true place of Mephistopheles, the perspective in which the Demon who denied Life could show himself paradoxically as its most valuable and tireless partner. Nor is it by chance that Balzac, the creator of the modern realistic novel, in his finest work of fantasy took up a myth that had obsessed humanity for countless thousands of years. Goethe and Balzac both believed in the unity of European literature, and considered their own works as belonging to that literature. They would have been even prouder than they were if they had realized that this European literature goes back beyond Greece and the Mediterranean, beyond the ancient Near East and Asia; that the myths called to new life in *Faust* and *Séraphita* come to us from a great distance in space and time; that they come to us from prehistory.

187. INDIA: "LIBERATED WHILE LIVING"

Clearly, this is only true from a transcendental and timeless viewpoint; in man's immediate experience, in his concrete, historical existence, the Devas and Asuras are opposed, and he must pursue virtue and combat evil. *What is true of eternity is not necessarily true in time.* The world came into existence as a result of the breaking of primordial unity. The world's existence, as well as existence *in* the world, presuppose a separation of Light from darkness, a distinction between good and evil, a choice and a tension. But, in India, the cosmos is not considered the exemplary and ultimate form of reality, and existence in the world is not thought of as the *summum bonum*. Both the cosmos and man's existence in the cosmos are particular situations—and no particular situation can exhaust the fabulous riches of Being. The Indian thinker's ideal is, as is well known,

Source: *TO*/94–97.

have discussed, to what sort of transcendence the abolition of contraries has led. Moreover, every attempt to transcend the opposites carries with it a certain danger. This is why the ideas of a *coincidentia oppositorum* always arouse ambivalent feelings; on the one side, man is haunted by the desire to escape from his particular situation and regain a transpersonal mode of life; on the other, he is paralyzed by the fear of losing his "identity" and "forgetting" himself.

the *jivan mukti*, the man "liberated while living," that is to say someone who, while living in the world, is not conditioned by the structure of the world, someone who is no longer "fixed in place" but, as the texts put it, "free to move at will" (*kamacarin*). The *jivan mukti* is simultaneously in time and in eternity; his existence is a paradox in the sense that it constitutes a *coincidentia oppositorum* beyond the understanding or the imagination .

The efforts a man makes to transcend the opposites cause him to leave his immediate and personal situation and raise himself to a suprasubjective viewpoint; in other words, to attain metaphysical knowledge. In his immediate experience, man is made up of pairs of opposites. What is more, he not only distinguishes the agreeable from the disagreeable, pleasure from pain, friendship from hostility, but comes to believe that these opposites hold also for the absolute; in other words, that ultimate reality can be defined by the same pairs of opposites that characterize the immediate reality in which man finds himself immersed by the mere fact of living in the world. Indian myths, rites and speculations shake this human tendency to consider the immediate experience of the world as a metaphysically valid knowledge reflecting, as one might say, the ultimate reality. Transcending the opposites, is, as is well known, a constant theme of Indian spirituality. By philosophical reflection and contemplation—according to the teaching of the Vedanta—or by psychophysiological techniques and by meditations—as recommended by Yoga—a man succeeds in rising above duality, that is to say in realizing the *coincidentia oppositorum* in his own body and his own spirit.

We will recall later some Indian methods of unification. Let us say for the moment that in India as in all traditional cultures the fundamental truths are proclaimed at all levels, though the expression varies at each, the terms used being suited to the level of knowledge. The principles clearly exposed and expounded in the Upanishads or the philosophic systems are also to be found in popular worship and religious folklore. It is significant, for example, that in certain texts of medieval Vishnu worship, the arch-demon Vritra has become a Brahman, an exemplary warrior and even a saint! The demon Ravana, who had captured Sita and taken her to Ceylon, is also considered to be the author of a treatise on magical child-medicine, *Kumaratantra*. A devil the author of a treatise containing antidemonic formulas and rituals! The goddess Hariti is said to have obtained the right to eat children as a consequence of merits gained in a previous existence.

And this is no exception: many demons are reputed to have won their demonic prowess by good actions performed in previous existences. In other words: *good* can serve to make *evil*. By his ascetic efforts, a devil gains the power to do evil; asceticism leads to the possession of a reserve of magical powers which allow any action to be undertaken without distinction of "moral" value. All these examples are only particular and popular illustrations of the fundamental Indian doctrine, that good and evil have no meaning or function except in a world of appearances, in profane and unenlightened existence. From the transcendental viewpoint, good and evil are, on the contrary, as illusory and relative as all other pairs of opposites: hot-cold, agreeable-disagreeable, long-short, visible-invisible, etc.

All the myths, rites and beliefs that we have just recalled have this essential feature in common: they compel a man to behave otherwise than he spontaneously would, to contradict by thought what immediate experience and elementary knowledge show him; in fact, to become what he is not—what he cannot be—in his profane, unenlightened state, in the human condition. In other words, these myths and their interpretation have an initiatory function. We know that in traditional societies initiation prepares the adolescent to assume adult responsibilities, that is to say introduces him to the religious life, to spiritual values. Thanks to his initiation, the adolescent attains more than personal knowledge, which was previously beyond his reach. Now, as we have just seen, the Indian myths of the *coincidentia oppositorum* help anyone who meditates on them to transcend the level of immediate experiences and uncover a secret dimension of reality.

188. REUNITING SHIVA AND SHAKTI: TANTRISM

It is well known that, according to Tantric yoga, the absolute reality, the *Urgrund*, contains all the dualities and contraries gathered into a state of absolute Unity (*advaja*). Creation represents the

SOURCE: *TO*/117–21.

explosion of the primal unity and the separation of the two contrary principles incarnate in Shiva and Shakti. All relative existence
implies a state of duality, and consequently implies suffering, illusion and "slavery." The final goal of the Tantricist is to reunite the
two contrary principles—Shiva and Shakti—in his own body.
When Shakti, who sleeps, in the shape of a serpent (*kundalini*), at
the base of his body, is awoken by certain yogic techniques, she
moves through a medial channel (*susumna*) by way of the *çakras*
up to the top of the skull (*sahasrara*), where Shiva dwells, and
unites with him. The union of the divine pair within his own body
transforms the yogin into a kind of "androgyne." But it must be
stressed that "androgynization" is only one aspect of a total process,
that of the reunion of opposites. Actually, Tantric literature speaks
of a great number of "opposing pairs" that have to be reunited.
The Sun and Moon must be made one, so must the two mystic
veins *ida* and *pingala* (which also symbolise these two heavenly
bodies) and the two breaths *prana* and *apana*. Above all *prajna*,
wisdom, must be joined with *upaya*, the means of attaining it,
shunya, the void, with *karuna*, compassion. *Hevajra Tantra* speaks
also of the state of "two in one," when the female element is transformed into the male principle.[1] This reunion of contraries corresponds also to a paradoxical coexistence of *samarasa* and *nirvana*.
"There is no *nirvana* outside *samarasa*" proclaimed the Buddha according to *Hevajra Tantra*, II, IV, 32.

All this amounts to saying that we are dealing with a *coincidentia
oppositorum* achieved on all levels of Life and Consciousness. As a
result of this union of opposites the experience of duality is abolished and the phenomenal world transcended. The yogin achieves
an unconditioned state of liberty and transcendence, expressed by
the word *samarasa* (state of bliss), the paradoxical experience of
perfect unity. Certain Tantric schools teach that *samarasa* is attain-
able principally by *maithuna* (ritual union of the sexes) and is char-
acterised by the "staying" or "immobilization" of the three principal
functions of a human being: breath, seminal ejaculation and
thought.[2] The unification of opposites is expressed by the cessa-

---

1. *The Hevajra Tantra*, ed. Snellgrove, II, IV, 2 vols. (London, 1959), pp.
40–47; 24 ff.
2. See selection 87, "Maithuna." Eds.

tion of the bio-somatic processes and also of the psycho-mental flux. The immobilization of those functions that are especially fluid is a sign that a man has left the human condition and come out on a transcendent plane.

Let us observe the religio-cosmic symbolism used to express the joining of contraries. The yogin stands both for a Cosmos and a pantheon; he incarnates in his own body both Shiva and Shakti and many more divinities who are ultimately reducible to this archetypal couple. The two principal phases of Yogo-Tantric *sadhana* are (1) the raising to the cosmic level of psychosomatic experience; (2) the abolition of this Cosmos and the symbolical return to the initial situation when primordial Unity had not yet exploded in the act of Creation. In other words, freedom and the bliss of absolute liberty are homologous with the fullness that existed before the Creation of the World. From one point of view the paradoxical state attained by the Tantricist during *samarasa* can be compared with ritual "orgy" and pre-Cosmic darkness: in both these states the forms are reunited, tensions and opposites are abolished. But it must be noted that *these resemblances are only formal, that in transcending the world the yogin does not rediscover the bliss of existence in the womb.* All these symbolisms of unification and totalization show that the yogin is no longer conditioned by cosmic rhythms and laws, that the Universe has ceased to exist for him, that he has succeeded in putting himself in the moment outside Time in which the Universe was not yet created.

To abolish the Cosmos is a means of saying that one has transcended all relative situations, that one has entered into nonduality and liberty. In classical Yoga the recovery, through *samadhi*, of the original nonduality introduces a new element in respect of the primordial situation (that which existed before the twofold division of the real into object-subject). That element is *knowledge* of unity and bliss. There is a "return to the beginning," but with the difference that the man "liberated in this life" recovers the original situation enriched by the dimensions of *freedom* and *higher consciousness*. To express it differently, he does not return automatically to a "given" situation, but he reintegrates the original completeness after having established a new and paradoxical mode of being: consciousness of freedom, which exists nowhere in the Cosmos, neither on the levels of Life nor on the levels of "mythological

divinity"—(the gods, *devas*)—but which exists only in the Supreme Being, Ishvara.

It is not without interest to remark that the paradoxical state of
a *jivan mukta*, of one who has realized the unconditioned state—
by whatever term that state is expressed: *samadhi, mukti, nirvana,
samarasa*, etc.—describes this state, which is beyond the imagination, by contradictory images and symbols. On the one side,
images of pure spontaneity and freedom (the *jivan mukta* is a *kamacarin*, "someone who moves at will"; that is why it is said of him
that he can "fly through the air"; on the other side, images of absolute immobility, of the final arrest of all movement, the freezing of
all mobility. The coexistence of these contradictory images is explained by the paradoxical situation of the man "liberated in this
life"; for he continues to exist in the Cosmos although no longer
subject to cosmic laws; in fact he no longer belongs to the Cosmos.
These images of immobility and completion express transcendence
of all relative conditions; for a system of conditions, a Cosmos,
must be defined in terms of becoming, by its continuous movement and by the tension between opposites. To cease moving and
no longer to be torn by the tensions between opposites is equivalent
to no longer existing in the Cosmos. But, on the other hand, no
longer to be conditioned by the pairs of opposites is equivalent to
absolute liberty, to perfect spontaneity—and one could not express
this liberty better than by images of movement, play, being in two
places at once or flying.

Once again, in fact, we are dealing with a transcendental situation which, being inconceivable, is expressed by contradictory or
paradoxical metaphors. This is why the formula of the *coincidentia
oppositorum* is always applied when it is necessary to describe an
unimaginable situation either in the Cosmos or in History. The eschatological symbol, *par excellence*, which denotes that Time and
History have come to an end—is the lion lying down with the
lamb, and the child playing with the snake. Conflicts, that is to say
opposites, are abolished; Paradise is regained. This eschatological
image makes it quite clear that the *coincidentia oppositorum* does
not always imply "totalization" in the concrete sense of the term;
it may equally signify the paradoxical return of the World to the
paradisaical state. The fact that the lamb, the lion, the child and
the snake *exist* means that the *World is there*, that there is a Cos-

mos and not Chaos. But the fact that the lion lies down with the lamb and the child sleeps beside the snake implies at the same time that this is no longer *our* world, but that of Paradise. In fact we are presented with a World that is paradoxical, because free of the tensions and conflicts which are the attributes of every Universe. . . .

189. *YANG* AND *YIN*

I have purposely left for the end the example of China. As in the archaic societies of the Americas and Indonesia, the cosmic polarity, expressed by the symbols *yang* and *yin*, was "lived" through the rites, and it also furnished quite early the model for a universal classification. Besides, as in India, the couple of contraries *yang* and *yin* was developed into a cosmology which, on the one hand, systematized and validated innumerable bodily techniques and spiritual disciplines, and on the other hand inspired rigorous and systematic philosophical speculations. I will not present the morphology of *yang* and *yin* nor will I retrace its history. It suffices to remark that polar symbolism is abundantly attested in the iconography of Shang bronzes (1400–1122 B.C., according to the traditional Chinese chronology). Carl Hentze, who has devoted a series of important works to this problem, points out that the polar symbols are disposed in such a way as to emphasize their conjunction; for instance, the owl, or another figure symbolizing the darkness, is provided with "solar eyes," while the emblems of light are marked by a "nocturnal" sign.[1] Hentze interprets the conjunction of polar symbols as illustrating religious ideas of renewal of time and spiritual regeneration. According to Hentze, the symbolism of *yang* and *yin* is present in the most ancient ritual objects, long before the first written texts.[2]

This is also the conclusion of Marcel Granet, though he reached it from other sources and by utilizing a different method. Granet recalls that in *Che King* the word *yin* evokes the idea of cold and

SOURCE: Q/170–72.
1. Cf. Carl Hentze, *Bronzegerät, Kultbauten, Religion im ältesten China der Shangzeit* (Anvers, 1951), pp. 192 ff.
2. Carl Hentze, *Das Haus als Weltort der Seele* (Stuttgart, 1961), pp. 99 ff.

cloudy weather, and also of what is internal, whereas the term *yang* suggests the idea of sunshine and warmth.[3] In other words, *yang* and *yin* indicate the concrete and antithetical aspects of the weather.[4] In *Kouei tsang*, a lost manual of divination known only from some fragments, it is a question of "a time of light" and "a time of obscurity," anticipating the saying of Tchouang tseu: "a (time of) plenitude, a (time of) decrepitude . . . a (time of) refining, a (time of) thickening . . . a (time of) life, a (time of) death."[5] Thus, the world represents "a totality of a cyclical order (*tao, pien, t'ong*) constituted by the conjugation of two alternate and complementary manifestations."[6]

Granet thinks that the idea of alternation seems to have entailed the idea of opposition.[7] This is clearly illustrated by the structure of the calendar. "*Yang* and *yin* have been summoned to organize the calendar because their emblems evoked with a particular force the rhythmic conjugation of two concrete antithetic aspects."[8] According to the philosophers, during the winter the *yang*, overcome by *yin*, undergoes below the frozen soil a kind of an annual trial from which it emerges invigorated. The *yang* escapes from its prison at the beginning of spring; then the ice melts and the sources reawaken.[9] Thus the universe shows itself to be constituted by a series of antithetic forms alternating in a cyclical manner.

Fascinated by the sociologism of Durkheim, Marcel Granet was inclined to deduct the conception and the systematic articulation of cosmic rotation from the ancient formulas of Chinese social life. We do not need to follow him on this path. But it is important to notice the symmetry between the complementary alternation of the activities of the two sexes and the cosmic rhythms governed by the interplay of *yang* and *yin*. And because a feminine nature was recognized in everything that is *yin*, and a masculine nature in everything that is *yang*, the theme of hierogamy—which, according to Granet, dominates the entire Chinese mythology—discloses a cos-

3. Marcel Granet, *La Pensée chinoise* (Paris, 1934), p. 117.
4. *Ibid.*, p. 118.
5. *Ibid.*, p. 132.
6. *Ibid.*, p. 127.
7. *Ibid.*, p. 128.
8. *Ibid.*, p. 131.
9. *Ibid.*, p. 135.

mic as well as religious dimension. The ritual opposition of the two sexes, carried out, in ancient China, as that of two rival corporations,[10] expresses simultaneously the complementary antagonism of two modes of being and the alternation of two cosmic principles, *yang* and *yin*. In the collective feasts of spring and autumn, the two antagonistic choirs, arrayed in lines face to face, challenged each other in verse. "The *yang* calls, the *yin* answers." These two formulas are interchangeable; they signify conjointly the cosmic and social rhythms.[11] The antagonistic choirs confront each other as shadow and light. The field where they meet represents the totality of space, just as the group symbolizes the totality of human society and of the realities belonging to natural realm.[12] A collective hierogamy ended the festivity. As we have noticed, such ritual orgies are well known in many parts of the world. In this case, too, the polarity, accepted as a fundamental rule of life during the year, is abolished, or transcended, through the union of contraries.

190. *COINCIDENTIA OPPOSITORUM—* THE MYTHICAL PATTERN

All these myths present us with a twofold revelation: they express on the one hand the diametrical opposition of two divine figures sprung from one and the same principle and destined, in many versions, to be reconciled at some *illud tempus* of eschatology, and on the other, the *coincidentia oppositorum* in the very nature of the divinity, which shows itself, by turns or even simultaneously, benevolent and terrible, creative and destructive, solar and serpentine, and so on (in other words, actual and potential). In this sense it is true to say that myth reveals more profoundly than any rational experience ever could, the actual structure of the divinity, which transcends all attributes and reconciles all contraries. That this mythical experience is no mere deviation is proved by the fact that it enters into almost all the religious experience of mankind,

Source: *PCR*/419–20.
10. *Ibid.*
11. *Ibid.*, p. 141.
12. *Ibid.*, p. 143.

even within as strict a tradition as the Judaeo-Christian. Yahweh is both kind and wrathful; the God of the Christian mystics and theologians is terrible and gentle at once and it is this *coincidentia oppositorum* which is the starting point for the boldest speculations of such men as the pseudo-Dionysius, Meister Eckhardt, and Nicholas of Cusa.

The *coincidentia oppositorum* is one of the most primitive ways of expressing the paradox of divine reality. We shall be returning to this formula when we come to look at divine "forms," to the peculiar structure revealed by every divine "personality," given of course that the divine personality is not to be simply looked upon as a mere projection of human personality. However, although this conception, in which all contraries are reconciled (or rather, transcended), constitutes what is, in fact, the most basic definition of divinity, and shows how utterly different it is from humanity, the *coincidentia oppositorum* becomes nevertheless an archetypal model for certain types of religious men, or for certain of the forms religious experience takes. The *coincidentia oppositorum* or transcending of all attributes can be achieved by man in all sorts of ways. At the most elementary level of religious life there is the orgy: for it symbolizes a return to the amorphous and the indistinct, to a state in which all attributes disappear and contraries are merged. But exactly the same doctrine can also be discerned in the highest ideas of the eastern sage and ascetic, whose contemplative methods and techniques are aimed at transcending all attributes of every kind. The ascetic, the sage, the Indian or Chinese "mystic" tries to wipe out of his experience and consciousness every sort of "extreme," to attain to a state of perfect indifference and neutrality, to become insensible to pleasure and pain, to become completely self-sufficient. This transcending of extremes through asceticism and contemplation also results in the "coinciding of opposites"; the consciousness of such a man knows no more conflict, and such pairs of opposites as pleasure and pain, desire and repulsion, cold and heat, the agreeable and the disagreeable are expunged from his awareness, while something is taking place within him which parallels the total realization of contraries within the divinity. . . .The neophyte begins by identifying all his experience with the rhythms governing the universe (sun and moon), but once this "cosmization" has been achieved, he turns all his efforts towards *unifying* the sun and moon, towards taking into himself the *cosmos as a whole*; he remakes in himself and for himself the primeval unity which was before the world was made; a unity which signifies not the chaos that existed before any forms were created but the undifferentiated *being* in which all forms are merged.

◆ ◆

Revalorization of Symbols

191. HISTORY INTO THEOPHANY: THE COSMIC TREE

It is striking that the symbol can contain or evoke so many interpretations: perhaps that is a characteristic of a true symbol! At any rate it is clearly the case that symbols are utilized differently at different stages of a culture's traditions, and it is this successive reinterpretation to which Eliade refers with the term revalorization. The example here is the Cosmic Tree, a symbol he has studied repeatedly,[1] and Eliade relates its valorization both to the universal and to the historic (using Joseph Campbell's terminology—Eliade himself refers to the question of the relationships between the "particular version" and the "universally attested formulas").

Certain Fathers of the Church have examined the interesting correspondence between the archetypal images evoked by Christianity and the Images which are the common property of mankind. One of their most constant concerns is, precisely, to make manifest to unbelievers the correspondence between those great symbols which the soul finds immediately expressive and persuasive, and the dogmas of the new religion. . . . For the Christian apologists, the Images were charged with signs and messages; they *showed forth* the sacred by means of the cosmic rhythms. The revelation conveyed by the Faith did not dispel the "primary" meanings of the Images; it simply added a new value to them. For the believer, it is true, this new meaning eclipsed all others: it *alone* valorized the Image, transfiguring it into Revelation. It was the Resurrection of the Christ that mattered, and not the "signs" that one could read in Nature: in the majority of cases, one did not understand the "signs" until after hav-

Source: *IS*/159–64; cf. *PCR*/52–54, 266 ff., and selection 153.
1. See the collection of illustrations by Peter Cook, *The Tree of Life: Image for the Cosmos* (New York, 1974).

ing found the Faith in the depths of one's soul. But the mystery of faith is a matter for Christian experience, for theology and religious psychology and surpasses our present research. In the perspective I have chosen, one thing alone is important: that *every new valorization has always been conditioned by the actual structure of the Image*, so much so that we can say of an Image that it is *awaiting* the fulfilment of its meaning.

. . . The Christian faith is dependent on a *historic* revelation: it is the manifestation of God in Time which, in the eyes of a Christian, ensures the validity of the Images and the symbols. We have seen that the "immanent" and universal symbology of water was not abolished nor dismembered in consequence of the local and historical Judaeo-Christian interpretations of baptismal symbolism. To put it in a rather simplified way: history does not radically modify the structure of an "immanent" symbolism. History continually adds new meanings to it, but these do not destroy the structure of the symbol. We shall see, later on, what consequences follow from this for the philosophy of history and the morphology of culture: but for the moment, let us look at [an example]. . . .

We have already discussed the symbolism of the Tree of the World. Christianity has utilized, interpreted and amplified this symbol. The Cross, made of the wood of the tree of good and evil, appears in the place of this Cosmic Tree; the Christ himself is described as a Tree (by Origen). A homily of the pseudo-Chrysostom speaks of the Cross as a tree which "rises from the earth to the heavens. A plant immortal, it stands at the center of heaven and of earth; strong pillar of the universe, bond of all things, support of all the inhabited earth; cosmic interlacement, comprising in itself the whole medley of human nature . . ." "And the Byzantine liturgy sings even now, on the day of the exaltation of the Holy Cross, of 'the tree of life planted on Calvary, the tree on which the King of ages wrought our salvation,' the tree which 'springing from the depths of the earth, has risen to the center of the earth' and 'sanctifies the Universe unto its limits.' "[2] The Image of the Cosmic Tree is preserved in astonishing purity. Its prototype is, very probably, to be sought in what Wisdom which, according to Proverbs 3:18, "is a tree of life to those who lay hold of her." Fr. de Lubac writes

2. Henri de Lubac, *Aspects du Bouddhisme* (Paris, 1951), pp. 57, 66–77.

of this Wisdom that "for Jews, this will be the Law; for Christians, it will be the Son of God."[3] Another probable prototype is the tree that Nebuchadnezzar saw in a dream (*Daniel*, 4:7–15): "I saw, and behold, a tree in the midst of the earth; and its height was great," etc.

Fr. de Lubac admits that, like the symbol of the Cosmic Tree of Indian tradition, the image of the Cross as the Tree of the World is a continuation into Christianity of "an old, universal myth."[4] But he is careful to draw attention to the innovations made by Christianity. We find, for instance, in the sequel to the homily of the pseudo-Chrysostom, that the Universe is the Church: "she is the new macrocosm, of which the Christian soul is the analogue in miniature."[5] And how many other striking differences there are between the Buddha and the Christ, between the pillar of Sanchi and the Cross.[6] For all his conviction that the utilization of such an image by both Buddhism and Christianity "is after all only a matter of language,"[7] the eminent theologian seems to exaggerate the importance of historical specificities: "The whole question is, in each case, that of finding out the kind and the degree of originality in the 'particular version.' "[8]

Is that really the whole question? Are we in fact condemned to be content with exhaustive analyses of "particular versions" which, when all is said and done, represent local histories? Have we no means of approach to the Image, the symbol, the archetype, in their own structures; in that "wholeness" which embraces all their "histories," without, however, confusing them? There are numerous patristic and liturgical texts which compare the Cross to a ladder, a column or a mountain.[9] And these, we may remember, are universally attested formulas for the "Center of the World." It is in this aspect, as a symbol of the Center of the World, that the Cross has been likened to the Cosmic Tree; which is a proof that the Image of the Center *imposed itself naturally* upon the Christian

3. *Ibid.*, p. 71.
4. *Ibid.*, p. 75.
5. *Ibid.*, p. 77.
6. *Ibid.*, pp. 77 ff.
7. *Ibid.*, p. 76.
8. *Ibid.*, p. 169, n. 101.
9. *Ibid.*, pp. 64–68.

mind. It is by the Cross (= the Center) that communication with Heaven is opened and that, by the same token, the entire Universe is "saved." . . . *But the notion of "salvation" does no more than repeat and complete the notions of perpetual renovation and cosmic regeneration, of universal fecundity and of sanctity, of absolute reality and, in the final reckoning, of immortality*—all of which coexist in the symbolism of the Tree of the World.

Let it be well understood that I am not denying the importance of history, or in the case of Judaeo-Christianity of faith, for the estimation of the true value of this or that symbol *as it was understood and lived in a specific culture*: we shall indeed underline this later. But it is not by "placing" a symbol in its own history that we can resolve the essential problem—namely, to know what is revealed to us, not by any "particular version" of a symbol but by the *whole* of a symbolism. We have already seen how the various meanings of a symbol are linked together, interconnected in a system, as it were. The contradictions one can discover between the various particular versions are in most cases only apparent; they are resolved as soon as we consider the symbolism as a whole and discern its structure. Each new valorization of an archetypal Image crowns and consummates the earlier ones: the "salvation" revealed by the Cross does not annul the pre-Christian values of the Tree of the World, that pre-eminent symbol of the total *renovatio*; on the contrary, the Cross comes to complete all its earlier valencies and meanings. Let us observe, once more, that this new valorization, brought about by the identification of the Cosmic Tree with the Cross, took place *in* history and through a historical event—the Passion of Christ. As we shall see, the great originality of Judaeo-Christianity was the transfiguration of History into theophany. . . .

◆ ◆

Modern Man: History, Death, A Regenerated World

192. RELIGIOUS SYMBOLISM AND MODERN MAN'S ANXIETY

We conclude the selections in this book with parts of the concluding chapter of Myths, Dreams, and Mysteries, *a work that demon-*

SOURCE: *MDM*/231–36, 238–45.

strates especially clearly Eliade's concern that comparative religious study not remain an exercise of the researcher alone, but become dialogue with one's own tradition.[1]

We propose now to consider the anxiety of the modern man as it appears in the light of the history of religions. To more readers than one, this project may seem singular, if not merely unnecessary. For some of us regard the anxiety of the modern world as a product of historical tensions, belonging specifically to our times, explicable by the fundamental crises of our civilization, and by nothing else. To what purpose, then, should we compare this historic moment in which we live with the symbolisms and religious ideologies of other epochs and other civilizations long since past? This objection is but half justified. There is no perfectly autonomous civilization, wholly unrelated to the others that preceded it. The Greek mythology had lost its reality some 2,000 years before it was found that some of the fundamental behaviour of the modern European could be explained by the myth of Oedipus. Psychoanalysis and depth-psychology have accustomed us to such comparisons—at first sight unverifiable—between historical situations apparently unrelated to one another. Some have compared, for example, the ideology of the Christian to that of the totemist; they have tried to explain the notion of the Father God by that of the totem. We will not now enquire how well-founded such comparisons are, or upon what documentary basis. Enough to point out that certain psychological schools make use of comparisons between the most varied types of civilization to gain a better understanding of the structure of the psyche. The directive principle of this method is that, since the human psyche has a history and, in consequence, cannot be wholly explained by the study of its present situation, all its history, and even its prehistory, should still be discernible in what we call its actual disposition.

This brief allusion to the methods employed by the depth-psychologists will suffice, for we have no intention of proceeding

1. See also: "Initiation and the Modern World," *Q*/112–26, and other chapters in *The Quest*. Eliade discusses modern psychological attempts to deal with personal cultural symbolism in several locations; see also selections 23, 31, 32, and 93. Eds.

in the same way. In saying that one can study the anxiety of modern times in the perspective of the history of religions, we were thinking of quite another comparative method, which we will now indicate in a few words. We propose to reverse the terms of comparison, to place ourselves outside our civilization and our own moment of history, and to consider these from the standpoint of other cultures and other religions. We do not think of rediscovering among ourselves, Europeans of the twentieth century, certain attitudes already known to the ancient mythologies—as, for example, Freud did with the Oedipus complex: our aim will be to see ourselves just as an intelligent and sympathetic observer, from the standpoint of an extra-European civilization, might see and judge us. For greater precision, we will imagine an observer who belongs to another civilization and judges us according to his own scale of values. . . .

. . . We need only instance one of the most specific features of our own civilization—namely, the modern man's passionate, almost abnormal interest in History. . . .

This is a fairly recent passion; it dates from the second half of the last century. It is true that, from the time of Herodotus, the Greco-Latin world knew and cultivated the writing of history: but this was not history as it has come to be written since the nineteenth century, the aim of which is to know and describe, as accurately as possible, all that has come to pass in the course of time. . . . Now, this is an interest we find nowhere else. Practically all the non-European cultures are without historic consciousness, and even if they have a traditional historiography—as in the case of China, or the countries under the Islamic culture—its function is always to provide exemplary models.

. . . In many religions, and even in the folklore of European peoples, we have found a belief that, at the moment of death, man remembers all his past life down to the minutest details, and that he cannot die before having remembered and relived the whole of his personal history. Upon the screen of memory, the dying man once more reviews his past. Considered from this point of view, the passion for historiography in modern culture would be a sign portending his imminent death. Our Western civilization, before it foundered, would be for the last time remembering all its past, from protohistory until the total wars. The historiographical consciousness

of Europe—which some have regarded as its highest title to lasting
fame—would in fact be the supreme moment which precedes and
announces death.

. . . It is, indeed, somewhat significant that judged from a wholly
external point of view—that of funerary rituals and folklore—this
modern passion for historiography reveals to us an archaic symbolism of Death.

. . . In all the other, non-European cultures, that is, in the other
religions, Death is never felt as an absolute end or as Nothingness:
it is regarded rather as a rite of passage to another mode of being;
and for that reason always referred to in relation to the symbolisms
and rituals of initiation, rebirth or resurrection. This is not to say
that the non-European does not know the experience of anguish
before Death; the emotion is experienced, of course, but not as
something absurd or futile; on the contrary, it is accorded the highest value, as an experience indispensable to the attainment of a new
level of being. Death is the Great Initiation. But in the modern
world Death is emptied of its religious meaning; that is why it is
assimilated to Nothingness; and before Nothingness modern man is
paralyzed.

Let us note, in a brief parenthesis, that when we speak of "modern man," his crises and anxieties, we are thinking primarily of one
who has no faith, who is no longer in any living attachment to
Judaeo-Christianity. To a believer, the problem of Death presents
itself in other terms: for him, too, Death is a rite of passage. But a
great part of the modern world has lost faith, and for this mass of
mankind anxiety in the face of Death presents itself as anguish before Nothingness. It is only that part of the modern world to which
we are referring, whose experience we are trying to understand and
interpret by situating it within another cultural horizon. . . .

* * *

Let us now try to decipher the anxiety of the modern world, using Indian philosophy as the key. An Indian philosopher would say
that historicism and existentialism introduce Europe to the dialectic
of Maya. His reasoning would be very much like this: European
thinking has just discovered that man is ineluctably conditioned, not
only by his physiology and his heredity, but also by History and
above all his personal history. This it is that keeps man for ever in

a predicament: he is participating all the time in History, he is a fundamentally historical being. And, the Indian philosopher would add: this "predicament" we have known for a very long time; it is the illusory existence in Maya. And we call it illusory precisely because it is conditioned by Time, by History. Furthermore, it is for this reason that India has never allowed philosophic importance to History. India is preoccupied with Being; and History, created by becoming, is just one of the forms of Nonbeing. But this does not mean that Indian thought has neglected the analysis of historicity: her metaphysics and spiritual techniques have long since included a highly refined analysis of that which, in Western philosophy, is now called "being in the world" or "being in a situation": Yoga, Buddhism and Vedanta have all demonstrated the relativity, and therefore the nonreality of every "situation," of all "conditions." Many centuries before Heidegger, Indian thought had identified, in temporality, the "fated" dimension of all existence; just as it had foreseen, before Marx or Freud, the multiple conditioning of all human experience and of every judgment about the world. When the Indian philosophies affirmed that man is "in bondage" to illusion, they meant to say that every existence necessarily constitutes itself as a rupture, a break-away from the Absolute. . . .

In other words, the discovery of historicity, as the specific mode of being of man in the world, corresponds to what the Indians have long called our situation in Maya. And the Indian philosopher would say that European thought has understood the precariousness and the paradoxical condition of the man who becomes aware of his temporality: his anguish follows from his tragic discovery that man is a being destined to death, issuing from Nothingness and on his way to Nothingness.

Yet the Indian philosopher would still be perplexed at the consequences that certain modern philosophers draw from this discovery. For, after having understood the dialectic of Maya, the Indian tries to deliver himself from its illusions, whilst these Europeans seem to be content with the discovery, and to put up with a nihilistic and pessimistic vision of the world. It is not for us here to discuss the why and wherefore of this tendency in European thought; we are only trying to submit it to the judgment of the Indian philosopher. Now, for an Indian, there is no sense in the discovery of the cosmic illusion if it is not followed by the quest of the absolute Being: the notion of Maya is meaningless without the notion of Brahman. In Occidental language, we might say that there is no point in becoming aware that one is conditioned unless one turns towards the unconditioned and seeks deliverance. . . .

. . . To become aware of the dialectic of Maya does not necessarily lead to asceticism and the abandonment of all social and historical existence. This state of consciousness generally finds expression in quite another attitude; the attitude revealed by Krishna to Arjuna in the *Bhagavad-Gita*: namely, that of remaining in the world and participating in History, but taking good care not to attribute to History any absolute value. Rather than an invitation to renounce History, what is revealed to us in the *Bhagavad-Gita* is a warning against the *idolatry* of History. . . .

. . . Now, it is significant that, whether we look at it from the standpoint of the archaic cultures or that of Indian spirituality, anxiety appears under the symbolism of Death. This means that, seen and evaluated by the *others*, by the non-Europeans, our anxiety reveals the same signification as we Europeans had already found in it: the imminence of Death. But agreement between our own view of it and that of the *others* goes no further. For, to the non-Europeans, Death is neither definitive nor absurd; on the contrary, the anxiety aroused by the imminence of death is already a promise of resurrection, reveals the presentiment of rebirth into another mode of being, and this is a mode which transcends Death. Viewed again in the perspective of the primitive societies, the anxiety of the modern world can be homologized with the anguish of death in initiation; seen in the Indian perspective it is homologous with the dialectical moment of the discovery of Maya. But, as we were saying just now, in archaic and "primitive" culture, as well as in India, *this anxiety is not a state in which one can remain*; its indispensability is that of an initiatory experience, of a rite of passage. In no culture other than ours could one stop in the middle of this rite of passage and settle down in a situation apparently without issue. For the issue consists precisely in completing this rite of passage and resolving the crisis by coming out of it at a higher level, awakening to consciousness of a higher mode of being. It is inconceivable, for example, that one could interrupt an initiatory rite of passage: in that case the boy would no longer be a child, as he was before beginning his initiation, but neither would he be the adult that he ought to be at the end of his ordeals.

We must also mention another source of the modern anxiety, our obscure presentiment of the end of the world, or more exactly of the end of *our* world, our *own* civilization. We will not consider how well-founded this fear may be: enough to recall that it is far from being a modern discovery. The myth of the end of the world is of universal occurrence; it is already to be found among primitive peoples still at a paleolithic stage of culture, such as the Australians, and it recurs in the great historic civilizations, Babylonian, Indian, Mexican and Greco-Latin. This is the myth of the periodic destruction and re-creation of worlds, the cosmological formula of the myth of the eternal return. One must immediately add, however, that the terror of the end of the world has never, in any non-European culture, succeeded in paralyzing either Life or Culture. The expectation of the cosmic catastrophe is indeed agonizing, but the anxiety is religiously and culturally integrated. The end of the world is never absolute; it is always followed by the creation of a new, *regenerated* world. For, to non-Europeans, Life and the Spirit are unique in this, that they can never definitively disappear.

. . . But this is as much as to say that a dialogue with the *true* Asiatic, African or Oceanian world helps us to rediscover spiritual positions that one is justified in regarding as universally valid. These are no longer provincial formulas, creations merely of this or that fragment of History but—one may dare to say—ecumenical positions. . . .

And this is the profound meaning of any genuine encounter; it might well constitute the point of departure for a new humanism, upon a world scale.

The Work of Mircea Eliade:
Implications for a Philosophy of Humankind[1]

WENDELL C. BEANE

The work of Mircea Eliade provides us with an opportunity to reconsider the vital relations that obtain between and among three longstanding and important areas of concern for us as scholars, teachers, students, and other value-sharing persons. These areas involve the relations of history and religion, humankind and nature, and religion and culture. It is out of Eliade's treatment of these realities both explicitly and implicitly that one may gather much food for intellectual and philosophical thought.

Let us consider at once the implications of his writings for the subject of history and religion. We infer from our author that in the final analysis history is not a mass of unrelated and sterile "facts" which merely ask and answer of "what happened" in the sense of human behavior. History is not, again, a concatenation of particular events in which humankind was present but had no intrinsic voluntary part to play; or, if a part were played, it constituted no predetermined role which meant the subjugation of the human spirit to the forces of nature at large. Yet what might seem unlikely to some, "primitive" persons were also not the incarnations of the rawest spontaneity of thought, speech, and action. Rather the earliest human beings who were to become history-makers were the

---

1. Cf. *MRS*/88: ". . . the historian of religions also is led to systematize the results of his findings and to reflect on the structure of the religious phenomena. But then he completes his historical work as phenomenologist or philosopher of religion"; *TO*/191: ". . . he is completing his task as historian by a task of phenomenology or religious philosophy."

result of the dynamic interplay of a history of nature, out of which they had come by evolutionary processes barely comprehended then (or now) and their own inherent religious tendency to be themselves creators of meaningful solitary and social situations that they would come to regard as sacred.

Thus when we look back upon either the religio-artifacts of peoples gone by or even upon others who may have remained as living vestiges of a past time, we cannot arrive at an authentic understanding of those sacred worlds by solely adopting the role of chroniclers of human events. We cannot do this because it appears that the history of human life includes a not completely calculable, indeed, an inexhaustible, factor (= Religion) which not only happens to be peculiar to human beings, but without which history itself becomes only a record of a people's past according to a particular scholar's intellectual disposition to affirm or deny the existence of the Sacred. It is, of course, religion's *sui generis* character, though no one faith is necessarily *the* meaning of all history, that has generally made spiritual meaning possible for the human species in history.

Yet it is more than mere meaning, alone, but *ultimate* meaning, which has enabled humankind to make sense out of history as existence: to tolerate, transform, and, ultimately, to transcend the ambiguities of both time and history. To be sure, if traditionalist peoples were in fact ahistorical in their bearing, it constituted on the one hand a constructive protest against the passive acceptance of their existential anxiety in the midst of an elusive evolutionary process; and on the other hand a thrilling prospect that involved the opportunity to make everyday life the occasion for discerning "times" (e.g., seasonal festivals, rites of passage) that symbolized the birth and rebirth of Sacred History beyond Profane Reality. Hence, in recognizing the ahistorical quality of so much of pre-historic and ancient religion we have to bear in mind that this ahistoricalism did not completely dehistoricize them in terms of their consciousness of the Profane. It really gave them access to a deeper dimension of spiritual involvement in history through which it became increasingly clear that sacred realities, mythically and ritually reexperienced, symbolized that not history alone but ultimate power had a decisive influence upon human nature and human destiny; so that in their seemingly "eternal return" to archetypal sacred myths, rites, and symbols, these pioneers of the Sacred were saying that the origins and destiny of their humanity lay not in the mere chance passage of time and circumstance but in the thoughts and gestures of beings, like themselves, yet Supernatural Beings even to those that conceived them. The periodic recourse, then, to a Primordial Time *before* profane time meant no surrender to the stark realities of natural existence. The recourse to the sacred past meant instead the affirmation of faith in humankind's own potential to *make* history, to *remake* human nature, indeed, to *revaluate* the relation between nature and humankind at the level of religious contemplation.

When we consider the relation between humankind and nature-at-large, Eliade's writings testify to a religious evaluation of nature by individuals and communities throughout practically all human history. This discovery marks a distinctive sense of religio-ecological adventure and responsibility in the human consciousness for nature both as the intimate source of all potential and actual symbolic forms and the ultimate resource for the re-creation of all discoverable and rediscoverable spiritual experiences. But what more can we say of this remarkable religious naturalism? First of all, the religious naturalism of such traditionalist men and women testifies not to their inherent mental inferiority as persons but to their achievement of a largely healthy understanding of the essential relation between myth (= thinking about the gods) and ecology (= following the way of the gods revealed in nature).

Second, the mythico-religious imagination of traditional societies marks their possession of an admirable courage and creativity in the face of what was largely for them scientifically incomprehensible (granting their pastoral and botanical knowledge) as well as a childlike humility and simplicity. Although this does not mean that the archaic world was devoid of complex systems of mythico-rituo-symbolic creations, it is that childlikeness before the Infinite which should remind us moderns of a capacity in ourselves that we have, perhaps, wrongfully discarded in favor of what appears more and more to be an uncreative security that brings no ultimate satisfaction at all. Finally, traditionalist human beings by their understanding of their place in nature are witnesses to us, again, that we, too, if we are to find our own places in the nature-of-the-future, may need to consider, as we continue to change the face of "mother earth" through technology, that the death of the gods does not necessarily mean the death of the Sacred; and the persistence of the Sacred always allows for the possible rebirth of genuine humility. Most important is the following question posed by Eliade's writings for the relation between humankind and nature. Are modern man and woman capable of struggling with nature and at the same time realizing with technocratic and philosophic realism that nature is never really conquered by them but ought finally to be understood as something from which to learn rather than as something from which to wrest sustaining economic realities for the sake of dominance alone? It is only a positive and cooperative answer to this question that could allow, for example, a modern "Earth Day" to become, let us imagine, an annual national, religio-ecological celebration in our time without literally returning to the mythic modes of past ages. Nonetheless myth we need, though more self-delusion we do not need. The persistent fable of today is our own self-delusion that throughout history myth was always a "false" way of apprehending the meaning of the world. Myth, in fact, was no futile wish so much as it was a creative framework for acknowledging our awareness in spiritual terms that our reach has always exceeded our grasp in history. Hence any new myth must transcend the faddism toward mythmaking for the sake of myth or demagoguery. And any nonreligious interpretation of history must answer the question of the meaning of the terror of history which has occurred under the form of efforts to prove that man is indeed the measure of all things. In a word, unless we overcome our fear of anamnesis as spiritual self-introspection, the threat of pollution, for instance, will remain a prophetic sign of the state of the land, human society, and, more basically, the state of the human mind.

The implications that Eliade's work has for humankind's religious consciousness in relation to culture are extremely important. The recognition of the ambivalence (= dialectic) of the sacred, therefore, culminates in our historian of religion's emphasis upon the fact that from the earliest cultural beginnings human beings found themselves unable—indeed they refused—to accept the historical "landscape" as they found it; they refused to see nature as mere stones, bones, and grass. They felt impelled by their unique sense of the numinous in nature and in themselves to envision, if not to *create*, a mythical geography which symbolized the cumulative traditional values whereby their sacred predecessors, they themselves, and their progeny could recurrently attain an ultimate mode of being in the world.

In this historico-religious perspective, then, man-the-hunter became man-the-*religious*-hunter; woman-the-agriculturalist became woman-the-*religious*-agriculturalist (though in these enterprises the sexes worked both cooperatively *and* in creative tension with each other). Through Eliade we learn that human culture, though capable of being understood and interpreted as comprising humankind's art, morals, government, etc., invites the paradoxical realization that man, indeed, "makes himself" (i.e., people create culture) *and* that man himself "is made" (i.e., in the myths by the Supernaturals). It is therefore this advent of culture as religious reality that imposes upon the scholar the obligation to recognize the ineradicable role which religion has played in the evolution of the human mind. To be sure, the historian of religions takes upon himself what seems a sacred trust comparable to the theologian of a particular faith—though the two fields differ—insofar as the former must see that the "true story" of myth, rite, and symbol is not lost in the passion to be forever modern. For the cumulative mythical, ritual, and symbolic heritage of humankind, after all, constitutes an indictment and a challenge to present and future members of our species. The indictment is that we have ignored the Holy, largely in the name of its mythical costume; but we have "done" the Unholy under the guise of "other" myths born out of a hunger for power and meaning—yet for profane ends. To be sure, we can only hope that we have not lost the capacity for a direct encounter with ultimate creative power. The challenge is tersely and paradoxically stated: humankind *can* save itself, if it would *be* saved.